# PUT YOUR
# BEST FOOT FORWARD

---

## EUROPE

# PUT YOUR
# BEST FOOT FORWARD

## EUROPE

*A Fearless
Guide to
International
Communication
and Behavior*

## MARY
## MURRAY
## BOSROCK

IES
International Education Systems

Published by International Education Systems.

This publication is designed to provide accurate and
authoritative information in regard to the subject matter
covered. It is sold with the understanding that the publisher is
not engaged in rendering legal, accounting or other
professional services. If legal advice or other expert assistance
is required, the services of a competent professional person
should be sought.

Information contained in this book does not necessarily reflect
the official views of any government. References to
organizations and publications are not endorsements. The
author alone is responsible for errors of omission or commission
in the contents of this book.

**Library of Congress Publisher's Cataloging-in-Publication Data**

Bosrock, Mary Murray.
      Put your best foot forward— Europe: a fearless guide
to international communication & behavior / Mary
Murray Bosrock.
         p. cm. — (Put your best foot forward; bk. 1)
         Includes index.
         Preassigned LCCN: 93-079392.
         ISBN 0-9637530-3-7
         1. Europe—Guidebooks. 2. Europe—Social life
and customs. I. Title. II. Series: Bosrock, Mary Murray. Put
your best foot forward; bk. 1.


D909.B67 1993                    914.04'559
                                    QBI93-1211


Printed in the United States of America
10 9 8 7 6 5 4 3 2 1

*To Ron,*

*who has given me the world—*

*our sons, Matt and Steve*

Look for other international education products from
IES, including European country brochures, *Put Your
Best Foot Forward–Asia,* Asian country brochures.

*Editor: Terry Wolkerstorfer
Design: Brett Olson
Illustrations: Craig MacIntosh
Research: Kristen Zuzek*

# TABLE OF CONTENTS

## PART III: COUNTRY INFORMATION

# i.
# ACKNOWLEDGMENTS

My thanks to the dozens of people, both
European and American—businesspeople,
diplomats, scholars and professionals—who
have drawn on their own experience to
contribute ideas to this book, and especially to
those who have helped review the manuscript.

Listed by their particular areas of expertise,
they include:

**Austria**
Franz Hutegger, Vice Consul, Austrian Embassy, Dublin
Klaus Janschek, Trade Commissioner and Director of
    Tourism, Chicago
Herbert and Erika Kahler
Monika Pacher, Director, ICD Austria-USA, New York

**Belgium**
Alain Genor, Counselor, Belgian Embassy, Dublin
Hans and Marjoleine Koppen
Patrick H. O'Neill, Honorary Consul, St. Paul
Piet Schiepers, President, Regional Development
    Authority, Limburg
Raymond Van Ballaer, Director General, Regional
    Development Authority Limburg/Flanders
    Investment Opportunity Council

### Denmark

Ib Alken, Counselor, Danish Embassy, Dublin
Bent Brogaard, Deputy Consul General/Commercial
    Counselor, Chicago
John Jensen, Investment Advisor, Danish Consulate,
    Chicago
Gordon A. Johnson, Honorary Consul, Minneapolis
Anette Petersen, International Trade Advisor,
    Minnesota Trade Office

### Finland

Marja Guercin, Secretary for Public Affairs, Finnish
    Embassy, Washington, D.C.
Mirja Lepistö-Wilson, Minnesota Trade Office
Guy Lindström, Commercial Counselor, Finnish
    Embassy, Dublin
David J. Speer, Honorary Consul, Minneapolis

### France

Lynn Franklin
Jasmine Z. Keller, Honorary Consul (retired)
Anne Schmidt, French Embassy, Dublin
Daniel van Ossten Slingeland, Honorary Consul,
    Minneapolis

### Germany

Franz-Josef Dicken, German Embassy, Dublin
Brian V. Dougherty, Deputy Director, Berlin Economic
    Development Corporation, Boston
Joseph E. Hamilton, Honorary Consul, Minneapolis
John Henzel
Robert C. Holtze, Honorary Consul (retired)
Karin Nelson, International Trade Advisor, Minnesota
    Trade Office

### Greece

Aris and Cassandra Apostolou
Anna Machairidis, Cultural Counselor, Greek Embassy,
    Washington, D.C.
Christos Salamanis, First Secretary, Greek Embassy,
    Dublin

**Ireland**
Hugh Brady
Ronan Deignan, Executive Director, International
    Development Ireland Ltd.
Godfrey Fitzsimons
Elaine O'Donovan

**Italy**
Stefano Cacciaguera, Consul General, Chicago
Italian Cultural Institute, Chicago
Ester MacDermot, First Secretary, Italian Embassy,
    Dublin
Alfredo and Denise Maselli
Sarah Rockler, Honorary Consul, Minneapolis

**Luxembourg**
Pierre Gramegna, Consul General, San Francisco
Paul R. Heinerscheid, Honorary Consul, Minneapolis
Egide Thein, Consul General, New York

**The Netherlands**
Johanna Delwiche
Lyle D. Delwiche, Honorary Consul, St. Paul
Julius B.E. Rellum, Commercial Attaché, Netherlands
    Embassy, Dublin
Inkie Rutgers, International Trade Advisor, Minnesota
    Trade Office

**Norway**
Steinar Bryn
Bjarne Grindem, Consul General, Minneapolis
Lars Loberg, Vice Consul, Minneapolis
Carl Platou

**Portugal**
Maria Paula de Brito, Foreign Investment Manager,
    PortugueseTrade Commission, New York
Mary Noonan, Portuguese Embassy, Dublin
Rita Varela Silva, Cultural Department, Portuguese
    Embassy, Washington, D.C.

**Spain**
F. Ochoa de Olza, Counselor, Spanish Embassy, Dublin
Fernando Die Ortega, Commercial Counselor, Spanish
    Embassy Commercial Office, Chicago
Jose L. Sastre, Director, Industrial Products Department,
    Spanish Embassy Commercial Office, Chicago

**Sweden**
Wendell R. Anderson, Honorary Consul General,
    Minneapolis
Phyllis E. Bakke, Consul, Minneapolis
Catherina Henzel

**Switzerland**
Anne Abele, Swiss Embassy, Dublin
Curt Felix Schneider, Consul, Minneapolis

**Turkey**
The American-Turkish Friendship Council,
    Washington, D.C.
Toni M. Cross, Director, American Research Institute in
    Turkey, Ankara
Dennis Osman, Turkish Embassy, Dublin
Turkish Embassy, Washington, D.C.

**United Kingdom**
Ruth McKenna, British Embassy, Dublin
Frank and Mary Skillern
    **⁃England**
    John, Sylvia, Katie and Emma Marshall
    Stephen Morris, Director, The English Unit,
        Department of Trade and Industry, London
    **⁃Northern Ireland**
    Pauline Brown, Vice President, Industrial
        Development Board for Northern Ireland, Chicago
    Heidi Christensen, Industrial Development Board
        for Northern Ireland, Chicago

**Europe/General**
Kimberly S. Adams, Tonja Berg, George Crolick, Manfred H. Fiedler, Dayton Gilbert, John Giordano, Howard and Betsy Guthmann, Heidi M. Hansel, David and Kathy Hyduke, Proctor Jones, Jim Lupient, Mary Bader Papa, Lewis E. Russell, Sarah E. Seeley, Boake and Marion Sells, Tim Smith.

A special thank-you to Dermot Moore of Dublin, who has supported this project in many ways from its inception.

And to all the others who helped and encouraged me in ways large and small, my sincere thanks.

—*Mary Murray Bosrock*
*St. Paul, Minnesota*
*Summer 1993*

Translation services provided by Global Language Institute, a Minnesota-based organization. GLI offers intensive English as a Second Language and foreign language instruction to high school, university, and business executive students at its language schools in Minnesota, Wisconsin and Florida. For further information about GLI language programs, please contact:
Global Language Institute, Galtier Plaza, 366 Jackson St. Suite 403, St. Paul, MN 55101. Phone (612) 228-1836; Fax (612) 228-0471.

*Put Your Best Foot Forward*

# ii.
# INTRODUCTION

This is a book about survival—for our companies, for our economy and for the way of life they support.

To survive, we must be able to compete in a truly global economy, and to compete effectively we must understand more about other countries, other cultures, other ways of doing business.

There was a time when such intercultural understanding was a nicety, a luxury for the idle rich. No longer. The world has changed dramatically.

For nearly 40 years after World War II, the United States was the world's preeminent military, political and economic power. We were the unchallenged leader of the Free World and, with rare exceptions, we got what we wanted.

That began to change more than a decade ago with the emergence of Germany and Japan as

*To compete effectively we must understand more about other cultures and other ways of doing business.*

economic superpowers. The change continued with the rapid industrialization of several countries on the Pacific Rim and accelerated with the end of the cold war and the dissolution of the Soviet Union.

Suddenly, we find ourselves in a global arena in which strategic military power is less important and economic power more important, and in which we are only one of several major players— the largest, to be sure, but by no means dominant.

*To succeed in the new global economy, we must understand both our potential customers and potential competitors.*

As mightily as we yearn for the good old days, it's unlikely in the foreseeable future that any country will dominate world affairs and the world economy as the United States did in the years after the war.

We need to make up our minds that we can and will compete successfully in this new, interdependent global economy. That means understanding both our potential customers and our potential competitors and the cultures in which they're rooted.

Everyone accepts the reality of interdependence; the challenge is to understand how that reality affects each of us, our companies and the ways we do business abroad.

In Europe, for example, the powerful winds of economic change are not blowing away the differences of history, language, culture and work habits that have bound nations together for centuries.

On the contrary, as the European countries move toward an economic and political alliance in which they will share a common currency and legal structure and make many decisions collectively, it's becoming apparent that each country is trying harder than ever to preserve its individual identity.

In short, it's more important than ever to understand and respect each European country's unique culture. Ignoring cultural differences isn't innovative or clever; it's arrogant. And it's bad for business.

This book includes material all of us should know when interacting with people from a European culture—whether they are guests in our country or we are guests in theirs.

It's really just a matter of putting yourself in your European colleague's place. When you're the host, you expect your European guest to have at least a rudimentary knowledge of your country and customs; the more knowledgeable your guest, the more favorably you're impressed.

Europeans feel exactly the same way about you when you're a guest in their country. If you're ignorant of their country and culture, you create

*It's more important than ever to understand and respect each European country's unique culture.*

the impression that you're boorish or, worse, that you don't care enough about them to spend a little time learning about their country.

That's not the kind of first impression that leads to a good business relationship.

On the other hand, the more you know about the history, culture and customs of the country you're visiting—even a few words of the language—the more favorable the impression you'll make, and the better your chances of doing business there.

Knowing your audience will allow you to be more sensitive, have more fun and quickly move on to the purpose of your meeting. The information in this book will allow you to understand and be understood more easily. You will make mistakes, but they will be sensitive mistakes—mistakes made as a result of trying, not out of ignorance. Remember, it's better to make mistakes by trying than not to try at all.

## FORMAT

Everyone who reads this book is busy. I've attempted to respect your time by organizing the book into easily accessible sections divided by country and by behavior. These quick-reference chapters give you a snapshot of each country that allows you to find the information you need in a matter of moments.

Although it was designed primarily as a resource for businesspeople, the book should be equally helpful for leisure travelers, students, teachers, people in the travel and hospitality industry, and hosts who regularly entertain European visitors.

Keep this book on your desk or tuck it in your suitcase. Before you meet or talk with someone from one of the countries included, you can quickly learn or review important facts that will assist you in communicating clearly.

The information in this book isn't just "nice to know." It's vital to your success and that of your company if you want to do business in Europe or with Europeans. The information in this book can be translated into increased revenues and earnings for your company. What you learn in this book literally will go to the bottom line.

# iii.
# THE WORLD
# ACCORDING TO ME

Before you read one word of this book, please understand that it reflects my experiences as an international businessperson.

All of us personalize our observations no matter where we are in the world. A half-dozen people on a street corner in Dayton, Ohio, will tell six different stories about the traffic accident they just witnessed. A half-dozen people in Delhi will do the same.

In general, this book is based on my observations; I'm simply "telling it as I see it."

In particular, however, each country chapter has been researched not only through personal observation but also through meetings with people from that country: diplomats, doctors, lawyers, businesspeople, teachers and students. This is my attempt to convey to you what I have learned and what other people with a great deal of international experience have passed on to me as important.

*This book is based
on my own
observations...and
what other
experienced people
have passed on to
me as important.*

The behaviors discussed in Part I are
the first, simplest and most basic rules for
communicating with someone from another
culture. This information should allow you to
move beyond the superficial so you can more
quickly and easily get to the purpose of your
international meeting.

In Part II, we'll talk about some important
customs that apply pretty much across the
board in Europe.

And in Part III, you'll find country-by-country
specifics on communication and behavior in 18
European countries.

# iv.
# LETTER FROM EUROPE

*Over the past several years, as I've collected material for this book, I've asked a number of Europeans how they view Americans and what points they'd like to make to Americans who'll be visiting Europe. The following letter is a compilation of some of their more poignant comments.*

Dear American Friends,

You asked what we Europeans think about you Americans. Honestly, we like America and Americans. We admire many things about you. You are open, friendly, gregarious, generous, optimistic, freedom-loving, independent and filled with a "can do" spirit like no other people in the world.

We know you go to church, volunteer your time and talent for worthy causes and fight for equality for all your people—especially your handicapped. How could anyone not like you?

We also admire the society and the economy you have created. You are clearly leaders in the aerospace, biomedical, pharmaceutical and telecommunications industries. You have physicians and medical facilities that are among the best in the world—as evidenced by the number of leaders from around the globe who come to your clinics for care, both critical and routine.

Your universities are excellent. Many of the younger leaders who are shaping Europe's future have been educated in your undergraduate and business schools.

And, yes, we'd probably even admit that we've come to like the cars that American companies are manufacturing for us here in Europe. They look great, run well, and we find them an excellent value.

Having said all that, however, perhaps there are a few things we don't understand about you. You have some habits we find curious and annoying. You say you "love" objects—food, clothing, cars or music. You call everything "cute," from the Eiffel Tower to our dogs. You say "Have a good day" and "Let's get together for dinner" to everyone you meet, and apparently don't really mean either. You talk too loudly—in other words, we hear you coming and going.

Sometimes you compare Europe to America and say what you have is bigger, better, prettier, faster or more expensive than what we have. You are monolingual and seldom attempt to speak our languages when you visit us. Sometimes you are even irritated when we don't speak English perfectly.

You think friendship comes instantly, while we think it takes time to mature. You appear to respect only the new and the young, while dismissing the old and traditional.

Your culture has infiltrated ours with fast food, rock music, movies and television shows, and yet you know little or nothing about our countries' history, culture or people.

Of course, many of us have a distorted image of what America is really like. We form our opinions by watching "Falcon Crest," "Beverly Hills 90210," Sally Jesse Raphael and Oprah.

When you come here to do business, you generally come with excellent products, competitively priced. However, you expect to walk in, slap us on the back and sign a contract—all in one visit. If you understood a little more about us and our customs, you'd be aware that we want to know you personally before we do business with you. When we do get to know you, we almost always like you a lot.

*"You are monolingual...and sometimes are even irritated when we don't speak perfect English."*

When you visit us, if you'd like to blend in, please take off your baseball caps, tennis shoes, running suits and yellow balloon pants at least while you are in our cities.

Try our food, enjoy our landscapes (even if they may be less spectacular than yours), visit some of our great museums. We're proud of our homes, our countries and our traditions and would like them respected.

Please visit us, but please come informed and with an open mind.

Respectfully,

*Your European Friends*

P.S. We have washers, dryers, televisions, VCRs, mobile telephones and computers. While we cultivate some Old-World customs, we are a late-20th-century, computer-literate, modern and well-educated society. Many of us have a higher standard of living than our counterparts in the United States. We are not quaint, backward, simple people. You might even learn something from us.

*"We're proud of our homes, our countries and our traditions and would like them respected."*

PART

I

*How To Go
International*

*Put Your Best Foot Forward*

# TAX LAWS VARY FROM COUNTRY TO COUNTRY.

# BUT YOUR BUSINESS DOESN'T.

DOING BUSINESS ACROSS NATIONAL BORDERS IS BECOMING MORE AND MORE COMPLEX EACH DAY. SO TOO IS MAINTAINING A CONSISTENT OPERATING STRUCTURE.

TAXES ADD TO THE CHALLENGE. FOREIGN TAX RATES AND REGULATIONS VARY AMONG JURISDICTIONS, WHICH COMPLICATES PLANNING FOR CASH FLOW, RETURN ON INVESTMENT AND PROFITS, AS WELL AS INTERCOMPANY PRICING AND THE EFFICIENT USE OF FOREIGN TAX CREDITS.

ARTHUR ANDERSEN RECOGNIZES HOW IMPORTANT IT IS FOR YOUR MULTINATIONAL BUSINESS TO MAINTAIN UNIFORMITY. OUR EXPERIENCED PROFESSIONALS SHARE CENTRALIZED TRAINING AND A COMMON METHODOLOGY IN EVERY OFFICE IN EVERY COUNTRY WHERE WE PRACTICE. THE RESULT: SEAMLESS INTERNATIONAL TAX MANAGEMENT FOR YOUR BUSINESS.

BECAUSE TAX LAWS VARY FROM COUNTRY TO COUNTRY. YOUR BUSINESS DOESN'T.

*For more information, please call John Mott, partner in charge, International Tax and Business Advisory Services – Americas at (713) 237-2945.*

ARTHUR ANDERSEN & CO, SC

If you're wondering where in the world you'll find the most accommodating hotels on earth...

**THIS** and

**CHICAGO**
RADISSON PLAZA AMBASSADOR WEST

**THIS** and

**ALEXANDRIA**
(WASHINGTON, DC AREA)
RADISSON PLAZA HOTEL AT MARK CENTER

**THIS** and

**BERLIN**
RADISSON PLAZA HOTEL BERLIN

From Minneapolis to Moscow.

Miami to Melbourne (Australia,

mate). Our Yes I Can® style of

**THIS MUST BE THE PLACE.**

hospitality will put you on cloud

nine. One call to your travel agent

tells you this must be Radisson.

This must be the place.℠

**CAIRNS**
RADISSON PLAZA HOTEL AT THE PIER

# Radisson
HOTELS INTERNATIONAL

FOR RESERVATIONS WORLDWIDE

# 1.
# NEVER GENERALIZE

Never, never, never generalize! Each of the world's nearly 6 billion people is a unique individual. People can't be stereotyped.

That's what makes going international so much fun. Even though people look alike, speak the same language, eat similar food, practice the same religion and live in the same country, each and every person you meet will be different.

Just about the time you're tempted to put labels on people, you'll meet a gregarious Finn, a humorless Irishman, an inhibited Italian, a rude Englishman or a lethargic German—and all your rules will go right out the window. So never, never, never generalize!

I have sat in homes, shops, offices and embassies with people of the same nationality and listened to them debate a particular custom or behavior. Women disagreed with men, older

*Just about the time you're tempted to use stereotypes, you discover that each of the world's nearly 6 billion people is unique.*

people disagreed with younger ones, and sometimes there was general disagreement. Only rarely did such a group reach consensus.

Trying to describe human behavior is tricky at best. No two people behave in exactly the same way; perhaps even more important, no two people interpret others' behavior in the same way.

Does this make intercultural communication impossible for the ordinary business traveler? Certainly not! Although you'll probably never meet a Belgian or Swede with all of the qualities I describe, after a quarter century of experience in Europe, I feel comfortable saying that in general there are certain qualities, customs and characteristics you'll encounter in dealing with people from a particular country.

Can you survive without this knowledge? Of course you can. Can this information help you understand and feel more comfortable with Europeans? Can it help you avoid misunderstandings? Can it help you communicate clearly and effectively what you really want to say? You bet it can!

Exotic places and the sights and activities they offer have been the subject of hundreds of travel books, but relatively little has been written about the people who live in these places and how we can relate to them.

This book is an attempt to make your interaction with Europeans easier, more comfortable and more fun.  It is intended to get you over some of the first cultural hurdles so you can establish productive business relationships—and eventually, I hope, friendships as well.

There isn't a country I've worked or traveled in that I haven't enjoyed.  And regardless of how dynamic the business environment or how beautiful the countryside, it is always the people—tens and hundreds and thousands of individuals—who hold my interest and eventually win my heart.

*This book is an attempt to make your interaction with Europeans easier, more comfortable and more fun.*

# 2.
# THE UGLY AMERICAN

I have rarely met an "Ugly American"!

The term became widely known as the title of
a 1963 movie starring Marlon Brando, based
on a 1958 book by William Lederer and
Eugene Burdick about the ignorant and
incompetent U.S. ambassador to a fictional
Southeast Asian country. It quickly became
an epithet for rude, self-centered people who
roamed the world with utter disregard—even
disdain—for other cultures.

*Most Americans
I know aren't
ugly—they're just
uninformed.*

The Americans I know, work with and meet on
my travels are quite the opposite. They want
very much to understand and appreciate other
customs and cultures. They're just uninformed
—not ugly.

It isn't easy to understand other languages and
cultures. We share this planet with nearly 6
billion people who speak 6,000 different
languages.

In the United States, most of us can travel thousands of miles in several directions without encountering significant cultural or linguistic differences. Is it any wonder we find it a little difficult to adjust our thinking to the European scale, where a journey of even a few hundred miles can take you through several countries, cultures and languages?

Obviously, most of us don't have the time or ability to learn dozens of languages or to become intimately familiar with scores of cultures. So how do we get started in this business of intercultural communication? By being willing to make mistakes.

An ambassador I know says his wife always learns the language of a new country faster than he does. Why? Because she's not worried about making mistakes as she shops, tours, visits and dines. He, on the other hand—with an official position to uphold—never speaks the language unless he's certain that he'll be correct.

There's a lesson in that story for all of us. We've got to be willing to take a chance—to make a mistake. It's important to understand that there are good mistakes and bad mistakes. Good mistakes are those that say clearly in any language, "I care, I'm trying, I'm sorry if I got it wrong." Sensitive imperfection can be endearing.

The high-water mark of American prestige in the postwar era probably came as a result of one of these good mistakes. President John F. Kennedy stood at the Berlin Wall in 1963 and said, *"Ich bin ein Berliner"* (I am a Berliner). The German people roared their approval.

After the event, it was noted that *ein Berliner* is a doughnut in Berlin. In proper German, the president would have said, *"Ich bin Berliner."* It was a mistake, but an inspired mistake. It said, "I, the president of the most powerful country in the world, care enough to try speaking your language." A good mistake? A great mistake!

Then there are bad mistakes—the ones that shout, "I don't care, I won't try and I'm not one bit sorry if I don't understand you." These are the mistakes that give us all a black eye—the ones we should never make.

For example, a member of the U.S. Congress traveled to Moscow in the winter of 1992— the worst winter many Russians had experienced since World War II. Food was scarce and people waited in long lines for everything. Fuel for heating and automobiles was nearly impossible to get.

*Sensitive imperfection can be endearing.*

Much to the shock of our representative's host (yes, he was representing us) and to the horror of his escorts, he complained because he couldn't get his bacon and eggs for breakfast! A bad mistake? You bet!

Approach going abroad as if you are being invited to your boss' home for a party, assuming you would like a raise or promotion. If you enter a host country with this attitude, you'll be sensitive, well dressed, bring an appropriate gift and take the time to learn the customs and behaviors that will make you a gracious guest.

*Put Your Best Foot Forward—Europe* invites you to a party. Please come! Europe is your host. Welcome—and don't be afraid to make a few mistakes.

# 3.

# CONSIDERATION

Consideration and respect are the qualities you most need to be a successful internationalist. Every behavior suggested in this book is, in essence, considerate and thoughtful. It is so easy! You can't go wrong if you always ask yourself, "Are my actions considerate?"

Most dictionaries define *considerate* as "having regard for the needs or feelings of others." It's interesting to think about how that word was derived from *consider,* one definition of which is "to examine, study, deliberate upon."

*"You see, but you don't observe."*

*—Sherlock Holmes*

It's clear in this context that examining, studying and preparing are what consideration is all about. You can't be considerate of others— especially in another culture— without taking the time to learn.

Doing your homework before you visit a new country is essential, but once you're on the ground, there are important ways to keep learning. Here are some of them:

**Observe** what the local people are doing. This is one of the safest and easiest ways to establish appropriate behavior. Quietly watch what others wear, how they greet each other, how they eat. Follow their example, and you'll usually be correct.

**Ask** whenever communication or expected behavior is unclear. Ask your host or business associate, the concierge at the hotel, a clerk in a shop. Ask quietly and politely. You may feel a little foolish at first, but people will appreciate that you're trying to learn.

Here are the kinds of things you'll want to ask if they're not absolutely clear:

- What is the expected attire for an event?

- What is the proper pronunciation of a name?

- What tip is expected?

- What is an appropriate gift for the occasion?

- What is the proper way of wrapping and presenting the gift?

- What flowers are appropriate for an occasion?

*"Consideration for others separates civilized man from the savage."*

*—Emily Post*

- When and where may I smoke?

- What time does an invitation really mean?

**Listen** actively and aggressively. Write down what you hear. When a person says his or her name, listen carefully to the pronunciation. Write down the phonetic pronunciation of the name. Listen for the title used.

In meetings or presentations, listen intently to what your hosts are saying, and take careful notes. You're sending them a signal that you're taking them seriously.

If they're speaking in English as a courtesy to you, remember that they may be speaking in their second or third language. This may require a little extra listening effort on your part. If you get impatient, just think about how well you'd be expressing yourself in *your* second or third language.

If there are ambiguities—linguistic or otherwise—ask politely for clarification. It's much better to ask a question than to risk misunderstanding.

At social functions, pay careful attention to what local people are saying to you and to each other. You'll learn a lot of things about their country and culture that will come in handy in future conversations, and you'll have many opportunities to ask informed questions.

Genuine interest is always appreciated.

We can learn a lot about appropriate behavior by observing, asking and listening. But especially in another culture, the ultimate learning technique is *trial and error*. We've got to be willing to *try* new things, and we've got to be willing to make our share of errors.

**Try** to speak a few words of someone's language, to taste the local food, to greet people properly, to learn others' behaviors, and you'll already be a success. To *try* is to show our vulnerability, our humanity.

Believe me, *trying* covers a multitude of errors! We all make mistakes when communicating in our own culture, so we certainly cannot expect to be perfect when communicating in someone else's. Remember, perfect is boring anyway! You never need to try for perfection—you just need to *try*.

When we *try*, people understand that we're taking a risk, that we're making a special effort to reach out to them. They give us credit both for being willing to take the risk and for being willing to make the effort.

On such credit are new friendships—and new business relationships—built.

# 4.
# RULES OF THUMB
## THE TEN COMMANDMENTS
## OF GOING INTERNATIONAL

1. Do your homework!

2. Ask, look and listen. You will be amazed what you learn.

3. Try! It is better to try and make a mistake than not to try at all.

4. When a problem develops, assume miscommunication was the cause.

5. Be patient. It generally takes much more time and effort to accomplish your goals in another country and culture.

6. Assume the best about people and their actions. Most people do what seems appropriate to them based upon their learned values, habits and traditions.

7. Always be sincere. It shows!

8. Keep your sense of humor.

9. Make people like you. Likability is the "magic wand." If people like you, they will forgive just about anything you might do wrong.

10. Smile.

> *Likability is achieved by sincere behavior and by showing a genuine interest in and concern for other people.*

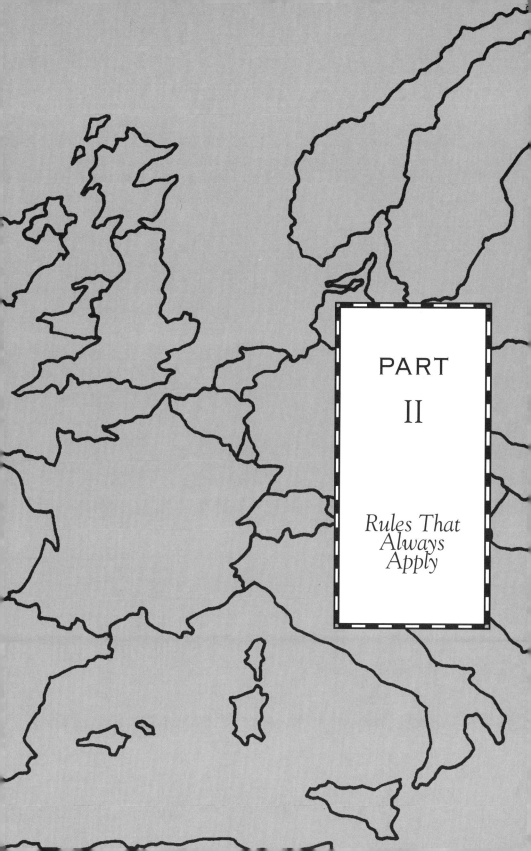

# PART

# II

*Rules That
Always
Apply*

# 5.
# VITAL STATISTICS

In 1985, the National Geographic Society commissioned the Gallup pollsters to find out how much Americans know about the world. One in five polled couldn't name a single country in Europe. One in four couldn't find the Pacific Ocean on a map, three of four couldn't find the Persian Gulf and 14 percent couldn't even find the United States.

The most common negative comment made in other countries about Americans is that we're ethnocentric. Americans often appear to know nothing about anyone, anywhere else in the world; even worse, they don't demonstrate much interest in learning.

Succeeding in the international arena doesn't require an M.B.A., foreign language training or cross-border experience. But it does require having respect for the people you deal with—and respect means taking the time necessary to develop at least a basic knowledge of your host

*"Judge a man by his questions rather than his answers."*

*—Voltaire*

Rule of Thumb

*Do your homework so you can ask sensitive, informed questions.*

country and the way your hosts live. Not knowing these fundamental facts is not only ignorant but also arrogant.

When visiting a country, please know the:

- President or prime minister's name.
- Political system.
- Language spoken.
- Official name of the country.
- The collective name for its people.

| A MAJOR GAFFE | *The Irish are irked when Americans ask (as they often do), "How do you like your new prime minister, Mr. Major?" Mr. Major is prime minister of the United Kingdom.* |
| --- | --- |

| COLD-WAR SHOULDER | *At a dinner party during the cold-war era, my dinner partner—a graduate of an elite East Coast university—asked, "Does your husband feel comfortable representing a Communist country?"*<br><br>*My husband represents Austria, a multiparty democracy with a market economy, as an honorary consul general. How do you answer that question diplomatically?* |
| --- | --- |

# 6.
# MEETING AND GREETING

The first impression is powerful! A good first impression creates the expectation of a positive relationship. A bad first impression, on the other hand, can be overcome only with a lot of work over a long period of time—and sometimes we don't get that chance.

Think about your own response to new people, especially in the work environment. Within a few minutes—maybe even seconds—most of us have developed a "gut feeling" about whether a new relationship will be positive or negative.

When you've traveled thousands of miles to develop a new business relationship, you need to make the best possible impression in those critical first few minutes.

Your chances of creating a good first impression improve enormously if you've done your homework. Knowing what initial behaviors you'll encounter when meeting a person or group allows you to relax and project a positive attitude.

*"You never get a second chance to make a first impression."*
—Anonymous

Rule of Thumb

*The American handshake, toned down a bit, is accepted worldwide.*

You'll also be well served by restraint, common sense and good taste. The "Well, I am here, folks" or "How y'all doing?" greeting combined with a knuckle-breaking, arm-pumping handshake is not common in other parts of the world and not likely to get a relationship off to a good start. It is much more acceptable to show a polite reserve combined with an open and friendly attitude.

### GENERAL RULES
### FOR MEETING AND GREETING

- Most Europeans shake hands with everyone present when arriving and again when leaving.

- Be prepared to give and receive a lighter, less firm handshake in many countries.

- Always remove gloves before shaking hands.

- Never shake hands with one hand in your pocket.

- Always use last names until you're invited to use first names.

- In some countries, gentlemen kiss a woman's hand when meeting. Women should accept this greeting graciously; never giggle or act self-conscious. *Visiting foreign men, on the other hand, should **never** attempt to kiss the hands of host-country women.*

# 7.
# NAMES AND TITLES
## "JUST CALL ME BILL"

For Europeans, a person's name and title express or imply a wealth of information about family history, education, profession, reputation and personal achievement.

In Europe, don't use first names until explicitly invited to do so by your host. The United States is definitely a "first name" country. We shift from last names to first names almost on first meeting. We consider it warm, comfortable and friendly to do so. We think everyone else would like to do the same. Europeans definitely do not! It is not a "Just call me Bill" world.

Asking most Europeans to call you by your first name is like inviting them to take their shirt off at your dinner table. First names make them feel uncomfortable. They seldom address each other by first names—even among close friends of long

*"You can't help but like someone who remembers your name, uses it often and pronounces it correctly."*

—Anonymous

standing. They do not want to call you by your first name, and they don't want you to call them by theirs.

For Americans who have been reared with a "Just call me Bill" attitude, the concern much of the world has about names and titles seems superficial. If this is your attitude, change it! In Europe, proper use or misuse of someone's name and/or title can make the difference between a successful negotiation and an international incident. That's just the way it is. Correct use of a person's name and title shows respect; incorrect use is an insult.

Correct use of names and titles is one of the most complicated and difficult things for an international traveler—even an experienced one—to learn. Many specifics vary from country to country. However, it's worth making the effort. Not only does it show consideration of your hosts, but you'll win friends and influence people. Here are some general rules that will help.

### GENERAL RULES FOR USING NAMES AND TITLES

- Do not use first names until invited to do so or until the other person repeatedly uses your first name.

- Do your homework. Know the correct rules of name usage in each country.

- Ask for a business card so you can see the correct spelling and correct title.

- Listen to the pronunciation of the name when you're introduced to someone. Ask for a name to be repeated if you didn't hear it.

- Ask each person by what name he or she prefers to be addressed.

- As soon as possible, jot down the phonetic pronunciation of a name.

- Err on the side of formality.

- When in doubt, use a title.

- If uncertain about the correct title, use a higher title but **never** a lesser title.

- Help the introducer or host with your name.

- Say your name slowly and pronounce it clearly.

Americans have plenty of status symbols. We judge each other by where we went to school, how big our houses are and what kinds of cars we drive, among other things. Many Europeans are less concerned with money and material possessions than are Americans, but their family history, social rank and educational level are all wrapped up in their names and titles. Their names and titles are a source of pride to them; foreign visitors need to realize that understanding and respecting this tradition is essential to doing business in Europe.

Just think of it as "The Comfort Zone." If your aim is to make your hosts comfortable—and amenable to doing business—respect their cultural comfort zone when it comes to using names and titles.

| ABOUT FORMALITY | *Many of my Austrian friends, whom I have known for 15 years, still refer to me and address me as "Mrs. Bosrock." Many of my Irish friends have referred to me and addressed me as "Mary" since we first met. It says nothing about the importance or sincerity of our friendship, only about their cultures and customs.* |
|---|---|

## A PRIMER:
## COUNTRY/PEOPLE/LANGUAGE

Once you've mastered your hosts' names and titles, the next hurdle is learning the proper use of the country's name and the ways its people are referred to collectively. Know and use the correct names of both.

| COUNTRY | PEOPLE | LANGUAGE |
|---|---|---|
| Austria | Austrians | German |
| Belgium | Belgians | |
| -Wallonia | -Walloons | French |
| -Flanders | -Flemings | Flemish/Dutch |
| Denmark | Danes | Danish |
| Finland | Finns | Finnish |
| France | French | French |
| Germany | Germans | German |
| Greece | Greeks | Greek |
| Ireland | Irish | English/Irish |
| Italy | Italians | Italian |
| Luxembourg | Luxembourgers | Luxembourgish/ French/German |
| Netherlands | Dutch/Netherlanders | Dutch |
| Norway | Norwegians | Norwegian |
| Portugal | Portuguese | Portuguese |
| Spain | Spanish/Spaniards | Spanish |
| Sweden | Swedes | Swedish |
| Switzerland | Swiss | French/German/ Italian/Romansch |
| Turkey | Turks | Turkish |
| United Kingdom | British | English |
| -England | -British/English | English |
| -Scotland | -Scots | English/Gaelic |
| -Wales | -Welsh | English/Welsh |
| -Northern Ireland | -Northern Irish | English |

## DIPLOMATIC TITLES

Finally, here's a short list of diplomatic titles common to the embassies of most countries, along with written forms of address and salutations:

| TITLE AND FORM OF ADDRESS | SALUTATION |
| --- | --- |
| **Ambassador** | |
| His/Her Excellency (name) The Ambassador of (country) | Excellency: (or) Dear Mr./Madame Ambassador: |
| **Chargé d'Affaires** | |
| The Honorable (name) Chargé d'Affaires of (country) | Dear Sir/Madame: |
| **Minister** | |
| The Honorable (name) The Minister of (country) | Dear Sir/Madame: Dear Mr./Madame Minister: |
| **Consul General** | |
| The Honorable (name) Consul General of (country) | Dear Mr./Ms.(name): |
| **Consul** | |
| The Honorable (name) Consul of (country) | Dear Mr./Ms.(name): |

In conversation, ambassadors may be addressed as "Excellency," as "Mister (or Madame) Ambassador," or simply as "Ambassador." In conversation, all other diplomatic personnel may be addressed simply as "Mister" or "Ms."

# 8.
# LANGUAGE
# AND BODY LANGUAGE

Language is a great gift! It is given not only with your mouth but with your eyes, your hands and your body. It is your initial act of sharing yourself. It is the best way to win friends for yourself, your country and your company. This is where you shout, "I care about you, your country and your culture."

To learn another's language is the greatest of compliments. The warmth, appreciation and welcome you will receive in return is incomparable. You will be richly rewarded. Nothing bespeaks your interest and concern more than taking the time to learn someone's language.

Realistically, however, most of us don't have the time to learn other languages fluently. What language would we learn if we did? The European Community alone has nine official languages. Americans are lucky! Due in part to Britain's earlier influence and in part to our postwar success, English is the second language in much of the world.

*"What you are speaks so loudly, I can't hear what you say."*

*—Ralph Waldo Emerson*

Rule of Thumb

*Attempt to speak the language of your host country, even if you can only manage a few polite phrases.*

Let's say you've just scheduled a business trip to Europe, and there's no time to become fluent in the languages of countries you'll be visiting—but you do care and don't want to appear arrogant.

What's the best approach? Learn a few simple, polite phrases—enough to show you are trying. Remember, trying counts and mistakes made while trying are good mistakes. When you speak at least a few words of another person's language, you're showing interest, effort and a positive attitude toward the people and their country.

Learn how to greet and thank your hosts in their language. Learn a short toast. It doesn't have to be perfect; the effort will be greatly appreciated.

When your hosts speak English as a courtesy to you, remember that English is usually their second or third language. To avoid misunderstandings:

- Speak slowly.

- Speak clearly.

- Use the simplest words possible.

- Never assume the listener understands your meaning; if there's any doubt, repeat what you said in a slightly different way.

- Never use slang terms, idioms, sports analogies or colloquialisms. Some examples of phrases not to use:

  -"I was tickled to death."

  -"We've got you covered."

  -"You can count on it."

  -"I got a kick out of it."

  -"We're batting a thousand."

- Leave room for error.

- Always be patient.

- Never jump to conclusions.

- Assume the best.

## USING INTERPRETERS

You've hired an interpreter. Your communication problems are solved, right? Watch out! Your problems may just be starting.

Clear communication of ideas in a business negotiation is difficult, even when the parties share a common tongue. When business is conducted in more than one language, misunderstandings cannot be avoided. Effective use of your interpreter is crucial to clear communication.

*"Your communications are as good or as poor as your interpreter's abilities."*

*—International business traveler*

Rule of Thumb

*Never assume communication has been clear and accurate. Always check and double-check.*

Here are some tips for using an interpreter:

- Ask your interpreter to advise you on expected meeting style—punctuality, preliminary small talk, getting down to the major issues, identity of key counterparts.

- Discuss with your interpreter in advance the subject of the meetings and the main points you plan to make.

- Look at and address your remarks to your counterpart, not the interpreter.

- Take your time; speak slowly and clearly.

- Keep language simple and direct.

- Pause frequently to allow for interpretation—after every verbal "paragraph" and, when the subject matter is especially important or complicated, after every sentence.

- Ask questions as your discussions proceed.

- Get feedback.

- Repeat main points.

- Assume your counterparts can understand English, even if they're using an interpreter; never say anything you don't want others to hear.

- Follow up with a written summary of what was said and agreed.

*Then:* In November 1956, at the height of the cold war between the United States and the Soviet Union, Nikita Khrushchev, at a reception for Western ambassadors in Moscow, said, "We will bury you." The Free World was shocked. Bomb shelters were constructed in private homes, the defense budget soared, schoolchildren practiced air raid procedures, and that quote was repeated over and over.

That statement once struck fear in the heart of every American. But what Khrushchev really meant was, "We will surpass you economically." The interpreter translated it as, "We will bury you." Was that a small communication error?

*Now:* At the April 1993 U.S.-Russia Summit in Vancouver, British Columbia, the relationship between presidents Boris Yeltsin and Bill Clinton nearly broke down over the misunderstanding of a pronoun. In their conversation regarding what the United States could do for Russia, President Clinton insisted on allocating each task to the vice president. President Yeltsin grew visibly upset as the translator continuously whispered in his ear the delegation of duties to the vice president. Finally, President Yeltsin announced his objection to assigning these important projects to his vice president and bitter rival, Aleksandr Rutskoi. The tension in the room relaxed after President Clinton explained that the problem was only in the translation—that the assignments were to be handled by Vice President Al Gore. (New York Times, April 5, 1993)

*"We will bury you."*

*—Erroneous translation of a remark by Nikita Khrushchev*

## BODY LANGUAGE

Eye contact, posture, where we put our hands, our feet, our arms, our legs, all send messages—positive or negative—to other people. We misread these signals constantly within our own culture. Can you imagine the mixed signals we can send and receive when dealing with another culture?

Behavioral scientists say there are 700,000 non-verbal signals given through body language. What one person views as proper behavior, another may consider an affront.

Surely, you say, there must be some common ground. How about the smile? It's the universally understood gesture. Not quite. By all means, smile. Smiling warms up any environment. However, be aware that your smile may not be returned; in some cultures, people don't smile at strangers. Also, the smile has different meanings in different cultures. It can be a coverup for embarrassment, confusion or anger. In some cultures, smiling at a person of the opposite sex may be interpreted as a "come-on" or an invitation. So even a smile can be misunderstood.

Rule of Thumb

*Never make assumptions or judgments based on the body language of someone from another culture.*

## GENERAL BODY LANGUAGE RULES

- Never mimic anyone's behavior.

- Never mimic what you think is a national gesture.

- Never slap people on the back.

- Don't display affection in public.

- Don't put your hands in your pockets.

- Cover your mouth when you yawn.

- Don't beckon someone with your index finger.

This matter of body language applies in reverse, too. The EuroDisney theme park outside Paris has been beset by problems, including some with their roots in cultural differences. The names of several attractions seemed to lose their magic when translated into French. And some observers have cited the difficulty of training European young people in the American style of service.

European youths, well-trained in manners and deportment, did and said everything correctly, but their body language was off. Disney likes to project the image of young people having fun while they deliver service with a smile, while many of these young people were reared in a culture where a cool and reserved attitude is the proper behavior toward strangers, especially adults. How do you teach a person to smile, to be enthusiastic, perky and cheery? The words are easy to learn, the body language more difficult.

And finally, a related matter: Don't be loud. A persistent criticism of Americans all around the world is that we're too loud and boisterous. Cultivate a moderate tone and volume in speaking with Europeans.

## TOUCHING

We all know the Italians, Greeks and Spanish are touchers. The English and Scandinavians are non-touchers. So why should you never touch?

Touching is a behavior reserved for friends and family members in almost all cultures. Touchers hug and kiss their children, spouses and close friends of the same or the opposite sex. They generally do *not* touch or want to be touched by strangers, people they meet occasionally, new business associates or new acquaintances.

As you establish a relationship with European associates, try to be sensitive to the dos and don'ts of touching in their particular culture. If a colleague or friend gives you a hug or a kiss on the cheek, to reject this touch could be just as offensive as touching too soon.

Faux Pas

*Do not initiate touching with anyone, anywhere, at any time, for any reason until a clearly understood friendship has been established.*

*In the spring of 1992, Queen Elizabeth of England
visited Atlanta and a friendly, vivacious woman
welcomed the monarch to her home by putting an
arm on the queen's back as a gesture of warmth
and friendship. Months of preparation and the
many positive aspects of the visit were almost
ignored because of a single, well-intentioned—but
inappropriate—gesture. The headline story of the
queen's visit to Atlanta, especially in Britain, was
"The Touch."*

The rule is *do not touch* anyone (except for a
handshake) when you first meet.

However, *expect* a hug, kiss or touch after a
relationship is established in:

- Greece.
- Italy.
- Portugal.
- Spain.

Do *not* expect hugs, kisses or touches in:

- Belgium.
- Denmark.
- England.
- Finland.
- Norway.
- Scotland.
- Sweden.
- Switzerland (except the Italian region).
- Wales.

Expect that some people will and some won't give hugs, kisses or touches in:

- France.
- Ireland.
- Switzerland (the Italian region).

## COMMON GESTURES
## WITH UNCOMMON MEANINGS

Rule of Thumb

*Do not make any gestures.*

Many gestures have different meanings in different countries. What may be appropriate in one country may be rude or have a completely different meaning in another. Such gestures include the OK sign, the forward-and-back head nod, the thumbs-up gesture and even a seemingly innocuous wave.

Because gestures can so easily be misunderstood, the best approach is to avoid them entirely if at all possible. Alternatively, check in advance on the local meaning of any gestures you consider absolutely essential to your business.

# 9.

# DINING/ENTERTAINING

Food—how you eat it and how you react to it—is essential to the art of diplomacy. Your behavior at the table also is one of the quickest ways to make or lose foreign friends.

When your hosts offer you a food that's a local delicacy or a national specialty, they are offering you a sample of their culture as well as their friendship.

They are giving you the best they have, and if you reject it, you are rejecting them, their culture and their friendship. This is not an auspicious way to begin a mutually beneficial relationship. So...

What's on your plate may swim, crawl, fly or look at you. Never mind! Taste it—you may even like it. If you don't, eat a reasonable portion anyway. I have eaten dozens of exotic dishes all around the world—a number of

*"What you put into your mouth may taste bad, but what comes out of your mouth may be in bad taste."*

—Anonymous

Rule of Thumb

*Food offered is friendship offered. To reject food is to reject friendship.*

which, I freely admit, I wouldn't choose to have in my own home—and I'm still here to write about it. What's more, I still enjoy eating. Eat what you're served. You'll survive, too, and eating those brains or that tongue just might seal the big deal.

## GENERAL EUROPEAN DINING/ENTERTAINING RULES

- Wait for your host to designate your seat at the table and invite you to be seated.

- Never begin eating until your hostess has begun.

- Never put your elbows on the table.

- Rest your hands and wrists on the table— never in your lap.

- Follow individual country rules regarding toasting and tasting.

- Sorbet or sherbet may be offered between courses to cleanse the palate.

- In many European countries, the salad is served after the main course.

- Each country has different rules for leaving food on your plate or eating everything served. It is not only polite but sometimes essential to your stomach to check these ahead of time.

- Never smoke at the table without asking permission of your host and other guests.

- Always write a thank-you note promptly.

## THE ART OF
## NOT EATING—POLITELY

If you have a weak stomach or really dislike the food served in a particular country, here are some helpful hints:

- Take a big gulp of the pink stuff (Pepto-Bismol) before you go to dinner.

- Prepare yourself mentally for the unexpected.

- Never ask what a dish is until you've finished eating it.

- Cut food into small bites.

- Don't chew particularly unpleasant food, just swallow fast. Sometimes the consistency is worse than the taste.

- Taste everything, and try to eat at least a little of it. If you truly can't eat something, a taste is polite.

- Never make a negative comment, joke or face about what is served.

- Engage in conversation with your dinner partners; it will get your mind off the food and take up time until the next course is served.

- When offered seconds of something you don't like, say "Thank you, but let me finish this portion first." Eat slower and talk more.

By and large, the food we're offered in other countries is marvelous and most of us find the major challenge of eating and drinking abroad is to limit our intake.

Be aware of the number of courses served in Europe. Pace your eating. Many of us have gotten caught thinking an appetizer was the main course. By the time the main course arrived, we were too full to eat it. The courses of a full European dinner may include soup, fish or pasta, meat, salad, cheese and fruit, and dessert.

### FORMAL DINING, EUROPEAN STYLE

Continental Style: The fork is held in the left hand, tines facing down. The knife is held in the right hand. The knife is used to cut and push food onto your fork.

- All silverware is arranged with the utensil to be used first laid on the outside, farthest from the plate (remember, the main course is often served before the salad).

- The butter knife is laid on the butter plate.

- Forks are always placed to the left of the plate. Spoons and knives are always placed to the right of the plate.

- If a fork is placed to the right of the spoons, it is a cocktail fork.

- Dessert silverware is brought on as dessert is served—or, in some countries, laid at the top of the plate.

- If your knife and fork are in any way open on your plate, it means that you would like more food or that you are not yet finished eating.

- When finished eating, place your knife and fork side by side on plate at the 5:25 position.

## FOR LESS FORMAL MEALS

- A bread and butter plate often is not used. Place bread directly on the table above your fork.

- Butter is usually served only with breakfast.

- In a restaurant, there may be a charge for each piece of bread and/or butter.

## TOASTING AT HOME AND ABROAD

If possible, make a toast in your host's or guest's language. Even if it isn't perfect, it will be enjoyed and appreciated by your foreign colleague.

- Make your toast short.

- An accompanying story (in English) is generally appreciated.

- Don't tell jokes— they seldom cross cultural lines.

- Use toasts to establish a closer, friendlier relationship.

- Enjoy toasting and being toasted. It is an offer of friendship.

## ENTERTAINING FOREIGN GUESTS

There is no place like home. Your city's best restaurants cannot compare to an invitation to your home. Visitors always enjoy seeing how you live, how you decorate your home, what music and art you enjoy and, especially, meeting your family. An invitation to your home is a special event not soon forgotten by your guests.

Some points to remember:

- Check for dietary restrictions.

- Serve American-style food.

- Avoid (huge) American-sized servings of beef. Most Europeans (and others, too) eat much smaller portions of meat than we do.

- Do not offer guests a tour of private areas of your home; they'll be more comfortable in "public" rooms like the living room, dining room and den.

- Always ask your guests if there is a particular event they would like to experience while in your city. Some suggested events:

  -Picnic or barbecue.

  -Baseball or American football game (if they like sports).

  -Concert or theater.

  -Museums.

  -Shopping.

  -Hiking.

  -Seeing local sights.

  -Boating or sailing.

  -Golf or tennis.

# 10.
# TIPPING

Americans are among the most generous people on earth. When Americans visit another country and throw money at service people, they're trying to be kind and appreciative, not abrasive or arrogant. But they often create the impression that they're boorishly flaunting their wealth—or worse, trying to take over the country!

Even people without material wealth have a sense of personal worth, and that sense can be violated by a tip that's inappropriately large or small.

Waiters and waitresses in Europe are generally professionals, not students working part time to pay their way through school. They consider what they're doing a career or profession, and they're proud of it. That makes tipping serious business.

*"Overtipping and undertipping are equally offensive. Both are in bad taste."*

*—European concierge*

Rule of Thumb

*Ask a local colleague or the concierge in your hotel whom to tip and how much.*

Tip too little, and a service person is likely to feel cheated out of fair compensation for his or her work. Tip too much, and a service person can feel like you're making him or her a charity case. But if you tip fairly and appropriately, it will be appreciated without being demeaning.

The key is to know both local customs and the value of what you're giving. Not only do rules for tipping vary from country to country, but inflation, fluctuating currency exchange rates and rapidly changing local attitudes all affect appropriate tipping.

Although the country information chapters in Part III of this book give guidelines for tipping, it is crucial to ask a local colleague or the concierge in your hotel for the current tipping practice. This simple step can save you considerable embarrassment—possibly in the presence of the local businesspeople you're trying to impress.

Most hotels and restaurants in Europe include a service charge of 10 to 20 percent. You may leave 5 percent extra if the service is exceptional, but it isn't mandatory. You look silly if you leave more.

That being said, it's worth noting that service personnel in hotels and restaurants that cater primarily to an American clientele may have come to expect somewhat larger tips.

If someone has performed an exceptional service for you, discreetly place a reasonable amount of money in an envelope and give it quietly to the person.

*Put Your Best Foot Forward*

# 11.
# MANNERS

As prehistoric people began to interact with one another, according to *World Book Encyclopedia*, they learned to behave in ways that made life easier and more pleasant.

The manners that developed had a practical purpose. For example, when two men met, they extended their right hands—and eventually shook them—to show that they were not carrying weapons. A handshake served as a display of friendship, or at least to demonstrate a lack of hostility.

Although the manners used in much of the Western world have common antecedents, they have evolved in different ways in different places. The following are some general guidelines on European manners; country-specific information is included in each of the country chapters in Part III.

*"Do unto others as you would have others do unto you."*

—*The Golden Rule*

Rule of Thumb

*If in doubt, ask, look or listen before acting.*

# EUROPEAN MANNERS GUIDELINES

- Quiet, modest behavior is always appreciated.

- Never meet, greet or talk to someone with your hands in your pockets.

- Humor is very local. It is best to avoid "telling a joke."

- Do not chew gum in public.

- Always use "please" and "thank you"—in the local language if possible.

- Never put your feet on furniture.

- Do not eat while walking in the streets.

- Show respect for others' habits and customs.

- Do not talk about money—yours or theirs.

- Do not point or beckon with your index finger.

- Do not ask for a tour of someone's home.

- Never wander uninvited into the "private" rooms of someone's home.

- Respect the privacy and dignity of others at all times; when in doubt, put yourself in their place.

- Never issue an invitation unless you genuinely intend to follow up with a specific time and date. This is quite different from the U.S. custom, where we casually say "Let's have lunch sometime" with no intention (or obligation) of following through.

## GETTING TO KNOW YOU

There is no better way to get to know and like people than to engage in a warm and friendly conversation. Most Europeans enjoy asking questions about America and most will be very well informed about current events in the United States.

Certain subjects are excellent icebreakers and will give you an opportunity to get acquainted and learn at the same time.

Holidays (as they call vacations) are a great source of pleasure and pride to Europeans. They like to travel to interesting places and enjoy sharing their experiences.

## SOME OTHER GOOD TOPICS OF CONVERSATION

- Food and wine.

- Art and music.

- Sports (European): Read the sports pages of the local paper if possible; at least know something about the local teams. Europeans are avid sports fans.

- Cars.

- Politics: Ask questions but never make a judgmental statement about their political system or a particular politician.

## DO NOT DISCUSS

- Salary.

- Where someone lives.

- Marital status.

- Educational level.

## USING THE TELEPHONE

Always ask before you use anyone's phone in an office or home. In many countries there is a charge for each local call as well as for long distance. Offer to pay any charges incurred as a result of your calls.

## SMOKING ETIQUETTE

Attitudes toward smoking are changing worldwide. While people in Europe continue to smoke in large numbers—proportionately larger than in the U.S.—many Europeans are increasingly aware of the health hazards associated with smoking and increasingly reluctant to subject themselves to secondhand smoke. The circumstances under which smoking is considered appropriate are changing. Always err on the side of consideration for your European hosts or colleagues.

# 12.
# THANK-YOU NOTES

Although the thank-you note was once a cornerstone of American civility, it's a custom that has fallen into widespread disuse in our society. In Europe, it continues to be a hallmark of culture and consideration.

The thank-you note, while not necessarily expected by your European hosts, will be appreciated by any host or gift-giver. Europeans generally phone to thank someone but always find a note especially nice. If they are potential customers or business partners whose opinion of you is important, you'll find it's well worth a few minutes to write a thank-you note.

## HELPFUL HINTS
## FOR THANK-YOU NOTES

- Write a prompt thank-you note to anyone who is your host for dinner, who entertains you, or who gives you a gift.

- Take your personal stationery with you when you travel, and try to write thank-you notes before you leave your host's country.

- Include a personal thought about the gift given or event attended.

- When you next write or see the giver, mention and wear or display the gift. For example, wear a scarf to your next meeting with the giver, or display a crystal bowl prominently in your home when the giver visits.

## REASONS FOR PROMPT THANK-YOU NOTES

- A thank-you received soon after the gift is received or the event attended shows genuine appreciation.

- The mailing of a note within the country is far less expensive than international postage from home.

- The memories of an event are vivid and can be recalled in detail when writing a note shortly after an event.

- The correct name, address and spelling are more likely to be at hand immediately after the event—and can be checked, if necessary, before you leave the country.

- Best of all, when you return home and your desk is piled high with work, you won't have a long list of thank-you notes to write!

# 13.
# DRESS

Dressing appropriately and attractively has two rewards. First, our appearance can and should say to our host that we have made an effort; it creates an opportunity to project what we are on the inside.

Second, and perhaps more important, we often behave like we think we look. There is no worse feeling than "sticking out"—calling attention to ourselves because we don't conform to local standards and expectations. It makes us uncomfortable and we generally project that discomfort to others, undermining the very impression we're trying to create with potential partners and customers.

Europeans do make judgments based on appearance and clothing. How you dress is seen as an indicator of your personality and social status.

*"When in doubt, dress up rather than down for any occasion."*

*—Anonymous*

Rule of Thumb

*Dress so as not to offend or stand out. Cover up what is inappropriate to expose.*

Europeans expect us to dress like Americans—within certain bounds of taste and judgment. So dress like an American—an American with classic, conservative tastes in styles and colors —a clean, neat, pressed, polished American.

## GENERAL RULES
## FOR DRESS IN EUROPE

- Good grooming is vital.

- Make sure nails are clean and manicured and shoes clean and polished.

- Shorts and jeans should be worn with caution. Always check to make sure they're appropriate.

- Never wear sloppy, dirty clothing.

- Avoid tennis shoes, sweatshirts and warm-up suits unless actually engaging in athletic activities. This attire should not be worn in restaurants, shops or for any business occasion; Europeans view it as being for athletic activities only—not as casual wear.

- Cover what is inappropriate to leave uncovered.

- When in doubt, button up. Err on the side of being conservative.

- Avoid funny hats, T-shirts, down vests and country-club attire.

- Avoid wearing polyester and other synthetic fabrics; stick with cotton and wool.

- Do not go native.  There is nothing that looks sillier or makes you more self-conscious than trying to look like a local and not succeeding.

- Avoid loud, flashy colors—plaid pants, bright colored sport coats.

- A dark suit and tie are always appropriate for a man.

- A dress or skirt is always appropriate for a woman.

- The "little black dress" is always appropriate evening attire for a woman attending a dinner, the opera, the theater or a concert.

Finally, if you happen to get caught sartorially short—relax, make a mental note for future reference, and then carry on with your business or fun.  If you conduct yourself with dignity, good taste and consideration for others, your behavior will overcome any temporary deficiency in dress.

*Put Your Best Foot Forward*

# 14.
# GIFTS

Knowing what gift to give and to whom, when to give it and under what circumstances, and how to present it are a vital part of doing business in Europe. Gift-giving customs vary from country to country, and observing them is important. It would be a shame to end up insulting someone you're trying to impress.

In general, gifts should:

- Never be cheap or tacky.

- Never be intimate items.

- Never be practical items.

- Never violate a tradition.

- Never be vulgar or insulting.

- Be appropriate to the relationship and culture.

- Be appropriately priced—neither demeaning nor extravagant.

Rule of Thumb

*Do your homework; ask a knowledgeable local source to suggest a gift. What is a great gift in one country may be an insult in another.*

- Be of good quality.

- Be brand names with international prestige.

- Be comparable in value to the gifts you receive.

## SUGGESTED GIFTS—MADE IN THE U.S.A.

- Local or regional arts or crafts.

- Native American arts or crafts.

- Photo books about your city, state or region.

- Candy from a local candymaker.

- Maple syrup, wild rice or other regional foods.

- Framed photos of your state or region.

- California wine.

- Lenox china.

- Amish handmade products.

- T-shirts/sweatshirts from universities in your state (for younger people).

- American cookbooks (if the recipient reads English and understands U.S. measurements).

High taxes on certain luxury items in many countries make them especially appreciated as gifts. These items usually include whiskey, cognac, cigarettes, cigars, perfume, jewelry, watches and lighters. It's especially nice if you know the fragrance, liquor or tobacco your hosts enjoy. (Many of these items are available in airport duty-free shops, and sometimes on international flights.)

Personalize a gift whenever possible. There is no nicer gift than one given because you took the time to listen and learn what someone enjoys—something that reflects their tastes, interests and personality.

---

*A friend of mine, whose parents were born in Italy, told me her mother wept uncontrollably the day my friend was born because the mother received a mum plant from a well-meaning acquaintance. In Italy, the mum is a symbol of death.*

A GIFT?

*Today, my Italian friend has just turned 40, and I think it is only now that her mother finally believes she will survive.*

---

## GENERAL GIFT GIVING AND RECEIVING RULES

- When invited to someone's home for a meal, always bring a gift for the hostess; it's thoughtful to send flowers the morning of a dinner party.

- Small gifts to the host family's children are always appreciated.

- Never give a gift that is noticeably inferior or superior to the one you've received from that person.

- Refusing to accept a gift can be a slap in the face.

- The wrong gift can ruin a business deal or a friendship.

- Follow local protocol for opening or not opening gifts in the presence of the giver.

- Wear or display the gift given at your next meeting with the giver.

- Always record the gift received on the back of the giver's business card, in your address book, or in a file.

- When you next see the giver, comment on the usefulness or your enjoyment of the gift you received.

- Write a thank-you note promptly.

## BUSINESS GIFTS

- Do not initiate gift giving or embarrass anyone by giving a gift if the person has nothing to give in return. Always save face for the giver and receiver.

- Tuck a wrapped gift in your briefcase, so if you are unexpectedly given a gift, you are able to reciprocate.

- In Europe, business gifts are generally not given at first meetings; they may even be considered crude.

- If there are several people present, give everyone a gift, give a group gift, or wait until the intended recipient is alone to give your gift.

- The U.S. government limits tax-deductibility to $25 for business-related gifts. A gift of greater value may be considered a bribe.

## GIFT TABOOS

- Most important: Read and observe the taboos noted in the various country chapters in Part III.

- Flowers are generally a lovely gift but the type and number of flowers given can have a symbolic meaning. Mums mean death and red roses mean romance in several European countries. An even number of flowers can mean bad luck in some countries. Giving 13 of anything can be taboo.

- Some colors have certain positive or negative meanings.

- Always write down the gift you give so as not to give it to the same person a second time.

*Put Your Best Foot Forward*

# The Optima℠ Card puts the right person in charge of your interest rate.

## You.

And who better? You know what you're doing when it comes to using a credit card.

That's why as an Optima Cardmember you can currently get a rate as low as **12%** for purchases.* All you need to do is pay your American Express bills on time and spend at least $1,000 in a year with the Optima Card.

And even if you don't get our lowest rate, you can have a rate that's lower than most—currently **14.25%** for purchases.*

Most credit card issuers give the same high interest rates to everyone. But we think you deserve more individual treatment—like the ability to control your own rate.

Of course, the full array of American Express benefits, and personal service, are always there for you. More than ever, the Optima Card is the credit card that puts you in control.

**Cards**

# ANNOUNCING A NEW WAY TO DO BUSINESS SUCCESSFULLY AND (ALMOST) FEARLESSLY IN RUSSIA TODAY.

United States/Russian
INFORMATION RESOURCE INSTITUTE

## UNITED STATES/RUSSIAN
# INFORMATION RESOURCE INSTITUTE

## IN COOPERATION WITH IMEMO

IMEMO is the Institute of World Economy and International Relations, Russia's most important business and economic research center. Its experts today specialize in helping Western business succeed in Russia and other republics. They are committed to the IRI/IMEMO working partnership.

### WHEN YOU NEED

- top-level contacts
- industry or project-specific expertise
- market research
- technical or geophysical research
- education & training
- database access (the best body of information on Russia today)
- meeting facilities (and support services including travel/translation/pr)
- investment/financial access
- continuing updates on overall and regional situations

### FOR MORE INFORMATION, CONTACT:

**IRI**
300 Central Ave.
Sandusky, Ohio 44871
Phone 419-626-6170
Fax 419-624-0707

**IRI**
23, Profsoyuznaya Str.
GSP-7, Moscow
117859, Russia
Phone 7-095-128-0716
Fax 7-095-310-7027

# 15.
# PUNCTUALITY
# AND PACE

In countries where being punctual is a habit, to be late says to people that you are:

- Lacking in respect (for them).

- Sloppy or undisciplined in your personal habits.

- Potentially unreliable as a partner or supplier.

If you are an "Oh well, what's a few minutes late?" person, I suggest you become an on-time person when traveling abroad.

Being "on time," however, means understanding and following local customs. What is late in one country may be early in another. "Seven o'clock" means seven on the dot in Germany, 15 minutes after in the United Kingdom, and up to an hour later for a social engagement in Italy, Greece or Spain.

*"Time and pace are among the most difficult cultural habits to learn and adapt to in business and social interaction."*

—Veteran business traveler

Rule of Thumb

*Be punctual for all meetings, business and social. Do not be irritated if others are not on time.*

The generally accepted attitude toward punctuality is covered in each country chapter in Part III. Follow this guide. If uncertain, ask! Ask your host, a friend or the hotel concierge. It is always better to err on the side of punctuality. You can expect the Germans, Austrians, Scandinavians and Scots to be on time.

On the other hand, be prepared to wait for Italians, Spaniards and Irish. Don't get angry or frustrated if they're late for an appointment; they probably won't understand your anger and

will not feel guilty or apologize for being late.

Be aware that Europe generally uses the 24-hour clock; 2 p.m., for example, would be 14:00; 6:30 p.m. would be 18:30; and 10 p.m. would be 22:00. Just add 12 hours to the time on your watch to get afternoon and evening times in the European system; or subtract 12 hours from (p.m.) times shown on a European itinerary or agenda to get afternoon or evening times as we normally express them. Morning times are the same.

Times are also spoken in ways we're unaccustomed to. In parts of Britain and Ireland, for example, 14:30 or 2:30 p.m. may be said "half two" (meaning half past two). In Germany, 2:30 could be said "halb drei" (meaning half before three). Always be alert to these different written and verbal ways of expressing time.

## PACE AND PATIENCE

Differences in pace are more difficult to learn and adjust to than differences in the sense of time. Pace deals with a sense of urgency (or the lack of it), with making or postponing decisions, getting the job done, keeping promises and making deadlines.

These differences in pace are not a matter of malice or incompetence. They have their roots in deeply ingrained habits and attitudes—in culture itself. The local pace seems natural and right to the person performing the task.

Europeans have a lot longer history than we do, and a correspondingly diminished sense that everything needs to be done in the current quarter. They truly understand that Rome wasn't built in a day. They believe it's important to spend time with their families, appreciate their culture and enjoy a good meal with a glass of wine. Their pace naturally tends to be a little slower than ours, their level of intensity a little lower.

This different sense of pace applies in the business arena as well. Europeans take a longer-term view of business results than Americans. They're not nearly as focused on the current quarter's results; they're more concerned about how all the company's stakeholders are going to fare in the long run.

Also—and I think there's a direct correlation to the European sense of history—they're not as concerned about growth as American business-people. If a European company has been profitable for several hundred years, and has done well by its owners, its employees and its customers, its managers don't necessarily think it has to be 10 or 20 percent bigger next year.

One of the greatest challenges you'll face in doing international business is understanding and accepting the local norms of pace—"getting the job done." It's important to understand that this different pace isn't necessarily better or worse—it's just different. This is where knowledge and patience are vital to the success of your project—and your sanity.

| THE LOCAL WORK ETHIC | *Consider the thought of C. William Carey, Town & Country's founder, chairman and CEO, who recently said after opening a highly successful foreign branch: "I don't believe in Americanizing. Employees in other countries don't want outside influences coming in that distort their values and work ethic."* (World Trade, *December 1992*) |

# 16.
# STRICTLY BUSINESS

In 1990, a major U.S. accounting firm surveyed CEOs of companies with $250 million or more in annual revenues. The companies agreed that the major obstacle to globalization is adapting to local cultures.

You have been asked by your company to go abroad. Consider yourself lucky! Someone thinks you have a skill worth exporting or an ability to sell your company in another land. You are on your way to the "international world," a world many businesspeople dream of and hope for, but never get a chance to enter.

Are you lucky? You bet you are! Are you nervous? I hope so! Nervousness means you won't be arrogant—the worst potential pitfall for the international business traveler.

Arrogance means you're likely to say, "I am an American. I'll do it my way. I'm paying the bill; let them adjust to me."

*"At least 30,000 American companies are capable of exporting and do not do so because they do not know how to deal in other markets."*

—U.S. Department of Commerce

Rule of Thumb

*Think globally, act locally.*

Nervousness means you might take the time and make the effort necessary to visit the library, read a few books on the countries you'll visit, and learn a few basic phrases in their languages.

Cultural differences affect every facet of doing business. Recognize and respect these differences. Remember, people have fought wars over such differences—and, it might well be argued, are still doing so. To ignore these conventions is to risk offending your potential partner or customer and embarrassing yourself and your country.

### SOME GENERAL RULES

- Avoid a "U.S.-centric" mind-set.

- Respect the local work ethic.

- Respect local customs and traditions.

- Do not attempt to Americanize the workplace. You'll be far more successful if you adapt to the local culture.

- Seek to build relationships.

- Show a sincere interest in people.

- Make employees glad they work for you by improving the quality of their life.

- Localize your marketing effort. What sells in Peoria doesn't necessarily sell in Paris, and what sells in Paris doesn't necessarily sell in Parma.

- An indigenous sales force is generally much more successful than a foreign one. Local people understand the market better and have better connections.

- Be flexible and willing to operate within the existing business and political structure.

- Emphasize compatibility.

- Be prepared for perception gaps. Ways of thinking and the approach to life and business may be different.

## CORPORATE CULTURE

The corporate culture, like everything else in Europe, differs from country to country. However, there are certain attitudes that apply at least in a general way to most companies in most European countries:

- The individual is respected. A person generally works for his personal gain rather than for group goals.

- A clear hierarchy exists. The boss is the boss and everyone knows who it is and responds accordingly.

- The organizational structure is generally vertical with decisions made at the top.

- Top managers dislike sharing information with subordinates.

- Participative management, although rapidly gaining adherents in Europe, still is a relatively new and not yet widely adopted practice.

- Communication from top to bottom is generally poor.

- Work life and private life are kept separate.

- Friendships are made slowly.

- In general, Europeans work toward developing relationships—not just doing business.

The Scandinavian countries are the exception to many of these rules. Companies in these countries are relatively egalitarian, with a more horizontal organizational structure, shared responsibility, relatively open communication and a more relaxed environment. Decisions are made by consensus.

## NAMES AND TITLES

All the general rules about using names and titles apply in business—only they're twice as important. Remember:

- Never use first names until invited to do so.

- Learn correct pronunciation of names and use them often.

- Ask a person what name and title he or she prefers.

- Use a person's proper title.

- If at all possible, learn names with proper pronunciation and usage before you meet. Underline the name that should be used in conversation.

*Jeffrey Swartz, Timberland's director of
international operations, shared this faux pas he
committed while working in Germany. "I am
paying the guy big bucks. He is my lawyer. He is
an older man. I got off the elevator and said, 'Hi,
Hans!' The entire room froze. He may be your
lawyer, but he ain't Hans. He's Herr Doctor, even
though you are paying the bills." (World Trade,
December 1992)*

## THE BUSINESS CARD

The business card is a very important
communication tool in many European
countries. The presentation of your card—and
the receiving of your counterparts'—is one of
your first opportunities to make a positive
impression on the people you are meeting. In
many countries, the business card and the ritual
of giving and receiving it will begin a
relationship on a positive or negative note.

The following rules will hold you in good stead
regardless of what European country you're in:

- Walk to the person to whom you are
  presenting the card.

- Shake hands and introduce yourself (if you
  haven't done so previously).

- Look at the person and hand him or her
  your card with your right hand; be prepared
  to receive your counterpart's card.

Rule of Thumb

*Present and receive
a business card
with care and
attention.*

• Treat your counterpart's business card with respect. Don't shove it in your pocket or write on it in the giver's presence.

• Never pass business cards out like you are dealing playing cards.

The business card can be one of your most valuable resources when meeting people. Use it well and you'll be amazed what it can tell you.

Look at a typical European business card. It tells you, in the correct form and with proper spelling:

• The company's name.

• The person's name.

• The person's corporate title (rank).

• The person's preferred professional title.

• The address of the company and person.

• Phone, fax and telex numbers.

After your meeting, turn the card over and write on the back important information to remember about the person you met. You will be amazed when you write a thank-you note, speak on the phone, correspond, or visit the person months later what this little card can help you recall. Your secretary also will appreciate this information.

Write on the reverse side:

- The person's name phonetically sounded out.

- Who introduced you to this person.

- His or her spouse's name.

- Children's names and ages.

- Gifts given and received.

- Birthday.

- Special interests.

- School or university attended.

- Home address.

- Home phone number.

- Date of meeting(s).

Caution: Writing on a business card (especially during a meeting) may be offensive in some countries. Do not write information on a business card until after the meeting has ended and you and/or the giver have departed.

## PERSONALIZING RELATIONSHIPS

- The "Hi, how are you? Let's sign the contract" approach will rarely work in Europe. If you want to get the business, you need to be prepared to take the time to personalize your relationships.

- Make personal visits as often as possible to countries and companies with which you hope to do business (Americans have a reputation for disappearing).

- Phone, write, fax often; stay in touch.

- Contribute to local charities.

- Join appropriate associations in the local community.

- Spend time on local issues.

- Don't come on too fast or too strong.

- Adjust your pace, if necessary.

- Maintain a low-key approach.

- Take time to build confidence.

- Make it clear you are there for the long haul.

- Be yourself—warm and friendly but initially more formal than you would be at home.

- Any knowledge you show about the local culture will be helpful in building closer and stronger business relationships.

## SOCIALIZING

When establishing, renewing or continuing a business relationship in a foreign country, be prepared to socialize. This is no time for a "No, thank you." Remember, most Europeans do business with people they know and trust. The time spent socializing will pay big dividends.

When socializing:

- Enjoy the local food—leave your diet at home.

- If drinks are being served, take one even if you only sip it or pretend to drink it.

- Do not talk business at dinner unless your host initiates the conversation.

- Respect local dining and drinking customs.

- Be prepared for long evenings and late hours. These may make or break a business deal.

---

**WOULD YOU LIKE FRIES WITH THAT?**

*Jeffrey Swartz, director of international operations for Timberland, says that "sales require sociability." In his view, Europeans say, "If you don't want to know my family, if you don't want to have dinner, if you don't want to do things differently, then you aren't going to do business with me. If you think you can just show up at my store and make a product presentation and ask for an order, you're crazy. You have to call up at least three or four or five times before I trust you enough even to talk about that kind of stuff."*

*But many people insist on learning the hard way. One of Swartz's salesmen said his entertainment of customers consisted of "'McDonald's, see you later, goodbye.' Not exactly the way to win over customers." (World Trade, December 1992)*

---

## CORRESPONDENCE

These general rules of correspondence are acceptable in all the European countries.

Envelope address: Use Mr., Mrs., Ms. or appropriate title + first + last name; street number often follows the street name—e.g., Kipplingerstrasse 45; postal code sometimes precedes city name, e.g. B-1020 Brussels; bottom line is always the country name, spelled out in full in block capital letters. Here are some examples:

> Mr. Dermot Moore
> Moore's China Shop
> 345 Rapidford Road
> London SW6 5DZ
> ENGLAND

> Dr. Walter Steinbauer
> General Director
> The Allied Group Europe
> Kipplingerstrasse 45
> 1010 Wien
> AUSTRIA

> Ms. Mary Wippermann
> Avenue Louise 720 Bte 6
> B-1020 Brussels
> BELGIUM

Date:  The date precedes the month.  Example:
17 June 1993 or 17/06/93.

Salutation:  Dear Sir; Dear Madam; or Dear
Mr., Mrs. or Ms. + last name.

Closing:  Yours truly, Sincerely, Yours
sincerely, or Very truly.

# 17.
# ESPECIALLY
# FOR WOMEN

Women worldwide are attaining prominence at a dramatic pace. As the new world order emerges, women are increasingly stepping forward to hold positions of power and prestige.

The attitude toward women is slightly different in each European country; prejudice still exists to some degree in a number of countries. However, as a rule, following a few simple behaviors can make being a woman a decided advantage when doing business in Europe.

Regardless of the attitude toward women in a given country, most foreign women are treated politely. Much of the resistance to women in business is directed at local women, not foreigners. As a woman doing business in Europe, I have generally found being a woman an advantage. It is sometimes easier for a woman to get in the door to tell her story.

*"Change creates opportunities. Women are transforming the world we live in."*

—Megatrends for Women, *Patricia Aburdene and John Naisbitt*

Working women worldwide have a lot in common. They struggle to meet the competing demands of family and career. The need for maternity leave, child-care facilities, equal work for equal pay and equal opportunity for raises and promotions all are issues in Europe just as they are in the United States. Some European countries have made greater progress on these issues than others; some, arguably, are well ahead of the United States.

## GENERAL RULES FOR WOMEN

- Establish your position and ability immediately.

- Define your role clearly.

- Never lose your cool.

- Do nothing that can be misinterpreted as a sexual invitation or a come-on.

- Be womanly.

- Allow men to open doors, light cigarettes, etc.

- Do not be embarrassed or angry if someone calls you "dearie" or kisses your hand.

- Aggressive behavior is frowned upon in most European countries. It is even more negative for a woman.

- Dress conservatively.

- Dress in a feminine style, but never with sexual overtones.

- Research local customs toward women and even if you think they are silly or antiquated, respect them.

- Expect cultural misunderstandings over interaction between genders; try not to be judgmental.

- It may be a new experience for some people to do business with women; be patient.

- Establish credibility by being introduced by a mutually respected person.

- Roll with the punches. If you are clearly dealing with someone who is incapable of working with a woman, consider asking a male colleague to join you or to handle that particular deal.

Scandinavia and Northern Europe are the leaders in accepting women in the top echelons of government and industry. Finland, where 40 percent of the seats in parliament are held by women, has Europe's only female defense minister. In Norway, the prime minister is a woman, three major political parties are run by women and almost half of the cabinet members are female.

Rule of Thumb

*Be 100 percent woman, with all the femininity and sensitivity that implies, but know your business.*

# 18.

# HEALTH AND SAFETY

## SECURITY

Be sure to take all the safety precautions you
would at home when traveling abroad. No
matter how safe a city or a country is reported
to be, there are potential dangers in any strange
city.

Remember that the time to make important
decisions is not after traveling seven to 10
hours in a crowded plane. Robert Burke,
director of corporate security for Monsanto,
says, "The fatigue and sleep deprivation caused
by jet lag, plus strange sights, sounds, smells
and customs, can add to disorientation and
make it easier to be victimized."

International travelers are advised by
Monsanto in its eight-page booklet to:

• Always have an escort who is a native of the
  country you are visiting.

- Know how to use public phones, and learn key phrases in the local language so you can communicate with the police if necessary.

- Carry with you at all times phone numbers and home addresses of local representatives of your employer, the nearest U.S. embassy or consulate and your principal business contacts in the cities you're visiting.

- Don't carry documents or packages for anyone else, and store your own important papers in a hotel safe.

- Always carry your passport on your person (not in a briefcase or purse) or leave it in the safe of a reputable hotel. Make photocopies of the identification pages of your passport and keep one copy in a separate place from your passport. Travel with several extra passport photos. The photos and a copy of the identification pages will make it much easier to get a replacement passport if the original is lost or stolen.

- Carry no papers that link you with the U.S. government or the military. Even a card that says you're an "honorary Kentucky colonel" could be misinterpreted by a terrorist.

## HEALTH AND SAFETY

- Check your medical insurance before you travel. Make certain it covers emergency care in a foreign country. If it does not, take out a policy that does.

- Keep medication in original, labeled containers to make customs processing easier.

- Take with you all prescription and non-prescription medication you may need.

- Pack a small first aid kit.

- Take your physician's phone number with you.

- Do not carry passport, identification, airline tickets or credit cards in your briefcase or purse. Hide valuables on your person.

- Do not wear a money belt or pouches outside your clothing or visibly hung around your neck; they could make you a target.

- Do not set your bag down at your feet while checking schedules or using a phone.

## HOTEL SAFETY

- Bring a little flashlight.

- Take note of fire exits.

- Upon entering your room, check emergency phone numbers; check to ensure that the phone line to the front desk works.

- Make sure that the safety lock on the door is locked at all times when you are in your room.

## DRUNK DRIVING

Most European countries have very stringent drunk driving laws, and they're strictly enforced. If your socializing involves alcohol, take a taxi back to your hotel; if your hosts are taking you home, they most likely have designated a non-drinking driver for the evening. In any case, do not drive after consuming alcohol.

# 19.
# HOLIDAYS
# AND FESTIVALS

Each country in Europe and many of the regions within countries have special holidays and holy days on which businesses close. There are typical vacation periods—such as August, the Christmas-New Year's holidays, and the week preceding Easter—during which it is virtually impossible to do business in Europe. Check before you schedule a business or pleasure trip to a particular region. If you plan to drop in on customers or shop in the city, a little-known holiday could ruin your plans.

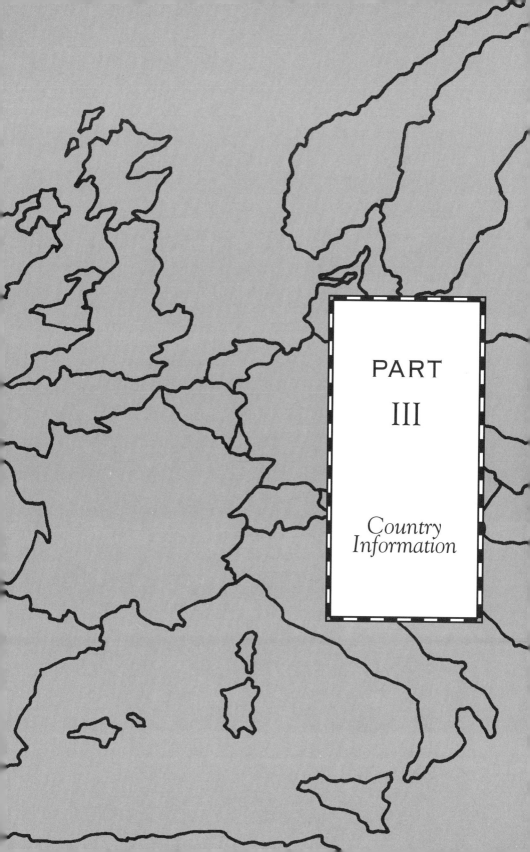

# PART

# III

*Country
Information*

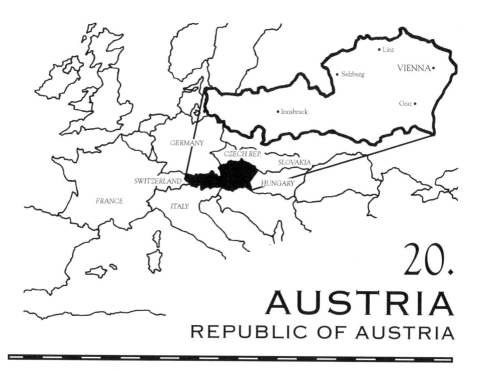

# 20.
# AUSTRIA
## REPUBLIC OF AUSTRIA

## VITAL STATISTICS

POPULATION:    7.9 million (1992).

CAPITAL:    Vienna, with a population of 1.5 million (1991).

LAND SIZE:    32,375 square miles, slightly smaller than Maine.

GOVERNMENT:    Federal republic consisting of nine states. Executive power lies with the chancellor, who leads the federal government. The head of state, the president, is elected every six years by direct popular vote. The Parliament consists of a 183-member *Nationalrat* (National Council) elected every four years through an electoral system and a 63-member *Bundesrat* (Federal Council) elected by the state assemblies.

| LIVING STANDARD: | GDP = US$23,700 per capita (1992). |
|---|---|

NATURAL
RESOURCES:     Timber, magnetite, aluminum, lead, coal, lignite, copper, hydropower.

AGRICULTURE:   Accounts for 3.2 percent of GDP (including forestry); principal crops and animals include grains, fruit, potatoes, sugar beets, finished wood, cattle, pigs, poultry; the country is 80 to 90 percent self-sufficient in food.

INDUSTRIES:    Processed foods, iron and steel, machinery, textiles, chemicals, electrical equipment, paper and pulp, tourism, mining.

CLIMATE:       Varies with altitude:  In the lowlands, average monthly temperatures are 30°F to 68°F (-1°C to 20°C); above 9,800 feet (3,000 meters), 12°F to 36°F (-11°C to 2°C).

CURRENCY:      Austrian schilling (ÖS). ÖS1=100 groschen. Bank notes are in denominations of ÖS5,000, 1,000, 500, 100, 50 and 20. Coins are in denominations of ÖS20, 10, 5 and 1, and 50, 10 and 5 groschen.

# THE PEOPLE

CORRECT
NAME: Austrians.

ETHNIC
MAKEUP: 99.4 percent Germanic, 0.3 percent Croatian, 0.2 percent Slovene, 0.1 percent other; 200,000 foreign workers from the former Yugoslavia and Turkey.

VALUE
SYSTEM: Austrians are proud of their contributions to world civilization. They value being cultured. They see themselves as modern and liberal. Regional pride is very strong. Austrians have a great love for the outdoors and such activities as walking, skiing and climbing.

FAMILY: The Austrian family is the fourth smallest in the world. The proportion of women working outside the home is one of the highest in the industrialized world. Traditional family values have been weakened by modern life and government legislation.

RELIGION: 89 percent Roman Catholic, 8 percent other Christian, 1 percent Muslim.

## MEETING AND GREETING

- Shake hands with everyone present—men, women and children—at a business or social meeting. Shake hands again when leaving.

- Handshake is firm, but not bone-crushing, with eye contact.

- Shake hands with ladies before gentlemen.

- A lady should offer her hand first.

- Viennese men may kiss the hand of a woman. Accept this tradition graciously. A foreign man visiting Austria should not kiss the hand of an Austrian woman; it is not expected and may come as a shock.

- Austrians, unlike Germans, greet people in public whether they know them or not.

- The most common greeting is *Grüss Gott* (grees gawt), "May God greet you."

## NAMES AND TITLES

- Use last names and appropriate titles until specifically invited by your Austrian hosts or colleagues to use their first names.

- First names among Austrians are used only for very close friends and family members.

- Titles are very important. Use them properly and at all times.

- *Herr* + professional title + last name are used when initially addressing a male professional.

**Example:** *Herr Doktor Bauer.*

- *Frau* + professional title + last name is used when initially addressing a female professional or the wife of a professional.

  **Example: *Frau Doktor Bauer* could be either a female physician or the wife of a physician.**

- After the initial meeting, you can drop the last names and address people using *Herr/Frau* + professional title alone.

  **Example: *Herr Doktor* or *Frau Doktor*.**

- All women over 18 are *Frau*, not *Fraülein*, even if they are not married.

| Mr. | *Herr* | hair |
|-----|--------|------|
| Mrs./Ms. | *Frau* | frrow |
| Miss | *Fräulein* | FROY-line |

---

## LANGUAGE

- German is the primary language.

- English is spoken by many people.

- Each region has its own dialect.

- Try to speak German. Austrians appreciate the effort.

---

## BODY LANGUAGE

- Austrians are reserved and formal.

- Kissing, hugging, touching and closeness in public are not common.

- Eye contact is very important to Austrians.

- Do not put your hands in your pockets while speaking to or greeting anyone.

## PHRASES

| English | German | Pronunciation |
|---|---|---|
| May God greet you | *Grüss Gott* | grees gawt |
| Good day | *Guten Tag* | GOOT-un taak |
| Good morning | *Guten Morgen* | GOOT-un MORG-un |
| Good evening | *Guten Abend* | GOOT-un AH-bent |
| Please | *Bitte* | BIT-uh |
| Thank you | *Danke* | DAHNK-uh |
| You're welcome | *Bitte* | BIT-uh |
| Yes | *Ja* | ya |
| No | *Nein* | nine |
| Excuse me | *Verzeihung* | fare-TSEYE-ung |
| Goodbye | *Auf Wiedersehen* | awf VEE-der-zay-un |
| Pleased to meet you | *Sehr erfreut* | zehr er-FROYT |
| How are you? | *Wie geht es Ihnen?* | vee gate es EE-nun |

- To beckon a waiter or waitress, raise your hand with your index finger extended. Do so quietly and never call or shout.

BREAKFAST (*Frühstück*): 6 to 9 a.m.

- Continental: Light meal of coffee, rolls, bread, butter and jam.

- Buffet-style breakfasts are becoming increasingly popular.

LUNCH (*Mittagessen*): noon to 2 p.m.

- Main meal of the day for most Austrians.

- Soup, meat, potatoes, vegetable, salad and dessert.

COFFEE BREAK (*Jause*): 3 to 4 p.m.

- Coffee or tea, cakes and pastries.

DINNER (*Abendessen*): 7 to 9 p.m.

- Main meal for business or entertaining.

- At home, cold meat, eggs, salad and cheese.

## DINING AND DRINKING

## MENU TERMS:

| | |
|---|---|
| *Vorspeise* | Appetizer |
| *Hauptspeise* | Main course |
| *Nachspeise* | Dessert |
| *Brot* | Bread |
| *Suppe* | Soup |
| *Gemüse* | Vegetables |
| *Fleisch* | Meat |
| *Rind* | Beef |
| *Schwein* | Pork |
| *Lamm* | Lamb |
| *Hähnchen* | Chicken |
| *Fisch* | Fish |
| *Ei* | Egg |

## TYPICAL FOODS

- *Wienerschnitzel:* Breaded and fried veal cutlet.

- *Wild:* Venison.

- *Knödel:* Bread or potato dumplings.

- *Gulasch:* Paprika beef with noodles.

- *Frittatensuppe:* Sliced pancake soup.

- *Griessnockerlsuppe:* Semolina dumpling soup.

- *Schweinsbraten:* Roast pork.

- *Tafelspitz:* Boiled beef.

- *Palatschinken:* Crepes.

- *Salzburger Nockerln*: Souffle from the Salzburg area.

- *Marillenknödel*: Apricot dumplings.

- *Apfelstrudel*: Apple strudel.

- *Milchrahmstrudel*: Cream cheese strudel.

- *Sachertorte*: Chocolate cake with apricot jam and chocolate icing.

- *Melange*: Coffee with hot milk.

- *Schlag*: Whipped cream. Viennese trademark served on cake, coffee, strudel, etc.

## DRINKING:

- Austria is known for wonderful *Wein* (wine), which is served with most meals.

- Austrians also enjoy drinking the good *Bier* (beer) produced in their country.

- *Heurigen*: The famous wine gardens in the Grinzing suburb of Vienna. Music, food and local wine are served with an abundance of ambience.

- *Kaffeehäuser*: Viennese coffeehouses are a culture in themselves. People sit for hours reading papers, talking and thinking. Some famous coffeehouse devotees were Sigmund Freud, Gustav Mahler and Leon Trotsky.

## TOASTS:

- Prost (prohst) or Prosit (PROH-zeet), "May it be good for you." Informal and formal.

- The host gives the first toast.

- The honored guest returns the toast later in the meal.

- Maintaining eye contact during a toast is very important.

- It is acceptable for a foreign woman to propose a toast.

---

## TIPPING

- Tipping is widespread but large amounts are not expected.

- Restaurants: A service charge of 10 to 15 percent is usually included in the bill (the bill will indicate *Bedienung*). As a rule, round up the bill to the nearest ÖS10 as an additional gratuity. If the service charge is not included, leave a 10 to 15 percent tip.

- Musicians: Tip ÖS50-ÖS100 if making requests. Otherwise, there's no need to tip.

- Porters: ÖS10 per bag.

- Taxis: ÖS5-10 for a short trip; 10 percent of the fare for a long trip.

- Cloakroom attendants: ÖS10.

- Washroom attendants: ÖS5 to 10.

- Airports and trains: Fixed price for porters.

- Austrians expect proper manners at all times.

- Eat only after the hostess has begun.

- Keep your hands on the table at all times during a meal—not in your lap. However, keep your elbows off the table.

- Use your fish knife to cut fish.

- Never cut a dumpling. You should hold a dumpling with your knife and break it apart with your fork.

- Break rolls apart with your fingers and eat them in small pieces.

- If your knife and fork are in any way open on your plate, it means that you would like more food or that you are not yet finished eating.

- Do not leave any food on your plate at a dinner party.

- When finished eating, place your knife and fork side by side on plate at the 5:25 position.

- Do not ask for a tour of your host's home; it's considered impolite. To Austrians, their home is a very private and personal place.

- Leave a party by 11 p.m.

- He who invites pays the bill in a restaurant. Austrians will not appreciate a struggle over the bill.

- Austrians seldom entertain business guests in their homes.

## DRESS

- Austrians dress in the European style, sometimes with an Austrian touch.

- Clothing is rather stylish, but never gaudy.

- Austrians take pride in dressing well regardless of where they are going or what position they hold.

- Austrians will judge you by your clothing. Dress well for all occasions.

- Clean, fashionable jeans are acceptable.

- Shopping is considered an event in Austria—not merely running errands. Dress appropriately.

BUSINESS

- Business attire is conservative.

- Men: Dark suits and ties.

- Women: Suits or dresses.

RESTAURANT

- Men: Suits.

- Women: Dresses or dressy pants.

## Theater or Opera

- Men: Suits. Tuxedos are worn for opening night.

- Women: Cocktail dresses. Black dresses are common for opening night.

## Casual:

- Men: Pants and shirts, sweaters.

- Women: Pants, skirts, dresses, sweaters.

---

- Gifts are opened immediately upon receipt.

**GIFTS**

### HOSTESS

- Always bring a gift for the hostess when invited to someone's home.

- Give: Flowers (in odd numbers only, except for the dozen; unwrap before giving them to the hostess), wine, pastries, chocolates, brandy, whiskey.

- Do not give: An even number of flowers (means bad luck), red roses (unless romance is intended), red carnations (official flower of the Social Democratic Party), perfume.

## BUSINESS

- Gifts are generally not expected, but come prepared in case a gift is presented.

- Give: Desk accessories, books, recorded music, a gift from your home country or region.

- Do not give: Personal gifts, gifts with sharp edges, gifts with your company logo (unless very subtle), or very expensive gifts.

## TOILET TIPS

| | |
|---|---|
| *Toiletten/WC* | Restrooms |
| *Frauen* | Ladies |
| *Herren* | Men |
| *Warm* | Hot water (red dot) |
| *Kalt* | Cold water (blue dot) |

## HELPFUL HINTS

DO:

- Be quiet and orderly in public.

- Recognize and use good manners at all times.

- Stand whenever a woman enters the room.

- Remain standing until invited to be seated.

- Greet salespeople when entering and leaving a shop.

- Check your coat into the cloakroom at a theater. Some theaters don't allow coats in the performance space.

Gemütlichkeit: *Relaxed and happy approach to life used to describe Austrians.*

## DO NOT:

- Do not ask to use the bathroom. Ask for the toilet or "WC" (water closet).

- Do not chew gum in public.

- Do not pick up fruit or vegetables from a stand. Point to your selections and allow the attendant to place them in a bag.

- Do not eat food while walking on the street.

- Do not offer personal compliments. An Austrian may find them embarrassing.

- Do not extend any invitation unless you plan to follow through.

- Do not drop in on anyone. Call in advance to set up a meeting.

- Do not make noise, talk or crinkle paper during an opera, concert or play.

*Never refer to an Austrian as a German; Austria and Germany have very different customs and cultures.*

- Austrians insist on punctuality for social occasions.

- Austrians take punctuality for business meetings very seriously and expect that you will do likewise; call with an explanation if you are delayed.

## PUNCTUALITY

# STRICTLY BUSINESS

## BUSINESS CARDS

- Business cards are given both to the secretary upon arrival and to businesspeople upon meeting.

- Business cards in English are acceptable.

- Austrian business cards may have several titles. Always use the higher-ranking title or the first title.

## CORPORATE CULTURE

STRUCTURE: Austrian companies tend to have a very vertical structure, with all real power held by a small number of people at the top. Deference and obedience are expected and given to those in authority; executives and managers are unlikely to be receptive to criticism from subordinates or outsiders. Bosses criticize poor performance but seldom, if ever, give compliments. Planning is cautious, conservative and risk-averse.

MEETINGS: Light conversation usually precedes the discussion of business. Decisionmaking in Austrian companies is slow, with a thorough analysis of all the facts—so don't expect an answer to your proposal on the spot. Be patient.

COMMUNICATION: Most businesspeople speak English, so an interpreter most likely won't be needed. Within companies, communication is from the top down on a need-to-know basis, so only a handful of people are likely to be aware of

*Austria has a well-educated and highly trained work force.*

your proposal to their company. It's important to correspond frequently by phone, fax and letter; Austrian businesspeople like a paper trail. On the phone or in letters, open and close with friendly comments to build a personal relationship. Do not call an Austrian businessperson at home except in an emergency.

BE AWARE:

- Rank and title are very important in business.

- Who you know is important to business success in Austria.

- Austrians may complain that they are overworked and cannot accomplish a task by a given date. In fact, they are reliable, do high-quality work and always meet deadlines.

- Never cancel an appointment at the last minute; it will damage your relationship with Austrian colleagues.

## ENTERTAINMENT

- Business entertaining is most often done in restaurants. Do not discuss business during a meal unless your host initiates the conversation.

- Business breakfasts and lunches are common.

- Business dinners often include spouses after a relationship is developed.

- Reciprocate with a lunch or dinner invitation before you leave the country.

APPOINTMENTS

| Office Hours: | Monday through Thursday<br>8 a.m. to 4 p.m. |
|---|---|
| | Friday<br>8 a.m. to 2 p.m. |
| Bank Hours: | Monday through Friday<br>8 a.m. to 12:30 p.m.<br>1:30 to 3:30 p.m. |

- Arrange business appointments in advance.

- Don't schedule appointments from mid-July to Sept. 1 or the Christmas to New Year's period.

## ESPECIALLY FOR WOMEN

- A foreign woman will not have a problem doing business in Austria, despite the fact that traditionally conservative attitudes toward women persist there. Today, there is an increasing number of women in politics and industry.

- A foreign businesswoman will have no problem inviting an Austrian businessman to dinner and paying the bill, but lunch is the most common setting for business discussions and she should stick with lunch until she gets to know him on a more personal level.

- Men enter restaurants before women.

- A woman should offer her hand first upon meeting or greeting a man.

- Do not plan to make a business visit or schedule any appointments during the following holidays or festivals. Be sure to check for the numerous regional and local holidays and festivals.

| | |
|---|---|
| January | New Year's Day (1), Epiphany (*Heilige Drei Könige* - 6). |
| March/April | Easter (Friday - Monday). |
| April/May | Ascension Thursday (40 days after Easter). |
| May/June | Whitsunday (Pentecost) and Whitmonday (49 and 50 days after Easter). |
| June | Corpus Christi (60 days after Easter). |
| August | Assumption (15). |
| October | National Holiday or Flag Day (26). |
| November | All Saints' Day (1). |
| December | Immaculate Conception (8), Christmas (25), Boxing Day and *Stephanstag* (26-Vienna). |

# 21.
# BELGIUM
## KINGDOM OF BELGIUM

## VITAL STATISTICS

POPULATION:     10 million (1992).

CAPITAL:     Brussels, with a population of 964,385 (1990).

LAND SIZE:     11,781 square miles, slightly larger than Maryland.

GOVERNMENT:     Parliamentary democracy under a constitutional monarch. The king holds executive power with the prime minister and his cabinet, with the latter two handling day-to-day affairs. The 212-member Chamber of Representatives is elected for four years, while the Senate has 106 directly elected members plus 50 from the provincial councils, 25 cooptees and the heir to the throne.

| LIVING STANDARD: | GDP = US$22,600 per capita (1992). |
|---|---|
| NATURAL RESOURCES: | Small amount of natural resources. Coal, natural gas, marble, sandstone, slate. |
| AGRICULTURE: | Accounts for 2.3 percent of GDP; emphasis on livestock production—beef, veal, pork, milk; major crops are sugar beets, fresh vegetables, fruits and grain; net importer of farm products. |
| INDUSTRIES: | Engineering and metal products, processed food and beverages, chemicals, tobacco, basic metals, textiles, glass, petroleum products and nuclear power. |
| CLIMATE: | Temperate with mild, foggy winters and cool summers. Monthly temperature range is 32°F to 73°F (0°C to 23°C). |
| CURRENCY: | Belgian franc (BF). BF1=100 centimes. Notes are in denominations of BF10,000, 5,000, 1,000, 500 and 100. Coins are in denominations of BF50, 20 and 1. |

# THE PEOPLE

CORRECT
NAME:            Belgians.  Residents of Wallonia are Walloons or
                 French-speaking Belgians.  Residents of Flanders
                 are Flemings or Dutch-speaking Belgians.

ETHNIC
MAKEUP:          55 percent Fleming, 33 percent Walloon,
                 1 percent German.

VALUE
SYSTEM:          Hard work and an appreciation for culture are
                 important values to Belgians.  Walloons and
                 Flemings love life, working and playing hard.
                 Walloons are traditionalists.  They are friendly
                 but may appear aloof.  Flemings are generally
                 more reserved, but also tend to be more open-
                 minded.

FAMILY:          Strong families are vital to Belgian society,  with
                 people often settling in the town where they
                 were raised.  Extended families often live on the
                 same street, with the grandparents playing  a
                 major role in the upbringing of their
                 grandchildren.

RELIGION:        90 percent Roman Catholic.

| MEETING<br>AND<br>GREETING | • Shake hands with everyone present—men, women and children—at a business or social meeting. Shake hands again when leaving. |
|---|---|
| | • Handshake is brief with light pressure. |
| | • Repeat your name when being introduced. |

| NAMES<br>AND<br>TITLES | • Use last names and appropriate titles until specifically invited by your Belgian hosts or colleagues to use their first names. |
|---|---|
| | • Professional titles are not important. |
| | • Be sure to address the Flemings and the Walloons correctly (in their language) or use the English Mr., Mrs., Ms. or Miss. |

|  | Flemings | Walloons |
|---|---|---|
| Mr. | *Mijnheer*<br>(muh-NAYR) | *Monsieur*<br>(meh-SYEUR) |
| Mrs. | *Mevrouw*<br>(muhv-ROW) | *Madame*<br>(mah-DAHM) |
| Miss | *Juffrouw*<br>(yuf-ROW) | *Mademoiselle*<br>(mahd-mwah-ZEHL) |

| LANGUAGE | • Flemings live in Flanders in the north, make up 55 percent of the population and speak Dutch. |
|---|---|
| | • Walloons live in Wallonia in the south, make up 33 percent of the population and speak French. |
| | • Brussels, located in Flanders, is inhabited by both Flemings and Walloons and maintains French as the main business language. |

*Even the song of the finch has two languages in this
small country. An ancient game in Flanders,*
vinkensport, *is a test of how many bird songs a
caged finch can sing in an hour. Vinkeniers want
only birds that sound Flemish; when a finch sings
with a French dialect from Wallonia, the song is
disqualified.*

- Dutch, French and German are the official
  languages.

- A small German minority (less than 1
  percent of the population of Belgium) lives
  in Eastern Belgium (within Wallonia) near
  the German border and maintains German
  as their first language.

- Many Belgians speak English.

- The language of choice for negotiators in
  Brussels is English and sometimes French.

- English is acceptable (and safe) for use in
  business and public places.

- In the past, Dutch was considered the
  language of servants and peasants and
  French the language of the upper-middle
  class. This is not true today.

- Belgian cities and streets have different
  names in Dutch and French.

*Beware! Speak
English if in doubt.
There is no place in
Europe you can get
in greater trouble
by using the
incorrect language
than Belgium.*

### FLEMINGS

- Dutch is spoken by Flemings.

- You may speak Dutch, German, English or French to Flemings.

- A Belgian dialect of Dutch was formerly called Flemish, but is now officially referred to as Dutch.

- People may be outwardly formal.

- Flemings maintain last-name relationships longer than the Dutch.

- Personal relationships are relaxed and low-key.

- Humor is mild and self-deprecating.

*Personal relationships are low-key.*

### WALLOONS

- French is spoken by Walloons.

- Most Walloons cannot speak Dutch.

- Walloons are not quaint Frenchmen and resent being treated as such.

- Etiquette is very traditional. Relationships are formal.

- Walloons maintain last-name relationships longer than the French.

- Humor is ironic and witty—usually at others' expense.

*Walloons are not quaint Frenchmen.*

- Do not snap your fingers.

- Never back-slap.

- Do not put your hands in your pockets when speaking to or greeting anyone.

- The "OK" sign (index finger and thumb made into a circle) means zero.

See Dutch, French and German phrases.

- To beckon a waiter or waitress, raise your hand and make eye contact. Do so quietly and never call or shout.

- There are more five-star restaurants in Brussels than in any European country except France.

BREAKFAST (French, *Petit Déjeuner*; Dutch, *Het Ontbijt*): 7:30 to 8:30 a.m.

- Bread, butter, jam and coffee.

LUNCH (French, *Déjeuner*; Dutch, *De Lunch*): noon.

- A business lunch could be several courses.

- Cities: Light meal. Cold cuts, rolls, or sandwich, fruit, dessert.

- Country: Main meal. Soup, meat, potatoes and vegetables, dessert.

DINNER (French, *Dîner*; Dutch, *Het Dîner*): 7 to 8 p.m.

- Appetizer, soup, fish dish, sherbet, main meat course, salad, dessert.

- Beer, wine, coffee, liqueurs.

## MENU TERMS

Please refer to the France and Netherlands chapters for translations of menu terms.

## TYPICAL FOODS

- *Moules* (French) or *Mosselen* (Dutch): Mussels.

- *Moules Marinière*: Mussels steamed in white wine, garlic and parsley with french fries.

- *Anguilles*: Eels.

- *Hochepot*: Stew of pork and mutton (a home-style country dish).

- *Carbonnades Flamandes*: Beef cooked in beer.

- *Civet de Lievre à la Flamandes*: Rabbit cooked in wine.

- *Waterzooi*: Stewed chicken in rich broth.

- Game, fish, cheese, fruit.

## DRINKING

- Be aware—Belgian beer has a much higher alcohol content than American beer.

- Vermouth or Cinzano are served before dinner.

- Scotch whiskey is served when you ask for whiskey. "Scotch" is a brand of beer.

- Beer and wine are served with meals.


## TOASTS

- *Op uw gezondheid* (op uv ge-ZOND-hite), "To your health" (Dutch). Formal or informal.

- *A votre santé* (ah vo-TRAH SAN-tay), "To your health" (French). Formal or informal.

- You should wait to drink until your host offers the first toast.

- The guest of honor is generally expected to give a toast.

- One generally stands for toasting.

- A woman may offer a toast.

## TIPPING

- Tipping is never required in Belgium.

- Tip only if you are very happy with service.

- Restaurants: A service charge of 15 percent is usually included in the bill; small change can be left as an additional gratuity for good service. If the service charge is not included, leave a 15 percent tip.

- In a restaurant if the service charge is included in the bill, it will read *dienst inbegrepen* (Dutch) or *service compris* (French). If the service charge is not included in the bill, it will read *dienst niet inbegrepen* (Dutch) or *service non compris* (French).

- Taxis: Tip is generally included.

- Cloakroom attendants: BF25. There is usually a sign posted.

- Ushers: BF25.

- Porters: BF25 per bag.

- Bathroom attendants: BF25.

- Gas station attendants: Token.

- Maids/doormen: Optional.

## MANNERS

- Keep your hands on the table at all times during a meal—not in your lap. However, keep your elbows off the table.

- Accept any drink offered by your host. Don't ask for a drink not offered.

- Hosts seat guests.

- Husbands and wives are not seated together.

- The host and hostess sit at opposite ends of the table.

- The female guest of honor is seated next to the host. The male guest of honor is seated next to the hostess.

- Fish course has a fish fork (left of plate) and a fish knife (right of plate).

- Bread plates are generally provided.

- Finish all the food on your plate. Belgians are thrifty and do not appreciate waste.

- Your knife and fork should be placed side by side on the dinner plate at the 5:25 position when you are finished eating.

- Stay about one hour after the meal ends.

- Do not ask for a tour of your host's home; it would be considered impolite.

*Meals are social and cultural events in Belgium. Belgians take great pride in their food. Do not plan to dine quickly.*

- Wear conservative clothing.

- Pack an umbrella and light sweater.

## DRESS

BUSINESS

- Men: Dark suits and ties.

- Women: Suits or dresses, skirts and blouses.

### Restaurant

- Men: Suits and ties may be required.
- Women: Dresses.

### Formal Dinner

- Men: Tuxedos or dark suits.
- Women: Evening dresses.

### Theater/Concert

- Men: Dark suits and ties.
- Women: Cocktail dresses.
- Young people wear colors and more casual clothing.

### Casual

- Young people wear jeans.
- Sweaters, sport coats, smart casual clothing are recommended.

---

## GIFTS

- Gifts are generally opened in front of the giver.

### HOSTESS

- When invited to someone's home, always bring flowers for the hostess. A small gift in addition to the flowers would be welcomed as well.

- Bring children a small gift or candy.

- Give a gift that is not too extravagant or expensive.

- Give: Quality chocolates, books, recorded music.

- Do not give: Chrysanthemums—a death reminder.

## BUSINESS

- Gifts are generally not exchanged in business or at the end of negotiations.

- It is common for Belgian companies to give small gifts at New Year's rather than Christmas.

- Give: Desk accessories, books, art from your home region.

- Do not give: Expensive or extravagant gifts.

## TOILET TIPS

|            | Dutch         | French        |
|------------|---------------|---------------|
| Restrooms  | *Toiletten/WC* | *Toilettes/WC* |
| Ladies     | *Dames*       | *Dames*       |
| Men        | *Heren*       | *Hommes*      |
| Hot water  | *Warm water*  | *Eau chaude*  |
| Cold water | *Koud water*  | *Eau froide*  |

## HELPFUL HINTS

---

*Belgians tell jokes about Dutch and vice versa. Avoid this rivalry.*

---

Faux Pas

*Do not ignore local tensions. The Walloons and Flemings coexist. Their rivalries dominate Belgian politics.*

---

**DO:**

- Rise when a woman enters the room.

- Allow women to enter the room, bus or elevator first.

- Stand on public transportation until women are seated.

- Maintain good posture.

- Try to sneeze and blow your nose in private.

**DO NOT:**

- Do not discuss personal matters or linguistic divisions.

- Do not flaunt wealth.

- Do not be noisy or loud in public.

- Do not ask personal questions about private lives.

- Do not behave too casually (considered rude).

- Never put your feet on chairs or tables.

- Do not use toothpicks in public.

- Do not yawn or scratch in public.

- Never back-slap.

- Belgians insist on punctuality for social occasions.

- Belgians take punctuality for business meetings very seriously and expect that you will do likewise; call with an explanation if you are delayed.

## BUSINESS CARDS

- Business cards are widely used.

- Business cards in English are acceptable.

- Present your business card upon meeting. It is often a time for discussing your company.

## CORPORATE CULTURE

*Belgians do business just about everywhere in the world.*

STRUCTURE: The structure and culture of Flemish companies differs sharply from that of Walloon companies.

Flemish companies tend to have a relatively horizontal structure; participative management is common, and decisions reached by consensus are preferred. Bosses are approachable, and perks are less important than pay.

Walloon companies, on the other hand, are much more formal and hierarchical. Rules and procedures are important, and decisions are made by the boss. Rank, job title, office size and elegance of furniture are taken seriously.

MEETINGS: Formality is the general rule. Belgians do business on the basis of personal trust, so initial meetings are for getting acquainted rather than serious discussion. Belgians tend to socialize for 15 minutes before they get down to business in meetings; it's considered rude to rush into business immediately.

Belgians are known as savvy, pragmatic businesspeople with a knack for negotiation. They look for practical solutions to issues or problems, so back up your proposal with clear facts and figures.

Especially in Wallonia, meetings are for the exchange of information and discussion of alternatives, not for making decisions. Don't press for one.

COMMUNICATION: English is widely used in business; you most likely will not need an interpreter. Don't call a Belgian businessperson at home except in an emergency.

BE AWARE:
- Belgians are hard-working, multilingual and cosmopolitan.

- Belgians have been involved in international commerce since the days of sailing ships. They do business just about everywhere in the world.

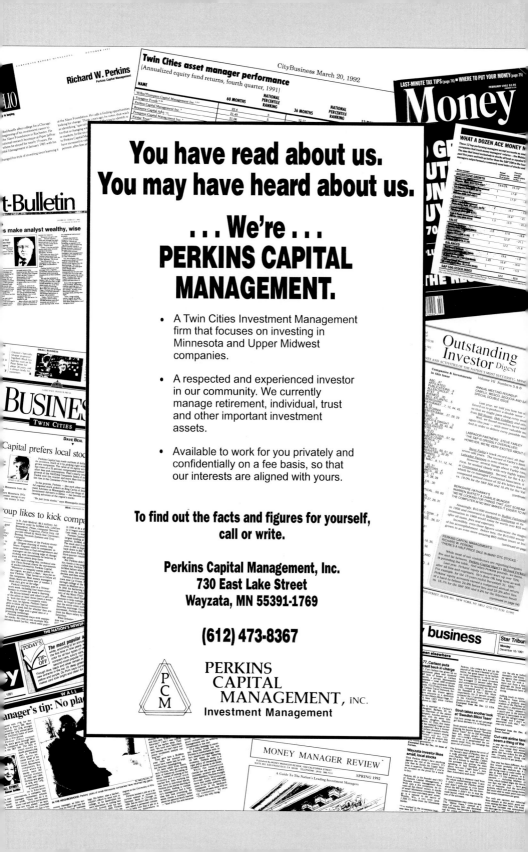

## ENTERTAINMENT

- Business entertaining is most often done in a restaurant.

- Don't suggest a business breakfast—it's generally not appreciated.

- Business lunches are preferred. There may be a lot of general chatting to get acquainted.

- Business dinners may or may not include spouses.

---

## APPOINTMENTS

**Office Hours:**     Monday through Friday
                     9 a.m. to noon.
                     2 p.m. to 5 or 6 p.m.

**Bank Hours:**      Monday through Friday
                     9:30 a.m. to 3:30 p.m.

- July and August are vacation months. Don't schedule business meetings during the Christmas/New Year's period or at Easter.

- Don't schedule appointments on Saturday.

- Book appointments at least one week in advance.

- Appointments made for 11:30 a.m. might include lunch.

## ESPECIALLY FOR WOMEN

- The role of women is viewed conservatively, but a foreign woman will have no problem doing business in Belgium.

- Many women are in the work force, but most are employed in support staff positions. Women are slowly moving into management positions.

- It is acceptable for a foreign woman to invite a Belgian man to dinner and she will not have a problem paying.

## HOLIDAYS AND FESTIVALS

- Do not plan to make a business visit or schedule any appointments during the following holidays or festivals. Be sure to check for the numerous regional and local holidays and festivals.

| | |
|---|---|
| January | New Year's Day (1). |
| March/April | Easter (Friday-Monday). |
| April/May | Ascension Thursday (40 days after Easter). |
| May/June | Whitsunday (Pentecost) and Whitmonday (49 and 50 days after Easter). |
| June | Corpus Christi (60 days after Easter). |
| July | Feast of the Flemish Community (11), Independence Day (21). |
| August | Assumption (15). |
| September | Feast of the French Community (27). |
| November | All Saints' Day (1), Veterans' Day (11), King's Day (15). |
| December | Christmas (24-26). |

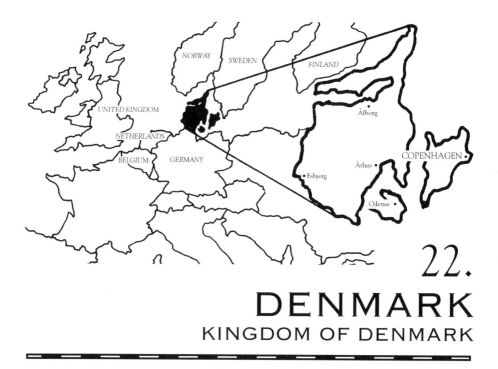

# 22.

# DENMARK
## KINGDOM OF DENMARK

## VITAL STATISTICS

POPULATION: 5.16 million (1992).

CAPITAL: Copenhagen, with a population of 1.8 million (1992).

LAND SIZE: 16,631 square miles, slightly more than twice the size of Massachusetts.

GOVERNMENT: Constitutional monarchy. The unicameral legislature, the *Folketing*, has 179 members elected for four years through an electoral system. The cabinet is headed by a prime minister responsible to the *Folketing*.

LIVING
STANDARD: GDP = US$28,500 per capita (1992).

| | |
|---|---|
| NATURAL RESOURCES: | Crude oil, natural gas, fish, salt, limestone. |
| AGRICULTURE: | Accounts for 4.5 percent of GDP and employs 6 percent of labor force; farm products account for nearly 15 percent of export revenues; principal products include meat, dairy, grain, potatoes, sugar beets, fish; self-sufficient in food production. |
| INDUSTRIES: | Food processing, machinery and equipment, textiles and clothing, chemical products, electronics, construction, furniture and other wood products. |
| CLIMATE: | Temperate and changeable, moderated by the Gulf Stream. Average temperatures are 61°F (16°C) in July and 32°F (0°C) in February. |
| CURRENCY: | Danish krone (DKK). DKK1=100 øre. Notes are in denominations of DKK1,000, 500, 100 and 50. Coins are in denominations of DKK20, 10, 5 and 1, and 50, 25 and 10 øre. |

# THE PEOPLE

CORRECT
NAME:                Danes.

ETHNIC
MAKEUP:              99 percent Danish.

VALUE
SYSTEM:              The Danes are respected for their literature, as
                     well as their accomplishments in science, art and
                     architecture.  They value tolerance and diversity.
                     Social welfare is highly valued despite the heavy
                     taxes imposed by this program.  The individual is
                     highly regarded in the Danish culture.  Danes are
                     very proud of their excellent school system, which
                     brings both professors and laborers to a cultural
                     level on which they can converse with ease.

FAMILY:              The Danes value close and stable family lives.
                     Most women work outside the home.  Children
                     are respected as individuals.

RELIGION:            96 percent Evangelical Lutheran.

## MEETING AND GREETING

- Shake hands with everyone present—men, women and children—at a business or social meeting. Shake hands again when leaving.

- A firm, short handshake with direct eye contact is appropriate.

- Shake hands with women first.

- Be sure to rise before shaking hands.

- *Goddag* (goh-DAH), "Good day," is a common greeting.

- *Davs* (daus), "Hi," is a frequent, informal greeting.

## NAMES AND TITLES

- Use last names and appropriate titles until specifically invited by your Danish hosts or colleagues to use their first names.

- Traditionally, only close friends and family addressed each other by first names; today, however, many people use first names.

- Use professional titles, especially with older people.

  **Example: *Professor Andersen.***

- If your colleague does not have a professional title, use *Hr.*, *Fru* or *Frøken*.

| Mr. | *Hr.* | hair |
|-----|-------|------|
| Mrs. | *Fru* | froo |
| Miss | *Frøken* | FRUH-ken |

  **Example: *Fru Andersen.***

- *De* (dee)—the formal "you"—used for older people and new acquaintances.

- *Du* (doo)—the informal "you"—used among younger people and close acquaintances.

---

- Danish is the official language.

- 60 percent of Danes speak and/or understand German; 85 percent of Danes speak and/or understand English.

- Danes are plain-spoken and respect frankness in conversation.

*Danes are plain-spoken and respect frankness in conversation.*

- Danes sometimes have an unusual way of expressing themselves. They may say, "It's wonderful weather," when it is pouring rain or, "It is a trifle chilly," when it's stifling hot.

- Danes say "Thank you" for everything— anytime, anywhere.

- Danes do not use the expression, "How are you?" as loosely as Americans. Stay away from this expression unless you have developed a personal relationship and truly wish to know how someone feels.

---

BODY LANGUAGE

- Danes are reserved and do not show affection in public.

- Do not touch Danes.

- Do not back-slap.

## PHRASES

| English | Danish | Pronunciation |
|---|---|---|
| Good morning | *Godmorgen* | goh-MORN |
| Good afternoon | *Goddag* | goh-DAH |
| Good evening | *Godaften* | goh-AHF-tehn |
| Please | *Vær sa venlig* | ver-sah-VEHN-lig |
| Thank you | *Tak* | tahk |
| You're welcome | *Velbekomme* | VEL-beh-kom-meh |
| Yes | *Ja* | yah |
| No | *Nej* | nigh |
| Excuse me | *Undskyld* | OON-skewl |
| Goodbye | *Farvel* | far-VILL |
| Pleased to meet you | *Gælder mig* | GLAY-ah-dar my |

- Summon a waiter/waitress by raising your hand and extending your index finger. Never shout—it's much better to catch his/her eye.

BREAKFAST (*Morgenmad*): 8 a.m.

- Cereal or porridge, yogurt, bread or rolls, Danish pastries, cheese, marmalade, eggs, coffee or tea. Some have bacon and eggs.

LUNCH (*Frokost*): noon to 2 p.m.

- Lunch breaks are generally short and most people do not go out to lunch.

- *Smørrebrød* (open-faced sandwiches) are a national institution.

- A *smørgåsbord* is common for a formal lunch buffet.

- Coffee is served after the meal only.

DINNER (*Aftensmad*): 6 to 8 p.m.

- Formal dinners of seven courses are common.

- Dinner is generally long and slow (up to four or five hours) with much conversation.

- Less formal: Sandwiches, beer or *snaps*, main course and dessert.

- It is common for a meal to begin with a single piece of *smørrebrød* (open-faced sandwich) as an appetizer, followed by a warm dish and then cheese, ice cream, fruit or cake as dessert. Coffee would be served after dessert, possibly with a pastry.

*Entertaining is generally informal with a "cozy" atmosphere.*

- The main dish is generally meat: beef, veal, pork or chicken.

- Fish is plentiful in Denmark and not considered special.

- Lobster and oysters are considered elegant, mussels and tripe are considered eccentric, and game and venison are enjoyed by everyone in the winter season.

## MENU TERMS

| | |
|---|---|
| *Forret* | Appetizers |
| *Hovedret* | Main course |
| *Dessert* | Dessert |
| *Brød* | Bread |
| *Suppe* | Soup |
| *Grønsager* | Vegetable |
| *Kødrete* | Meat |
| *Oksesteg* | Beef |
| *Svinekød* | Pork |
| *Lam* | Lamb |
| *Høne, Kylling* | Chicken |
| *Fisk* | Fish |
| *Æg* | Egg |

## TYPICAL FOODS

- *Kogt Torsk*: Boiled cod.

- *Flæskesteg med Rødkål*: Roast pork with red cabbage.

- *Røget Fisk*: Smoked fish — many types.

- *Engelsk Bøf*: Steak.

- *Gule Ærter*: Soup of dried peas served with pork, sausage or pickled goose.

- *Frikadeller*: Meatballs.

- *Stegt Ål*: Fried eel.

- *Øllebrød*: Rye bread mixed with black beer, sugar, lemon and cooked.

- *Rødspætter*: Sole.

- *Sild*: Herring (most often pickled).

- *Lagkage*: Sponge cake with custard, strawberries and whipped cream.

- *Rødgrød*: Fruit compote.

*"The Danish national drink is beer. The Danish national weakness is another beer."*

*—The National Travel Association of Denmark*

## DRINKING

- *Øl* (beer) and *akvavit* (a clear or slightly colored, very potent alcohol) are the national drinks.

- If you ask for *snaps* (a shot), you will get a small, ice-cold glass of *akvavit*. Be careful not to drink too many *snaps*.

- The Danes particularly like their local beers.

- Beer is drunk with *smørrebrød* and to wash down *snaps*.

- Ice cold *akvavit* is an essential accompaniment to pickled herring and smoked fish.

### TOASTS

- *Skål* (skohl), "Cheers." Widely used for formal and informal occasions.

- Toasting can be a very formal process.

- Never sip your drink until the host says *Skål*.

- Never toast your hosts until they have toasted you.

- Never toast anyone senior to you in rank or age.

- Propose a toast by tapping your glass with a spoon.

- The person seated at the hostess' left (guest of honor) proposes a toast during dessert and makes a short "thank-you" speech to the hostess.

- It is not customary for women to propose toasts in Denmark, other than *Skål*. However, you may find more women doing this in modern society.

- Tipping is not customary in Denmark. A token tip is appreciated.

- Restaurants: A service charge of 12.5 to 15 percent is always included in the bill, but it is customary to also round up the bill to the nearest DKK1-5 when paying your bill. The bill is usually paid directly to the waiter or waitress at the table.

- Taxi fares include tip.

- Washroom attendants: DKK5.

- Ushers: Small change.

- Porters: DKK5 to 10 per bag.

- There is no need to tip gas station attendants, hairdressers, barbers, hotel maids or doormen. They receive good salaries.

## MANNERS

- Politeness is very important.

- The host and hostess sit at either end of the table.

- At a formal dinner, name cards may be presented to each man with the name of his female dinner partner, who will be seated to his right. He should escort her to the table at dinner.

- The female guest of honor sits next to the host. The male guest of honor sits next to the hostess.

- The guest of honor is served first.

- Wait for everyone to be served before eating.

*Danes love making speeches for their guests, for others and for themselves.*

- Home entertaining presupposes only half the food is to be eaten, after which the family proceeds to enjoy the "leftovers" for the next few days.

- Guests are expected to "eat up" what they have taken on their plate.

- Partake sparingly of the first dish served. It will be passed once or twice again.

- Try everything passed to you.

- Keep your hands on the table at all times during a meal—not in your lap. However, keep your elbows off the table.

- Værsgo (VER-skoh) means "please" when passing food.

- Place your knife and fork side by side on the dinner plate at the 5:25 position when you are finished eating.

- Conversation extends long after the meal is finished.

- Don't get up from the table until the hostess does.

- Never leave directly after a meal. Plan to stay at least one hour after a meal ends.

- Thank the hostess before leaving the table.

- Dinner parties end as late as 1 a.m.; some hosts do not consider the party successful if the guests leave before midnight.

- An invitation to a Danish home for the evening may not include dinner. An invitation after 7:30 generally would not include dinner.

- There is no obligation to reciprocate by entertaining your hosts within a short time.

- Do not ask for a tour of your hosts' home until a friendship is well-established.

- *Tak* (which means "Thank you") may be accompanied by a prolonged and hearty handshake given after a dinner or other meal.

---

- European fashions are the norm.

## DRESS

- Never dress sloppily.

- Dress for rain and cool weather; coats and woolens are essential.

### BUSINESS

- Men:  Sport coats or suits and ties.  Neat appearance is a must.

- Women:  Suits or dresses and heels.

### RESTAURANT

- Men:  Jackets and ties.

- Women:  Dresses, dressy pants.

- Black-tie events are common for the business community.

### CASUAL AND BEACH

- Topless bathing on beaches is common; some beaches have sections for nude bathers.

- Bathers change clothes on the beach with a towel around them.

## GIFTS

- Gifts are opened immediately upon receipt.

### HOSTESS

- Always bring a small gift for the hostess when invited to someone's home.

- Gifts should not be lavish.

- Give: Bouquet of flowers (wrapped), liquor (very expensive in Denmark).

- Do not give: Sharp objects.

### BUSINESS

- Gifts are normally not exchanged at business meetings, but small gifts may be appropriate at the successful conclusion of negotiations. It is acceptable but not expected to give a Christmas gift to a Danish colleague.

- Give: Liquor, wine, chocolates, whiskey. A gift with a company logo is acceptable.

### TOILET TIPS

| | |
|---|---|
| *Toilet/WC* | Restroom |
| *Damer* | Ladies |
| *Herrer* | Men |
| V | Hot water |
| K | Cold water |

## DO:

- Use proper etiquette with Danes. Relaxed, polite manners are appreciated.

- Wait to be invited before entering a home.

- Wait to sit until your host invites you to sit.

- Treat everyone equally.

- Refrain from abundantly complimenting or commenting on anyone's clothing.

## DO NOT:

- Do not ever call a Dane a Swede or a Norwegian.

- Do not show emotions.

- Do not be ostentatious, displaying outward trappings of success.

- Never follow the host into the private rooms of a house.

- Do not discuss your personal life.

# HELPFUL HINTS

- Danes insist on punctuality for social occasions.

- Danes take punctuality for business meetings very seriously and expect that you will do likewise; call with an explanation if you are delayed.

# PUNCTUALITY

# STRICTLY BUSINESS

## BUSINESS CARDS

- Business cards are given to everyone at a meeting.

- Business cards in English are acceptable.

## CORPORATE CULTURE

STRUCTURE: The structure of Danish companies tends to be functional and relatively horizontal. Authority is earned by competence, and the boss is viewed as the group leader. Decisions are made after consulting with everyone involved, but accountability lies with the individual. Authoritarian behavior is not acceptable.

MEETINGS: Danes are famous for their informality, and that style definitely applies to business meetings. In most companies, meetings are frequent, and all participants are encouraged to voice their opinions.

Meetings begin and end punctually, but Danes generally engage in 15 minutes of casual conversation before getting down to business. Agendas are clearly defined, and participants know in advance whether the purpose of the meeting is to share information, discuss an issue or make a decision.

*Danes are more interested in success than money and care more about ability than titles.*

COMMUNICATION: English is the language of business in Denmark, and you'll almost certainly not need an interpreter. There is good horizontal communication between functional areas of Danish companies. It's acceptable to call a Danish businessperson at home on important matters.

BE AWARE:

- Although Denmark is a social welfare state, industry and agriculture are 100 percent privately owned.

- Independence and the entrepreneurial spirit are greatly admired by Danes.

- Agendas are clearly set for meetings with a stated purpose to brief, discuss or decide an issue.

- Meetings begin and end punctually.

- It is acceptable to call a Danish businessperson at home on important matters.

## ENTERTAINMENT

- Business entertaining is more common in restaurants, even though they are very expensive in Denmark.

- Business breakfasts are not common.

- Business lunches are common and preferred over business dinners, but foreigners are often invited to dinner.

- Business dinners are more social, but business could be discussed.

- Spouses are not commonly invited to a business dinner.

---

## APPOINTMENTS

**Office Hours:**    Monday through Friday
9 a.m. to 5 p.m.

**Bank Hours:**    Monday through Friday
9:30 a.m. to 4 p.m.

- Schedule appointments well in advance.

- July and August are vacation months. Don't schedule business meetings during the Christmas/New Year's period or at Easter.

- Weekends are for family. Don't set a business meeting for Saturday or Sunday.

---

## ESPECIALLY FOR WOMEN

- There is little discrimination against women in Denmark, and a foreign woman will have no problem doing business there.

- Denmark has the highest proportion among EC countries of women who work outside the home. Many women hold managerial and professional positions.

- Excellent maternity benefits, paternity leave and child care are provided. Women generally go back to work after having children.

- It is acceptable for a foreign woman to invite a Danish man to dinner, but his wife may come along. A traditional Danish man may insist on paying, but the younger generation has no problem with a woman paying. It is better for a woman to schedule a business lunch rather than dinner with a man.

- Women do not smoke in the streets in Denmark. They do smoke everywhere else—some even smoke cigars.

- It is acceptable to go to a restaurant that offers dancing to meet members of the opposite sex.

---

## HOLIDAYS AND FESTIVALS

- Do not plan to make a business visit or schedule any appointments during the following holidays or festivals. Be sure to check for the numerous regional and local holidays and festivals.

| | |
|---|---|
| January | New Year's Day (1). |
| March/April | Easter (Friday - Monday). |
| April/May | Ascension Thursday (40 days after Easter). |
| May | Great Prayer Day (7). |
| May/June | Whitsunday (Pentecost) and Whitmonday (49 and 50 days after Easter). |
| June | Constitution Day (5). |
| July | Industrial Summer Holiday (first three weeks— most common period in which companies close down their offices. Dates vary). |
| December | Christmas (24-26), New Year's Eve Day (31). |

# 23.

# FINLAND
## REPUBLIC OF FINLAND

## VITAL STATISTICS

POPULATION:   5 million (1992).

CAPITAL:   Helsinki, with a population of 497,000 (1991).

LAND SIZE:   130,119 square miles, slightly smaller than Montana.

GOVERNMENT:   Republic since 1919. The chief executive is the president, who is elected every six years by a college of 301 electors chosen by popular vote. The 200-member unicameral legislature, the *Eduskunta*, is elected through an electoral system for a four-year term, subject to dissolution by the president.

| | |
|---|---|
| LIVING STANDARD: | GDP = US$21,700 per capita (1992). Finland's economy has been hurt considerably by the collapse of the former Soviet Union. |
| NATURAL RESOURCES: | Timber, copper, zinc, iron ore, silver. |
| AGRICULTURE: | Accounts for 8 percent of GDP (including forestry); livestock production, especially dairy cattle, predominates; forestry is an important export earner and a secondary occupation for the rural population; main crops include cereals, sugar beets, potatoes; 85 percent self-sufficient, but with a shortage of food grains and fodder grains; annual fish catch about 160,000 metric tons. |
| INDUSTRIES: | Metal products, shipbuilding, forestry and wood processing (pulp, paper), copper refining, foodstuffs, chemicals, textiles, clothing. |
| CLIMATE: | In the far north temperatures range from -22°F (-30°C) to 81°F (27°C); extremes are less marked further south. The Baltic freezes most years. |
| CURRENCY: | Finnish markka (FMK) or Finmark. FMK1 = 100 penniä. Notes are in denominations of FMK1,000, 500, 100, 50 and 10. Coins are in denominations of FMK10, 5 and 1, and 50, 20, 10 and 5 penniä. |

# THE PEOPLE

CORRECT
NAME:            Finns.

ETHNIC
MAKEUP:          94 percent Finn; Swedish and Lapp minorities.

VALUE
SYSTEM:          Loyalty, reliability, self-sufficiency and
                 independence are highly valued.  Finns are proud
                 of their heritage and current society.  They are
                 leaders in peace conferences and international
                 peace initiatives.  They enjoy nature and proudly
                 protect their environment, which is one of the
                 cleanest in the world.  Finns value their privacy
                 and appreciate others respecting it.

FAMILY:          Average family size is three, which gives Finland
                 one of the slowest-growing populations in
                 Europe.  Both parents often work outside the
                 home.  Many young people live together before
                 or instead of marriage.

RELIGION:        88 percent belong to the Evangelical Lutheran
                 Church, but the government has an official
                 policy of religious neutrality.

## MEETING AND GREETING

- Shake hands with everyone present—men, women, and children—at a business or social meeting. Shake hands again when leaving.

- Handshake is firm with eye contact.

- Children will shake hands upon meeting guests.

- Finns are very friendly to foreigners.

- *Hyvää päivää* (WYHO-vah PAY-vah), "Have a good day," is a common Finnish greeting.

## NAMES AND TITLES

- Use last names and appropriate titles until specifically invited by your Finnish hosts or colleagues to use their first names.

- It is quite common to use first names during a first meeting, but be sensitive to status.

- Academic and professional titles are used instead of Mr., Mrs. or Miss. This is not as important in speech but very important in correspondence.

  **Examples: *Professor Nieminen.***
  ***General Director Jokela.***

- Foreigners may use Mr., Mrs. or Miss, but an attempt to use *Herra/Rowva/Neiti* is appreciated.

  | Mr. | *Herra* | HAIR-rah |
  | Mrs. | *Rowva* | ROW-vah |
  | Miss | *Neiti* | NAY-tee |

  **Example: *Herra Jokela.***

- Finnish and Swedish are both official languages of Finland.

- Finns are linguistically different from Scandinavians, but racially many have Scandinavian roots.

- Most Finns are bilingual; many speak English.

- Finns tend to be quiet, reserved, unemotional and sincere. They value their privacy—and silence. Don't intrude by making small talk with Finns on a bus, in a line or other public place.

## BODY LANGUAGE

- Kissing, hugging and touching are not done in public. Finns are seldom physical, even among very close friends and relatives.

- Men remove hats when meeting or talking, or when entering an elevator, church or home.

- Maintain eye contact when talking with someone.

- Cover your mouth when yawning.

## TANGO FINLANDIA

*In a country where body language is virtually unknown, the tango has captured Finns' bodies and souls. There are more than 2,000 tango dance halls in Finland, frequented by men and women of all ages. Unlike the hot and heavy Latin dance, the Tango Finlandia is more like a waltz. The music is sad and melancholy, featuring songs about lost love. An upbeat tango would be unthinkable. These dance halls help the Finns overcome their shyness by flashing "ladies' choice" or "men's choice" signs.*

## PHRASES

| English | Finnish | Pronunciation |
|---|---|---|
| Good morning | *Hyvää huomenta* | WYHO-vah WHO-o-men-teh |
| Good afternoon | *Hyvää ilta päivää* | WYHO-vah EL-teh PAY-vah |
| Good evening | *Hyvää iltaa* | WYHO-vah EL-teh |
| Please | *Pyydän* | POOH-dahn |
| Thank you | *Kiitos* | KEY-eat-ohs |
| You're welcome | *Ole hyvä* | OH-leh WYHO-vah |
| Yes | *Kyllä* | COOL-lah |
| No | *Ei* | a |
| Excuse me | *Anteeksi* | awn-TEK-see |
| Goodbye | *Näkemiin* | KNACK-eh-me-een |
| How are you? | *Kuinka voitte* (formal) | KWIN-kah VOY-teh |
|  | *Kuinka voit* (informal) | KWIN-kah voyt |
| Pleased to meet you | *Hauska tavata* | HOW-skeh tah-VHAT-ah |

## DINING AND DRINKING

BREAKFAST (*Aamiainen*): 7:30 to 9 a.m.

- Hot cereal, eggs, bread and open-faced sandwiches, yogurt and fruit, coffee.

LUNCH (*Lounas*): 11 a.m. to 1 p.m.

- In general, a lighter meal.

- Soup, sandwiches, salad and milk or buttermilk.

DINNER (*Illallinen*): 5 to 6 p.m.; dinner party, 7 to 8 p.m.

- Main meal.

- Soup, fish dish, main course, cheese and dessert.

- The main course is generally veal, chicken or fish—only rarely beef. Potatoes are a common side dish.

- You may be invited to a *voileipapöyta* (smorgasbord), a buffet-style meal which is popular for business.

COFFEE

- A favorite way of entertaining in Finland.

- This is served between meals or after dinner.

- Cookies and cakes are served with coffee.

- Once you have taken a pastry or food from the tray, be sure to eat all of it.

- Finns are among the biggest coffee drinkers in the world.

*To beckon a waiter or waitress, wave your hand and make eye contact.*

## MENU TERMS

| | |
|---|---|
| *Alkujuoma* | Appetizers |
| *Lämpimät ruoat* | Main course |
| *Jälkiruokia* | Desserts |
| *Leipää* | Bread |
| *Keittoja* | Soups |
| *Vihanneksia* | Vegetable |
| *Lihaa* | Meat |
| *Häränlihaa* | Beef |
| *Sian* | Pork |
| *Lampaan* | Lamb |
| *Kananpoikaa* | Chicken |
| *Kala* | Fish |
| *Kananmunia* | Eggs |

## TYPICAL FOODS

- *Voileipäpöytä*: Cold table or smorgasbord.

- *Kesäkeitto*: Summer vegetable soup (family dish in autumn).

- *Kalakukko*: Fish and pork in a rye crust shaped in a ball (specialty in Kuopio).

- *Rusipiirakka*: Rye pastry with rice.

- *Perunapiirakka*: Rye pastry with mashed potatoes.

- *Merimiespihvi*: Beef chunks with onion, potatoes, beer (family dish).

- *Poronliha*: Reindeer meat.

- *Lohi*: Salmon.

- *Riista*: Wild game.

- *Rapuja*: Crayfish (in July and August).

- *Kiisseli*: Fruit pudding.

- *Rahkapiirakka*: A dessert similar to cheesecake.

### DRINKING

- Milk, water and home-brewed beers are served with meals.

- Vodka, beer and *aquavit* (a clear, hard liquor) are favorite drinks.

- Finns have a great appreciation for *sahti* (homemade beer).

- Finns drink a lot of homemade hard liquor.

- *Marskin ryyppy: Snaps* of *aquavit* or *Koskenkorva* vodka. Glass is filled to the rim. Named after Marshal Mannerheim, Finland's national hero.

- *Kalja* (beer) or *olut* (low-alcohol beer) are drunk often and *viiniä* (wine) is drunk occasionally.

- *Marjalikööri* (berry), *mesimarja* (arctic bramble) and *lakka* (cloudberry) liqueurs are local specialties.

Snaps: *A small shot glass. If a Finn says, "Let's go have a* snaps,*" it means, "Let's go have a shot," usually vodka or aquavit.*

## TOASTS

- *Kippis* (KEE-pees), "Cheers." Informal.

- *Maljanne* (MAHL-ya-neh), "Your glass." Formal.

- *Terveydeksi* (ter-VAY-deck-say), "To your health." Formal toast in business setting.

- *Skål* (skohl), "Cheers." Popular Swedish toast.

- Do not drink until the host has proposed a toast.

- A guest can propose a toast to the host or hostess.

- It is acceptable for women to propose a toast.

---

## TIPPING

- Tipping is not widespread; a service charge is included in most bills.

- Restaurants: A service charge of 15 percent is always included in the bill; small change can be left as an additional gratuity for good service. If the service charge is not included, leave a 10 to 15 percent tip.

- Taxis: Rounding the fare up to the nearest markka is optional.

- Cloakroom attendants: Price listed.

- Washroom attendants, hairdressers, ushers: No tip.

# MANNERS

*It is considered bad luck to pass salt hand-to-hand. Put the shaker down on the table and let the next person pick it up.*

- Finns appreciate good manners.

- Finns behave very informally at home.

- The host and hostess sit at opposite ends of the table.

- The host will tell guests where to sit. Guests are seated without fuss.

- Children are often included in dinner parties.

- Do not drink until the host offers a toast. A toast is generally made with a *snaps* of vodka, *aquavit* or *Koskenkorva*.

- Wait for the hostess to start eating before you begin.

- Keep your hands on the table at all times during a meal—not in your lap. Keep your elbows off the table at all times.

- Do not eat anything with your fingers (except crayfish and shrimp).

- Take second helpings when offered.

- It is rude not to finish all the food on your plate.

- It is impolite not to compliment the hostess.

- When finished eating, place your knife and fork side by side on the plate at the 5:25 position.

- Do not leave the table before your host.

- Never leave until coffee/dessert/cognac are finished.

- Conversation may continue approximately one to two hours after dinner.

- Thank your hostess before saying goodbye to other guests.

- A sauna may precede or follow dinner.

- Restaurant checks are never split. If you invite, you pay.

- Finns may give you a tour of their home, but do not ask for a tour; it is considered impolite.

*A guest may be invited to sit in a sauna with the host. This is a special honor. Do not refuse except for health reasons.*

## DRESS

- Fashion is of a very high standard; dress is conservative and fairly formal.

- Winter is very cold. Bring warm clothing.

- Summer: Sweater, raincoat, insect repellent (generally provided by host).

BUSINESS
- Men: Suits and ties or sportcoats and ties. In summer, men may remove jackets if Finnish colleagues remove theirs. Often a jacket is not worn in the summer.

- Women: Dresses or suits.

RESTAURANT
- Better restaurants require jackets and ties, except in the summer.

- Men: Formal—Dark suits and ties. Tuxedos are seldom worn.

- Women: Dresses or dress pants; cocktail dresses for a formal dinner.

- Men: Suits.

- Women: Nice dresses.

---

## GIFTS

- A gift is opened as soon as it is received.

### HOSTESS
- Always bring a small gift for the hostess when invited to someone's home.

- Give cut flowers in odd numbers.

*Give tulips. They are a favorite flower.*

- Tulips are a favorite flower.

- Flowers may be sent the following day as a "thank you."

- Give: Flowers (odd number), wine, chocolates.

- Do not give: Potted plants, white or yellow flowers or an even number of flowers.

### BUSINESS
- Gifts are normally not exchanged in business meetings, but small gifts may be appropriate at the successful conclusion of negotiations. It is acceptable but not expected to give a small Christmas gift to a Finnish colleague.

- Give: Books, cognac, local/national gifts, records, art, glass, liquor (very expensive in Finland).

## TOILET TIPS

| | |
|---|---|
| WC | Restrooms |
| *Naiset* | Ladies |
| *Miehet* | Men |
| *Kuuma vesi* | Hot water |
| *Kylmä vesi* | Cold water |

DO:

- Observe all hiking, fishing or hunting rules.

- Maintain eye contact when speaking to someone.

- Speak quietly in restaurants.

- Expect that strangers may be seated at your table in a crowded restaurant, but not in more upscale establishments. You do not need to have a conversation with them. They may even resent an invasion of their privacy.

DO NOT:

- Do not eat while walking in the street.

- Do not show emotions in public.

- Never ask personal questions about someone's religion, job or political party.

- Never strike up a conversation with anyone on a bus, train or while waiting in line. Finns do not like their privacy invaded.

Faux Pas

*Don't interrupt silence. Don't make small talk or use animated gestures.*

### SAUNA ETIQUETTE

- The sauna is a venerated Finnish tradition.

- The sexes have separate saunas.

- All Finns sauna naked.

- You do not have to sauna naked, though it is considered strange not to; you may wrap a towel around yourself or wear a bathing suit.

- Shower before entering the sauna.

- Feel free to leave when you have had enough. Don't be macho.

- Snacks are generally served during and after the sauna.

## PUNCTUALITY

- Finns insist on punctuality for social occasions.

- Finns take punctuality for business meetings very seriously and expect that you will do likewise; call if you are delayed.

## STRICTLY BUSINESS

### BUSINESS CARDS

- Business cards are exchanged when meeting. No ritual exists.

### CORPORATE CULTURE

STRUCTURE: The managing director is the decisionmaker.

MEETINGS: Meetings are held to get ideas to managers. Finns do not make small talk in meetings—they get right down to business. Two- to three-minute pauses are common; don't interrupt silence.

COMMUNICATION: Most Finns speak English, so you shouldn't need an interpreter. It is acceptable to call a Finn at home for important business.

BE AWARE:

- Finland is a liberal society with no class distinctions. Bricklayers and managers may socialize.

- Doing business in Finland takes time and patience.

- Finns have been the link between the former Soviet Union and the Western World since the end of WWII.

### ENTERTAINMENT

- Business entertainment is mostly in restaurants.

- Business breakfasts are not very common.

- Business is commonly discussed over lunch.

- A business lunch may be preceded or followed by a sauna; it is preferable to sauna before lunch.

- Most businesspeople are invited to a sauna at some point in their visit.

- Business discussions may be held in a sauna.

*Finland has a rigorous work and play ethic—work at work, play at home.*

- Spouses are often included in business dinners.

- Business is not discussed during dinner— only after coffee.

- Business is not discussed at dinner when spouses are present.

---

APPOINTMENTS

**Office Hours:**   **Monday through Friday 9:15 a.m. to 4:15 p.m.**

**Banks Hours:**   **Monday through Friday 9:15 a.m. to 4:15 p.m.**

- Make appointments in advance.

- July/August is the most popular vacation period.

- On days preceding holidays, most businesses close at 1 p.m.

---

## ESPECIALLY FOR WOMEN

- Women are treated as equals in business and at home; 70 percent of women work outside the home.

- Finland was the first European country to grant women the right to vote (1906).

- Of 200 members of parliament, 77 are women.

- A foreign businesswoman can invite a Finnish man to dinner and pay without difficulty.

- Women can safely go to bars or restaurants alone.

- Take a taxi after dark.

---

- Do not plan to make a business visit or schedule any appointments during the following holidays or festivals. Be sure to check for the numerous regional and local holidays and festivals.

HOLIDAYS

AND

FESTIVALS

| | |
|---|---|
| January | New Year's Day (1), Epiphany (6). |
| March/April | Easter (Friday - Monday). |
| April | May Day Eve (30). |
| April/May | Ascension Thursday (40 days after Easter). |
| May | May Day (1). |
| May/June | Whitsunday (Pentecost) and Whitmonday (49 and 50 days after Easter). |
| June | Midsummer's Eve and Day (Friday-Saturday, summer solstice). |
| November | All Saints' Day (First Saturday). |
| December | Independence Day (6), Christmas (24-25), Boxing Day (26). |

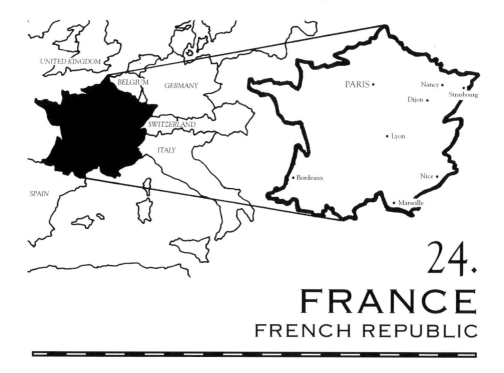

# 24.

# FRANCE
## FRENCH REPUBLIC

POPULATION:   57.2 million (1992).

CAPITAL:   Paris, with a population of 2.1 million (1990).

LAND SIZE:   212,918 square miles, slightly more than twice the size of Colorado.

GOVERNMENT:   Republic. The head of state and chief executive is the president, elected by a simple majority in a two-round election every seven years. The president appoints the prime minister and the rest of the council of ministers. The 577-member National Assembly is elected for five years; the current system is based on single-member constituencies. The second chamber, the Senate, is elected by a college of local councillors and members of the National Assembly.

LIVING STANDARD:   GDP = US$23,500 per capita (1992).

| | |
|---|---|
| NATURAL RESOURCES: | Coal, iron ore, bauxite, fish, timber, zinc, potash. |
| AGRICULTURE: | Accounts for 4 percent of GDP (including fish and forestry); one of the world's top five wheat producers; other principal products include beef, dairy products, cereals, sugar beets, potatoes, wine grapes; self-sufficient for most temperate-zone foods; shortages include fats and oils and tropical produce; France is a net exporter of farm products. Fish catch of 850,000 metric tons, ranking among world's top 20, all used domestically. |
| INDUSTRIES: | Steel, machinery, chemicals, automobiles, metallurgy, aircraft, electronics, mining, textiles, food processing and tourism. |
| CLIMATE: | Temperate and wet on the north coast; long, hot summers and dry winters in the south; wet springs and autumns in the west; a continental climate in the center and east. Temperatures in Paris are generally between 32°F (0°C) and 75°F (24°C). |
| CURRENCY: | French franc (FF). FF1=100 centimes. Notes are in denominations of FF500, 200, 100, 50 and 20. Coins are in denominations of FF10, 5, 2 and 1, and 50, 20, 10 and 5 centimes. |

# THE PEOPLE

CORRECT
NAME:            French.

ETHNIC
MAKEUP:          93 percent French, 1.5 percent Algerian. Other
                 foreign communities include Portuguese, Spanish,
                 North African. The French have a strong
                 attachment to their home regions.

VALUE
SYSTEM:          The French adhere to a strong and homogeneous
                 set of values. They take their culture and history
                 quite seriously. Cooking is
                 considered an art; good food and
                 wine are symbols of this country.
                 The French remain world leaders
                 in fashion, food, wine, art and
                 architecture. The French
                 embrace novelty and new ideas
                 and manners with enthusiasm, as
                 long as they are elegant.

FAMILY:          Family life is still very important. However, many
                 young people are moving to other areas for work or
                 schooling. Many couples are choosing not to have
                 families. Many couples live together before
                 marriage or as an alternative to marriage. Most
                 families are small, with no more than two children.

RELIGION:        Majority Roman Catholic.

## MEETING AND GREETING

- Shake hands with everyone present—men, women and children—at a business or social meeting. Shake hands again when leaving.

- Handshake may be quick with a light grip.

- A man may initiate a handshake with a woman.

- A Frenchman may kiss the hand of a visiting woman; accept this gesture graciously. A foreign man should never kiss the hand of a Frenchwoman.

- When family and close friends meet, they use first names and kiss both cheeks.

## NAMES AND TITLES

- Use last names and appropriate titles unless specifically invited by your French hosts or colleagues to use their first names.

- First names usually are used only for close friends and family.

- Colleagues on the same level generally use first names in private but always last names in public. At the same time, *vous*—the formal "you"—is used, even after a 20-year relationship.

- Allow the older person to suggest the use of first names or *tu,* the informal "you."

- Address people as *Monsieur/Madame/ Mademoiselle* without adding the surname.

| Mr. | *Monsieur* | meh-syeur |
| Mrs. | *Madame* | mah-dahm |
| Miss | *Mademoiselle* | mahd-mwah-zehl |

- *Madame* is used for all adult women, married or single, age 18 or older (except for waitresses, who are addressed as *Mademoiselle*.)

- Academic titles and degrees are very important. You are expected to know them and use them properly.

  **Examples:**

  | | |
  |---|---|
  | University professor | *Madame la Professeur* |
  | Lawyer | *Maître* |
  | Ph.D. | *Monsieur le Docteur* |
  | M.D. | *Docteur* |

---

## LANGUAGE

- French is the official language.

- Many French are able to speak and understand English.

- Use French only for greetings, toasts and occasional phrases unless your French is perfect.

- Accent marks are for correct pronunciation of vowels, not to stress syllables.

- When writing, be sure grammar and usage are perfect. Writing properly is a sign of education and breeding in France.

---

## BODY LANGUAGE

- Entrance to a room and seating is done by rank.

- Do not sit with legs spread apart.

- Sit straight with legs crossed at the knee or knees together.

- Feet are never placed on tables or chairs.

- Toothpicks, nail clippers and combs are never used in public.

- Keep your hands out of your pockets when speaking to or greeting someone.

- Sneeze or blow your nose as quietly as possible using a handkerchief or tissue. If possible, leave the room.

- Do not slap your open palm over a closed fist (a vulgar gesture).

- The "OK" sign (with your index finger and thumb making a circle) means "zero."

## PHRASES

| English | French | Pronunciation |
|---------|--------|---------------|
| Good morning, day, afternoon | *Bonjour* | bone-ZHOOR |
| Good evening | *Bon soir* | bone-SWAR |
| Please | *S'il vous plaît* | seel voo PLEH |
| Thank you | *Merci* | mare-SEE |
| You're welcome | *De rien* | duh ry-EHN |
| Yes | *Oui* | wee |
| No | *Non* | no |
| Excuse me | *Pardon* | pare-DONE |
| Goodbye | *Au revoir* | o reh-VWAHR |
| How are you? | *Comment allez-vous?* | kom-oh-tah-lay-VOO |
| Pleased to meet you | *Enchanté* | ahn-shan-TAY |

# DINING AND DRINKING

- The modern way to beckon a waiter is to quietly say *Monsieur* or *S'il vous plaît* rather than *Garçon*. You say *Mademoiselle* to summon a waitress.

BREAKFAST (*Petit Déjeuner*): 7 to 8 a.m.

- Bread, butter, jam and croissant, coffee, tea, hot chocolate.

LUNCH (*Déjeuner*): 1 p.m.

- Could be either the main meal of the day or a light meal.

- Main meal: *Hors d'oeuvres*, fish course, meat and vegetable course, salad, cheese, fruit or pastries, coffee (*demi-tasse*).

- Wine accompanies meal.

DINNER (*Dîner*): 8 p.m.

- Could be either main meal or a light meal. If it is a dinner party, it is the main meal of the day.

- Light meal: Soup, cold meat/cheese, casserole and bread.

- Wine accompanies meal.

## MENU TERMS

| | |
|---|---|
| *L' entrée* | Appetizers |
| *Le plat principal* | Main course |
| *Le dessert* | Dessert |
| *Le pain* | Bread |
| *La soupe/Le potage* | Soup |
| *Les legumes* | Vegetables |
| *Le boeuf* | Beef |

| | |
|---|---|
| *Le porc* | Pork |
| *L'agneau* | Lamb |
| *Le poulet* | Chicken |
| *Le poisson* | Fish |
| *L'oeuf* | Egg |

## TYPICAL FOODS

- *Patisseries* (pastries) and *pain* (bread).

- *Vin* (wine) and *fromage* (cheese).

- *Pâté*: Goose and/or duck paste.

- *Quiche*: Pastry filled with bacon, eggs, cream and cheese.

- *Crêpes*: Paper-thin pancakes with filling.

- *Escargots*: Snails in garlic butter.

- *Bouillabaisse*: Seafood stew.

- *Omelette*: Eggs fried with meat, vegetables and cheese.

- *Les Truffes*: Truffles.

*Do not ask for a martini or whiskey before dinner.*

## DRINKING

- Do not ask for a martini or whiskey before dinner—they are viewed as palate-numbing.

- Before dinner: Pernod, kir, champagne or vermouth may be offered.

- Wine is always served with meals.

- After dinner: Cognac, Grand Marnier or other liqueurs are served.

## TOASTS

- A *votre santé* (ah vo-TRAH SAN-tay), "To your health." Formal and informal.

- The host offers the first toast.

- Wait until everyone is served wine and the toast proposed before drinking.

- It is acceptable for women to propose a toast.

---

## TIPPING

- Restaurants: A service charge of 10 to 15 percent is usually included in the bill (bill will read *service compris*). Small change can be left on the table as an additional gratuity for good service. If the service charge is not included (bill will read *service non compris*), leave a 10 to 15 percent tip.

- Taxis: 5 francs or 10 percent.

- Ushers: 3 francs.

- Bellboys: 5 francs per bag.

- Hotel maids: Tip according to length of stay—approximately 20-25 francs.

- Bathroom attendants: 3 francs (price usually posted.)

- Gas station attendants: 5 francs (optional).

- Tip hairdressers, barbers and guides according to service rendered. They will expect a tip.

- Airport and railway porters charge by the item.

- The French are traditional, formal and appreciate good manners.

- Proper attention to and appreciation of food is a must.

- Conversation is a vital part of dinner in France.

- The female guest of honor is seated next to the host. The male guest of honor is seated next to the hostess.

- Never start eating until your host and hostess have begun.

- Keep your hands on the table at all times during a meal—not in your lap. However, keep your elbows off the table.

- Fold your salad onto your fork by using your knife. Do not cut your salad with a knife or fork.

- Never cut bread. Break bread with your fingers.

- There usually are no bread/butter plates. Put bread on the table next to your dinner plate above your fork.

- Cut cheese vertically. Do not cut off the point of the cheese.

- Almost all food is cut and eaten with a knife and fork.

- Never eat fruit whole. Fruit should be peeled and sliced before eating. Do as much as possible with your knife and fork.

- Bread is used to enjoy gravy and to help push food onto your fork—but not at a formal restaurant or party.

- Cross your knife and fork across your plate to signify that you would like more food.

- The spoon and fork above the plate are for dessert.

- Do not smoke between courses.

- Leave your wine glass almost full if you don't care for more wine.

- Mineral water is served with wine at meals.

- Taste everything offered.

- Leaving food on your plate is impolite.

- When finished eating, place knife and fork side by side on the plate at the 5:25 position.

- Send a thank-you note or telephone the next day to thank the hostess.

- Do not ask for a tour of your host's home, or wander into rooms uninvited; that would be considered very impolite.

- Dress is conservative and understated, but always fashionable. Be clean and well dressed at all times.

## DRESS

### BUSINESS

- Men: Conservative suits and ties. Colored, white or striped shirts are appropriate.

- Women: Conservative suits, pant suits and dresses.

- Suit coats stay on in offices and restaurants.

*The French are the world leaders in fashion.*

### RESTAURANT

- Better restaurants require a coat and tie.

- Always dress smartly.

### THEATER OR OPERA

- Men: Dark suits and ties.

- Women: Cocktail dresses/dinner dresses.

### CASUAL AND BEACH

- Casual attire is inappropriate in cities.

- Dress jeans are OK for weekends or the country; high-style casual clothing is worn.

- You may change into a swimsuit on the beach by holding a towel around yourself.

- Nude and topless bathers are not uncommon.

# GIFTS

## HOSTESS

- Always bring a small gift for the hostess when invited to someone's home.

- If possible, send flowers the morning of the party (popular in Paris).

- A gift to the hostess will probably not be unwrapped immediately (unless no other guests are present or expected).

- A gift should be of high quality and wrapped beautifully.

- Give: Candy, cookies, cakes, flowers.

- Do not give: Gifts of six or 12 or red roses (for lovers only); gifts of odd numbers, especially 13; chrysanthemums (for funerals); wine, unless it is of exceptional quality (French pride themselves on their wine cellars).

## BUSINESS

- Small business gifts may be exchanged but usually not at the first meeting.

- It is acceptable, but not expected, to give a Christmas gift.

- Never send a business gift for a French colleague to his or her home.

- Enclose a personal note, not a business card, with your gift.

- Give a good quality gift or none at all. Some possibilities are records, CDs, art, books or office accessories.

- Do not give: Gifts with your company logo stamped on them (the French consider this garish).

---

## TOILET TIPS

| | |
|---|---|
| *Toilettes/WC* | Restrooms |
| *Dames/Femmes* | Ladies |
| *Messieurs/Hommes* | Men |
| *Eau chaude* | Hot water |
| *Eau froide* | Cold water |

---

# HELPFUL HINTS

**DO:**

- Show knowledge of history, politics and French culture.

- Lower your voice a little and behave graciously and you will enjoy a warm response from the French.

- Close doors behind you when entering or leaving a room.

- Greet clerks when you enter or leave shops with *Bonjour* and *Au revoir*.

Faux Pas

*Never violate the French sense of privacy! Never ask personal questions such as income, address, job, etc.*

**DO NOT:**

- Do not expect a thank you when you compliment someone. Compliments may be appreciated but usually are received by denial.

- Do not chew gum in public.

- Do not select fruit or vegetables from stands. The vendor serves you. Vendors are likely to become angry if you pick up fruit or vegetables.

- Do not discuss politics or money.

- Do not ask about a Frenchman's occupation, salary, age, family or children unless you have a well-established friendship.

- French do not tell or like to hear jokes. They prefer intelligent and satirical humor. Funny stories of real-life situations are appreciated.

- For social occasions:  Arrive 15 minutes late for a house party but on time at a restaurant.

- The French take punctuality for business meetings very seriously and expect that you will do likewise; call with an explanation if you are delayed.

- The French consider punctuality a sign of courtesy.

## BUSINESS CARDS

- Give business cards to the receptionist or secretary upon arrival.

- Give business cards properly to each person you meet.

- Print cards in English or French.  Include academic degree and/or title.

- Carry a good supply of business cards.  They are exchanged often.

## CORPORATE CULTURE

STRUCTURE:  Organizations are highly centralized with a powerful chief executive; a vertical structure with a rigid chain of command is the norm.  Middle management is multilayered.  Rules and procedures are set and followed.  The team approach is rare.

Work actually gets accomplished through a network of personal relationships and alliances; this subculture is flexible, informal and energized to get the job done. Spontaneity and creativity take place at lower levels among peers who trust each other.

Company loyalty is highly valued, and job-hopping is uncommon. Technical competence is admired; rivalry and competition are encouraged.

MEETINGS: There generally is an established format and a detailed agenda. Meetings are an opportunity for the boss to assert authority; the purpose of meetings is to brief or coordinate and to clarify issues—not to discuss or debate. Suggestions are sometimes offered. The French get down to business quickly but make decisions slowly and only after much deliberation.

Presentations are made with great style and drama. Yours should be well-prepared and well-written, clear, comprehensive, informative and presented in a formal, rational and professional style that appeals to the intellect.

COMMUNICATION: Many French speak and understand English; an interpreter probably will not be necessary, but it's always good to check ahead of time. Communications exist on two levels, formal and informal, corresponding to the hierarchy and the working subculture. Don't discuss your personal life with French businesspeople; personal lives are kept separate from business relationships. Do not call a French businessperson at home except in an emergency.

BE AWARE:

- There are close links between government and business; both public and private sectors are strong.

- Businesspeople tend to be formal and conservative, and business relationships are proper, orderly and professional.

- The French are world leaders in economic planning, and that quality carries over into business, where plans are detailed and far-reaching.

ENTERTAINMENT

- Business entertainment is done mostly in restaurants.

- Business breakfasts are rare.

- Lunch is still considered a private time. However, the working lunch or breakfast is becoming more common.

- The French do not like to discuss business during dinner. Dinner is more of a social occasion and a time to enjoy good food, wine and discussion. Be prepared to discuss French culture, heritage and government.

*Senior managers socialize only with those of equivalent status.*

- Show proper respect and attention to your food and wine—an art in France.

- Spouses are not included in business lunches. Spouses may be included in business dinners.

---

APPOINTMENTS

**Office Hours:**  **Monday through Friday 9 a.m. to 12:30 p.m. 2:30 to 6 p.m.**

**Bank Hours:**  **Monday through Friday 9 a.m. to 4 p.m.**

- Make appointments at least two weeks in advance.

- Avoid planning business meetings during August or the weeks before and after Christmas and Easter.

---

ESPECIALLY FOR WOMEN

- Foreign women are generally accepted in business though they may be flirted with on occasion.

- Women are better accepted in management positions in the major cities than in the provinces. An increasing number of women hold management jobs in retail and service sectors, law, finance and personnel. However, considerable bias exists toward women in industry.

- Businesswomen can invite a Frenchman to lunch or dinner and should have no problem paying.

- Dress well but conservatively for business meetings.

- Inquire about the safety of the area where you are staying.

- Avoid using the Paris Metro after dark; take a taxi.

- Be careful of petty theft, especially in Paris.

---

- Do not plan to make a business visit or schedule any appointments during the following holidays or festivals.  Be sure to check for the numerous regional and local holidays and festivals.

## HOLIDAYS AND FESTIVALS

| | |
|---|---|
| January | New Year's Day (1). |
| March/April | Easter (Friday - Monday). |
| April/May | Ascension Thursday (40 days after Easter). |
| May | May Day (1), V-E Day (8). |
| May/June | Whitsunday (Pentecost) and Whitmonday (49 and 50 days after Easter). |
| July | Bastille Day (14). |
| August | Assumption (15). |
| November | All Saints' Day (1), Armistice Day (11). |
| December | Christmas (24-25). |

# ALSACE: Invest in Your Future

## A line drawn from London in the northwest to Milan in the southeast forms what is known as the "backbone" of today's Europe. This is where the wealth is concentrated. Where technology is equated with growth. Where the infrastructure and transportation systems are state-of-the-art. And, where education and research are held in the highest esteem.

## Alsace lies in the heart of this new European megalopolis. Its proximity to Europe's major markets is unparalleled: 75% of all purchasing power of the EC – $5 trillion – is within a 500 mile circle. As close to Prague as it is to Paris, Alsace is strategically located between Eastern and Western Europe.

*In the last 25 years, over 600 companies have moved into Alsace, France. More than half of these companies are based outside of France, coming from such diverse countries as the United States, Germany, Sweden, and Japan. In fact, more that 40% of the workforce in Alsace is employed by companies headquartered outside of France.*

### The "Golden Triangle" of research and education.

Basel, Switzerland. Baden-Wurtemburg, Germany. And Alsace, France. Together these three areas form what is known as the "Golden Triangle" of European research. No other place in Europe boasts a higher concentration of research capabilities.

With 4 major universities, 250 laboratories and more than 4,600 researchers, Alsace offers today's forward-thinking business the entire spectrum of technological research.

Almost every field of science is represented. The Center for Macromolecular Research, the Center for Nuclear Research and the Center of Sedimentology and Geochemistry are just a few of the facilities in Alsace.

### Reliable infrastructure and transportation network.

Alsace is blanketed with an efficient electrical power grid. The grid is fully interconnected, linking up numerous modern power stations – including natural gas, oil, hydroelectric, nuclear, and coal – giving it the advantage of multiple feeders.

This wide range of energy sources ensures that electrical supplies remain stable and secure. No other place in Europe has the reliable, low cost diversity and quantity of energy resources that Alsace offers.

Throughout history, Alsace has been a crossroads whose connections are vital arteries of the European community. Today, Alsace boasts an efficient transportation network – road, rail, water and air – that is exceptionally well maintained and constantly being improved.

*For Information in the United States Contact:*

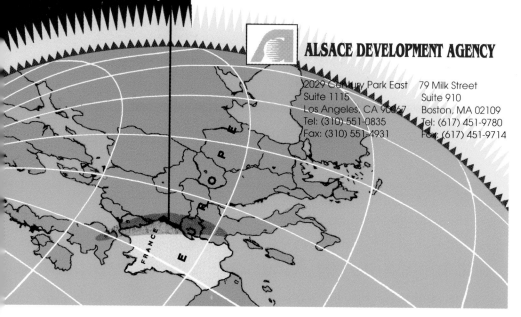

## ALSACE DEVELOPMENT AGENCY

2029 Century Park East
Suite 1115
Los Angeles, CA 90067
Tel: (310) 551-0835
Fax: (310) 551-4931

79 Milk Street
Suite 910
Boston, MA 02109
Tel: (617) 451-9780
Fax: (617) 451-9714

# Good things come to those who wait.

# Great things come to those who don't.

World Trade.
The magazine for America's global companies.
For subscription information, call 714-640-7070 ext. 105

# 25.

# GERMANY

## FEDERAL REPUBLIC OF GERMANY

## VITAL STATISTICS

POPULATION: 80.3 million (1992).

CAPITAL: Berlin, with a population of 3 million (1991).
Note that the shift of the capital from Bonn to
Berlin will take place over a period of years, with
Bonn retaining many administrative functions
and several ministries.

LAND SIZE: 137,838 square miles, slightly smaller than
Montana.

GOVERNMENT: Federal republic, consisting of 16 regions
(*Länder*). The federal government deals only
with defense, foreign affairs and finance. The
legislature has two houses: the *Bundesrat* (upper

house), a 45-member council appointed by the governments of the *Länder*; and the *Bundestag* (lower house), a 663-member federal assembly, 519 from the west, 144 from the east, elected through both an electoral system and single-member constituencies. The assembly elects the chief executive, the federal chancellor, who appoints the cabinet. The head of state is a president elected by a college of the assembly and regional legislatures.

LIVING
STANDARD:     GDP = US$24,000 per capita (1992). Germany is one of the top five economic powers in the world.

NATURAL
RESOURCES:    Iron ore, coal, potash, timber, lignite, uranium, copper, natural gas, salt, nickel.

AGRICULTURE:  West—Accounts for about 2 percent of GDP (including fishing and forestry); diversified crop and livestock farming; principal crops and livestock include potatoes, wheat, barley, sugar beets, fruit, cabbage, cattle, pigs, poultry; net importer of food. East—Accounts for about 10 percent of GDP (including fishing and forestry); principal crops include wheat, rye, barley, potatoes, sugar beets, fruit; livestock products include pork, beef, chicken, milk, hides and skins; net importer of food.

INDUSTRIES: West—Iron, steel, coal, cement, chemicals, machinery, vehicles, machine tools, electronics, food and beverages. East—Metal fabrication, chemicals, brown coal, shipbuilding, machinery, food and beverages, textiles, petroleum refining.

CLIMATE: Temperate and variable. Temperatures range from 27°F to 34°F (-3°C to 1°C) in January, 61°F to 66°F (16°C to 19°C) in July. Temperatures higher in southern valleys and lower on highlands with more rain. Spring and autumn are often overcast.

CURRENCY: Deutsche mark (DM). DM1 = 100 pfennig. Notes are in denominations of DM1,000, 500, 200, 100, 50, 20, 10 and 5. Coins are in denominations of DM10, 5, 2 and 1, and 50, 10, 5, 2 and 1 pfennig.

# THE PEOPLE

CORRECT
NAME:                  Germans.

ETHNIC
MAKEUP:                93 percent German.

VALUE
SYSTEM:                Germans value order, privacy and punctuality.
                       They are thrifty, hard-working and industrious.
                       Germans respect perfectionism in all areas of
                       business and private life.  There is a sense of
                       community and social conscience and a strong
                       desire for belonging.  To admit inadequacy—even
                       in jest—is incomprehensible.  There is an innate
                       distaste for stepping out of line.

FAMILY:                The father is the head of the family.  Both
                       parents often work outside the home.  Family
                       size is generally small.  Responsibility and
                       achievement are family values.  It is common for
                       young people to live together before or instead of
                       marriage.  There is a greater variety of lifestyles
                       in Germany today than in the past.

RELIGION:              44 percent Protestant, 37 percent Roman
                       Catholic.

Regionalism is very strong in Germany.  People
tend to be more loyal to and proud of their region
than Germany as a whole.

- Shake hands with everyone present—men, women and children—at a business or social meeting.  Shake hands again when leaving.

- When introducing yourself, never use your title.  Introduce yourself by your last name only.

  **Example:  *"Guten Tag, Schmidt"* or just *"Schmidt."***

- Men rise when women enter a room (not in a business meeting).

- Women should extend their hand to a man.

- Never shake hands with one hand in your pocket.

- There is no need to shake hands when meeting someone on the street.

- *Sehr erfreut* ("Pleased to meet you") is not considered "proper" etiquette, but many Germans do use it.

- Germans say *Wie geht es Ihnen?* ("How are you") only to people they know and in whom they are genuinely interested—not when being introduced.  It is an invitation to begin a discussion.

- Greeting:  *Guten Tag* (GOO-tun tahk), "Good day."

- Bavarian greeting: *Grüss Gott* (grees gawt), "May God greet you."

*Germans do not say, "Pleased to meet you," upon being introduced. Instead, they wait to see if they will be pleased to have met you.*

## NAMES
## AND
## TITLES

---

*Titles are very important. Never use titles incorrectly.*

---

- Use last names and appropriate titles until specifically invited by your German hosts or colleagues to use their first names.

| Mr. | *Herr* | hair |
|------|----------|------------|
| Mrs. | *Frau* | frow |
| Miss | *Fräulein* | FROY-line |

- *Fräulein* was traditionally used for women under 18, but it is going out of style even for young women. *Fräulein* is used to address a waitress.

- Address Germans as *Herr/Frau/Fräulein* + title and/or last name.

**Example:** *Herr Schmidt* or *Frau Schmidt.*

**Example:** *Herr Doktor Schmidt* or *Herr Doktor.*

**Example:** *Frau Direktor Schmidt* or *Frau Direktor.*

- If unsure of someone's title, err in favor of a higher title.

- Though at times it is used, it is not correct to address a married woman by her husband's title, such as *Frau Direktor*. When addressing a woman of status, it is always correct to address her as *Gnädige Frau* (ge-NAY-dig-ah frow) which means "madam."

- A *Doktor* can be either a medical doctor or a holder of a Ph.D. degree.

- A university professor is called *Herr/Frau Professor* without using the last name.

**Examples:** *Herr Professor.*
*Frau Professor.*

- Two titles should not be used at the same time, except when addressing a letter to someone. If a person does hold several titles, the higher one is used in speaking to him or her.

  **Example: In the address block, one would write *Herr Prof. Dr. Franz Schöll*. The salutation would read *Sehr verehrter Herr Professor*.**

- *Sie* (formal "you") is almost always used in conversation and is a must when addressing a professor, doctor or those with academic rank.

- *Du* (familiar "you") traditionally is used only among close friends by mutual agreement, but is being used more frequently today by the younger generation.

- The senior person initiates the use of *du* and a ritual may mark the occasion—this is a symbolic entry into each other's guarded private life and an offer of friendship. Never take this invitation lightly.

---

- German is the official language of Germany.

- Regional dialects are strong and spoken in most regions.

- English is widely understood and spoken.

- Any attempt to speak German is appreciated.

- Germans answer the phone mostly with their last name (i.e., "*Schmidt*").

**LANGUAGE**

# BODY LANGUAGE

---

*Never put your hands in your pockets when talking with someone.*

---

- Germans may appear reserved and unfriendly until you get to know them better.

- The "thumbs up" gesture means "one" (as in "one beer") or may be a sign of appreciation or agreement.

- Making your hands into fists, thumbs tucked inside, and pounding lightly on a surface expresses "good luck."

- Never use the "OK" gesture (index finger and thumb joined together to make a circle)—it is considered very rude.

- Don't point your index finger to your own head—this is an insult.

# PHRASES

| English | German | Pronunciation |
| --- | --- | --- |
| Good morning | *Guten Morgen* | GOO-tun MAWR-gun |
| Good afternoon/day | *Guten Tag* | GOO-tun tahk |
| Good evening | *Guten Abend* | GOO-tun AH-bent |
| Please | *Bitte* | BIT-uh |
| Thank you | *Danke* | DUNK-uh |
| You're welcome | *Bitte* | BIT-uh |
| Yes | *Ja* | ya |
| No | *Nein* | nine |
| Excuse me | *Verzeihung* | fare-TSY-oong |
| Goodbye | *Auf Wiedersehen* | owf VEE-der-zeyn |
| How are you? | *Wie geht es Ihnen?* | vee gate es EE-nun |

# DINING
# AND
# DRINKING

BREAKFAST (*Frühstück*): 6 to 9 a.m.

- Generally light: Soft boiled eggs, rolls, marmalade, coffee, hot chocolate or tea; possibly also sausages and cheese.

LUNCH (Mittagessen): noon to 1:30 p.m.

- Main meal: Soup, meat, potatoes, vegetables and salad.

COFFEE: 4 p.m.

- Coffee and pastry.

DINNER (*Abendessen*): 6 to 7:30 p.m.

- Light meal: Sandwiches, salads, cold cuts, cheese, sausages, pastries.

- For social occasions, dinner is the main meal.

*To beckon a waiter, raise your hand and say, "Herr Ober." To beckon a waitress, raise your hand and say, "Fräulein."*

## MENU TERMS

| | |
|---|---|
| *Vorspeise* | Appetizer |
| *Hauptspeise* | Main course |
| *Nachtisch* | Dessert |
| *Brot* | Bread |
| *Suppe* | Soup |
| *Gemüse* | Vegetable |
| *Fleisch* | Meat |
| *Rind* | Beef |
| *Schwein* | Pork |
| *Lamm* | Lamb |
| *Hähnchen* | Chicken (male) |
| *Huhn* | Chicken (female) |
| *Fisch* | Fish |
| *Ei* | Egg |

## TYPICAL FOODS

- *Würste:* Sausages—Germans have numerous varieties.

- *Kartoffeln:* Potatoes.

- *Nudeln:* Noodles.

- *Bratwurst:* Fried sausage.

- *Leberwurst:* Liver sausage.

- *Wienerschnitzel:* Breaded and fried veal.

- *Knödel:* Dumplings made of *Leber* (liver), *Semmel* (rolls) or *Kartoffeln*.

- *Torten:* Decorated cakes.


## IN BAVARIA

- *Züngerl:* Pig's tongue.

- *Wammerl:* Pig's stomach.

- *Schweinebraten:* Roast pork.

- *Schweinshaxen:* Roast knuckle of pork.

- *Weisswurst:* White sausage served between breakfast and lunch.

- *Spätzle:* Small, heavy egg noodles.

- *Sauerkraut:* Shredded cabbage that has been soaked, pickled or marinated in vinegar or wine.

- *Zwetschenkuchen:* Plum cake.

- *Eisbein:* Knuckle of pork.

- *Erbsensuppe:* (yellow split pea soup) served mostly with *Bockwurst* (venison sausage).

- *Gans:* Goose.

## DRINKING

- Beer, wine, mineral water, lemonade and cola are served with meals.

- Drinks are served without ice.

- Germans like beer cool—not ice cold.

- German beers and white wines are world-famous.

- Brandy is served after dinner.

- There are no long cocktail hours in Germany.

- Germans consume large amounts of strong coffee.

## TOASTS

- Prosit (PROH-zeet), "May it be good for you." Informal.

- *Zum Wohl* (tsoom vohl), "To your health." More formal, but can be said for all occasions.

- Nobody drinks at a dinner party before the host has drunk. The host will raise his glass to the woman on his right and then toast to the health of the group. Thereafter, people may drink as they see fit.

*Bier (beer) is Germany's trademark. Germany has more breweries than the rest of Europe combined.*

- When toasting as a guest, hold the glass only at the stem, clink your glass with everyone near you at the table and say *Prosit*, then take a drink. Then look into the eyes of someone at your table, lift your glass just slightly, and bring your glass down to the table.

- *Guten Appetit* is said before eating and means "Enjoy your meal." It is the host's way of saying, "Please start." Guests can respond with *Guten Appetit* or *Danke ebenfalls*, which means "Thanks, likewise."

- A person of higher rank initiates the toast towards his lower-ranked colleague, who is expected to return the toast later.

- A guest returns the host's toast later in the meal. This should be done by the leader of the delegation or the highest-ranking person.

- A woman can propose a toast if she is the highest-ranking person or the leader of the delegation.

## TIPPING

- Restaurants: A service charge of 10 to 15 percent is usually included in the bill (the bill will read *Bedienung*) but round the bill up to the nearest full DM when you pay the waiter or waitress at the table (minimum of DM1 or 2). If the service charge is not included, leave a 10 to 15 percent tip.

- Cloakroom attendants: 50 pfennig-DM1.

- Porters: Tip DM1. Tip is included in their salary.

- Taxi drivers: 10 to 15 percent. Round out the fare to nearest full DM. Give more if you have luggage. Generally, drivers charge 50 pfennig extra per bag.

- Toilet attendants: 50 pfennig.

- Hairdressers, barbers and maids: Optional.

## MANNERS

- Germans are very formal socially; politeness and good manners are a must.

- An invitation to a home is seldom given and considered a great honor.

- The female guest of honor is seated next to the host; the male guest of honor is seated next to the hostess.

- Keep your hands on the table at all times during a meal—not in your lap. However, keep your elbows off the table.

- Use a knife and fork to eat sandwiches, fruit and most food.

- A few foods are eaten with your fingers, such as asparagus and chicken wings.

- Do not use a knife to cut potatoes or dumplings; it suggests the food is not tender. In general, whatever doesn't need to be cut with a knife shouldn't be.

- Never cut fish with anything but a fish knife. If a fish knife is not offered, however, two forks are acceptable.

- If you are taking a break during the meal, but would like to continue eating or would like more food, cross the knife and fork on your plate with the fork over the knife.

- Do not leave any food on your plate when you are finished eating.

- Do not smoke until dinner is finished and coffee is served. Then ask permission.

- When finished eating, place knife and fork side by side on the plate at the 5:25 position.

- The honored guests are expected to make the first move to leave.

- Germans don't tend to stay long after dinner.

- A "thank you" is usually done in person or with a telephone call.

- Do not ask for a tour of your host's home; it would be considered impolite.

*When a German issues an invitation, it is always sincere and he expects it to be accepted. Never invite a German to your home or to dinner unless you're willing and able to follow through.*

## DRESS

- Dress is similar to that in the U.S., but with a European flavor.

- Being well and correctly dressed is very important.

- Casual or sloppy attire is frowned upon.

### BUSINESS

- Men: Dark colors, suits with ties.

- Women: Dresses, suits, pant suits or skirts and blouses.

### RESTAURANT

- Inquire about required dress.

- Usually dress well. Some restaurants are smart casual and some are very formal.

### THEATER/OPERA

- Men: Suits and ties.

- Women: Dresses or dress pants.

- Ask what attire is suggested for a particular event. You will see everything from formal attire to jeans.

## GIFTS

### HOSTESS

- Always bring a small gift for the hostess when invited to someone's home.

- For a large party, it is nice to send flowers on the morning of the party or the next day.

- Give: An uneven number of flowers (unwrapped, not 13), yellow roses, tea roses, chocolates.

- Do not give: Red roses (love symbol) or carnations (mourning). Yellow and white chrysanthemums and calla lilies are given for funerals only.

## BUSINESS

- Gifts are normally not exchanged at business meetings, but small gifts may be appropriate at the successful conclusion of negotiations.

- It is acceptable but not expected to give a Christmas gift to a German colleague.

- Give: Books, bourbon, recorded classical music. American-made gifts are very appropriate.

- Do not give: Pointed objects like knives, scissors, umbrellas (considered unlucky), personal items, extravagant gifts, wine (Germans are very proud of their wine cellars).

## TOILET TIPS

| | |
|---|---|
| *Toiletten/WC* | Restrooms |
| *Frauen* | Women |
| *Herren* | Men |
| *Warm* | Hot water |
| *Kalt* | Cold water |

# HELPFUL HINTS

---

*Germans are more formal and punctual than most of the world. They have prescribed roles and seldom step out of line.*

---

DO:

- Understand and respect cultural, political and economic differences between Germany's various regions.

- A man or younger person should always walk to the left side of a woman.

- Traditional manners call for the man to walk in front of a woman when entering a public place.

- Compliment carefully and sparingly—it may embarrass, not please.

- Stand when an older or higher-ranking person enters the room.

- Turn lights off if leaving a room.

- Always close inside doors behind you (bedroom, living room, etc.).

DO NOT:

- Do not expect quick friendships. However, once friendship is offered, it is maintained much longer than in "instant friendship" societies.

- Do not expect compliments.

- Never lose your temper.

- Never shout or be loud.

- Do not dress or behave in an eccentric manner. Eccentricity will attract criticism.

- Never violate privacy; never enter a room without knocking.

- Never make any noise in an opera, concert or play—unwrapping paper, fingering through program, opening purse, etc.

- Do not object if strangers are seated at empty places at your table in a restaurant. There is no obligation to converse with strangers who may be seated with you.

- Never put your feet on furniture.

- Never chew gum in public.

- Don't be offended if someone corrects your behavior (such as taking your jacket off in a restaurant or parking in the wrong spot). Germans see policing each other as a social duty.

---

- Punctuality is a German trademark.

**PUNCTUALITY**

- Germans take punctuality for business meetings and social occasions very seriously and expect that you will do likewise; call with an explanation if you are delayed.

- Tardiness is viewed as thoughtless and rude.

# STRICTLY BUSINESS

## BUSINESS CARDS

- Bring plenty of business cards.

- Present business cards properly.

- Business cards in English are acceptable.

## CORPORATE CULTURE

STRUCTURE: A strict vertical hierarchy exists, and power is held by a small number of people at the top. The corporate organization is logical, methodical and compartmentalized; procedures and routines are done "by the book."

The boss is respected for being strong and decisive and working hard; subordinates rarely contradict or criticize the boss publicly. The boss gives unequivocal direction and may make even minor decisions. Objective criticism isn't given or received easily; compliments are seldom given for work accomplished.

No dominant elite exists, but who you know is very important. Rank is also important, and it would be a mistake to set up a meeting between two people of different ranks. Fast-track promotions are rare; steady progress and job security are considered more important than rapid promotion. Car, size of office and holiday venues are all important symbols of individual success.

MEETINGS: Meetings are formal and scheduled weeks in advance with a set agenda. The primary purpose of a first meeting is to get to know one another, to evaluate the visitor, to gain trust and to check the chemistry. Germans usually begin to discuss business after a few minutes of general discussion.

People come to meetings well-prepared; reports, briefings and presentations should be backed up by numerous facts, figures, charts and tables. Avoid hard-sell tactics and surprises. Germans have an aversion to divergent opinions, but will negotiate and debate an issue fervently. Decisions often are debated informally and generally are made before meetings, with compliance rather than consensus expected in the meeting.

COMMUNICATION: Most Germans speak and understand English. An interpreter is generally not needed, but check in advance. Communication within German companies tends to be from the top down, with information shared on a need-to-know basis only. However, Germans produce massive written communications to elaborate on and confirm discussions.

Send personal and company profiles to German colleagues before your visit to establish credibility. Never call a German at home unless it is an emergency.

*Germans take business very seriously. Pride in German ability and achievement may be misinterpreted as arrogance.*

BE AWARE:

- Germans are competitive, ambitious and hard bargainers; perfectionism is respected in business and private life.

- Contacts are vital to business success. Use a bank, German representative or the *Industrie und Handelskammer* (Chamber of Industry and Commerce) to provide introductions when possible.

- Never lose your temper publicly—it is considered a sign of weakness.

- Always deliver information and products to clients on time.

## ENTERTAINMENT

- Business entertaining is usually done in restaurants.

- Business breakfasts can be arranged, but a business lunch is usually preferred.

- Lunch with business colleagues generally includes social conversation, not business.

- Germans enjoy fine cuisine and wine and view dinner as an occasion to enjoy food and drink with good conversation. Join in this spirit if you hope to establish a relationship. Do not discuss business during dinner unless your German host initiates the conversation.

- Germans are very hospitable toward foreign business partners.

- Germans behave in a reserved manner in the presence of their bosses or superiors when socializing. Privately, and among close friends, Germans joke, laugh, banter and have a good time (*Gemütlichkeit*).

- Older people tend to socialize with others of their own social level. The younger generation tends to socialize with anyone at any level.

- Spouses are generally not included in business dinners. However, if your spouse is traveling with you, it is appropriate to ask if he or she can join you for dinner.

---

## APPOINTMENTS

**Office Hours:**  **Monday through Friday 8:30 a.m. to 4 p.m.**

**Bank Hours:**  **Monday through Wednesday and Friday 8:30 a.m. to 12:30 p.m. 1:30 to 3:30 p.m.**

**Thursday only 8:30 a.m. to 12:30 p.m. 1:30 to 5:30 p.m.**

- Make an appointment well in advance.

- Avoid rescheduling or canceling an appointment.

- Avoid July, August and the Christmas season for business appointments.

- Avoid Friday afternoon appointments.

---

## ESPECIALLY FOR WOMEN

- Women, especially foreign women, must establish their position and ability immediately in order to successfully do business in Germany. Traditionally, there has been little acceptance of women in positions of responsibility and power in business.

- Older Germans hold more traditional views on the role of women in society. The younger generation has more open attitudes about women's advancement into higher positions in the business world.

- A woman should not feel inhibited about inviting a German man to dinner for business and will not have any problems paying.

- Sex discrimination is unlawful in Germany, but it is difficult to pursue such a case.

- Do not plan to make a business visit or schedule any appointments during the following holidays or festivals. Be sure to check for the numerous regional and local holidays and festivals.

| | |
|---|---|
| January | New Year's Day (1), Epiphany (6—some regions). |
| March/April | Easter (Friday - Monday). |
| April/May | Ascension Thursday (40 days after Easter). |
| May | Labor Day (1). |
| May/June | Whitsunday (Pentecost) and Whitmonday (49 and 50 days after Easter). |
| June | Corpus Christi (60 days after Easter). |
| August | Assumption (15—some regions). |
| October | National Day (3—Day of German Unity). |
| November | All Saints' Day (1), Day of Prayer and Repentance (third Wednesday in November). |
| December | St. Nicholas Day (6), Christmas (24-26). |

# 26.
# GREECE
## HELLENIC REPUBLIC

## VITAL STATISTICS

POPULATION: 10 million people (1992).

CAPITAL: Athens, with a population of 3 million (1992).

LAND SIZE: 50,961 square miles, slightly smaller than Alabama.

GOVERNMENT: Republic. The president is the ceremonial head of state, but the prime minister is the head of government. The president is elected by parliament for five years; he appoints the majority leader in parliament as prime minister and chief executive. A 300-member parliament is elected for a four-year term.

| | |
|---|---|
| LIVING STANDARD: | GDP = US$6,500 per capita (1992). |
| NATURAL RESOURCES: | Bauxite, lignite, magnetite, crude oil, marble. |
| AGRICULTURE: | Accounts for 17 percent of GDP and 27 percent of the labor force; principal products include wheat, corn, barley, sugar beets, olives, tomatoes, wine, tobacco, potatoes; self-sufficient in food except meat, dairy products and animal feedstuffs; fish catch of 115,000 metric tons in 1988. |
| INDUSTRIES: | Food and tobacco processing, textiles, chemicals, metal products, tourism, mining, petroleum. |
| CLIMATE: | Mediterranean, with hot, dry summers. Average temperatures in Athens 82°F (28°C) in July, 48°F (9°C) in January; cooler in the north. |
| CURRENCY: | Drachma (Dr). Dr1 = 100 lepta. Notes are in denominations of Dr5,000, 1,000, 500, 100 and 50. Coins are in denominations of Dr50, 20, 10, 5, 2 and 1. |

# THE PEOPLE

CORRECT
NAME:            Greeks.

ETHNIC
MAKEUP:          98 percent Greek.

VALUE
SYSTEM:          The Greeks believe you should "pass" time, not
                 "use" it.  Pretentiousness and standoffishness are
                 not appreciated.  Greeks are proud of their culture
                 and history and take pride in their country's many
                 accomplishments in establishing the foundation of
                 modern civilization.  In keeping with their
                 Olympic tradition, they love sports, including
                 soccer, basketball, swimming and sailing.

FAMILY:          The family is very important in Greece.  No
                 Greek should ever bring shame or dishonor to his
                 family.  Elders are highly respected and elderly
                 parents are cared for by their children.  Children
                 are disciplined firmly.  However, parents (even
                 the poor) spend a great deal of their income on
                 feeding, clothing and educating their children.
                 Men consider it a personal honor and
                 responsibility to care for their family.

RELIGION:        98 percent Greek Orthodox, 1 percent Muslim,
                 0.4 percent Roman Catholic.

## MEETING AND GREETING

- Shake hands with everyone present—men, women and children—at a business or social meeting. Shake hands again when leaving.

- Handshake is warm and friendly with a firm grip and direct eye contact.

- Good friends would be more likely to embrace and kiss.

- *Kaliméra sas* (kahl-ee-MER-ah sahs), "Good morning."
  *Kalispéra* (kah-lee-SPEH-rah), "Good evening."

- *Giá sou* (GYA-su), "Hello" or "Goodbye."

- Greeks say *Embros* (em-BROS), which means "Go ahead," instead of "Hello" when they answer the phone. This is a signal to start conversation.

## NAMES AND TITLES

- Use last names and appropriate titles until specifically invited by your Greek hosts or colleagues to use their first names.

- Formality rapidly moves to informality when interacting with Greeks.

- General titles used to address Greeks:

| | | |
|---|---|---|
| **Mr.** | *Kyrios* | **KEE-ree-ohs** |
| **Mrs.** | *Kyria* | **KEE-ree-yah** |
| **Miss** | *Despinís* | **theh-speen-EES** |

- *Kyrios/Kyria* + last name is the formal way to address Greeks.

  **Example:** *Kyrios Apostolou.*

- *Kyrios/Kyria* + first name + last name is a common, less formal way to address Greeks.

  **Example:** *Kyrios Pedros Apostolou.*

- If you do not know a Greek person's name, you can use *Kyrios/Kyria* by itself.

- Use professional titles. Greeks are proud to carry titles, especially doctors and lawyers. Use professional title + last name.

  **Example:** *Dr. Apostolou.*

---

## LANGUAGE

- Greek is the official language, but English and French are widely understood.

- Greeks will be very patient with any attempt to speak their language. Speaking even a few words of Greek will reap rich rewards.

---

## BODY LANGUAGE

- Greeks are very demonstrative and affectionate.

- "Yes"—Slight downward nod of the head. This gesture alone is not polite. Say "Yes."

- "No"—Slight upward nod of the head.

- Greeks today often use North American gestures, which could cause confusion. Say "Yes" or "No" and ask for a verbal response to be certain everyone understands.

## GESTURES

- A wave with the palm of hand out and fingers spread (*mountza*) is a rude gesture.

- Do not wave by raising your index finger and keeping your palm closed.

- The "OK" sign (index finger and thumb making a circle) does not mean OK. It is a rude gesture.

- "Thumbs up" means OK.

- "Thumbs down" (hand out with thumb pointing down) is a rude gesture.

- Putting hand out, palm down and middle finger extended downward means "up yours."

# PHRASES

| English | Greek | Pronunciation |
| --- | --- | --- |
| Good morning | *Kaliméra* | kah-lee-MEH-rah |
| Good evening | *Kalispéra* | kah-lee-SPEH-rah |
| Good day/<br>evening/night | *Chérete* | [CH]EH-reh-teh |
| Please/<br>You're welcome | *Parakaló* | pah-rah-kah-LOW |
| Thank you | *Efcharistó* | ef-kah-ree-STOW |
| Yes | *Ne* | neh |
| No | *Óchi* | O-[ch]i |
| Excuse me | *Me sinchórite* | may seen-[CH]O-ree-tay |
| Goodbye (one person)<br>(two or more, formal) | *Geea sou*<br>*Geea sas* | GYAH su<br>GYAH sas |
| Pleased to meet you | *Poli or Hareka* | pol-EE or HAH-ree-kah |
| How are you? (formal) | *Ti kanatey* | tee kah-nay-TAY |
| How are you?(informal) | *Ti kanees* | tee kah-NEES |

# DINING AND DRINKING

- To beckon a waiter or waitress raise your hand, quietly saying *Parakaló* (please).

- Greeks are extremely generous hosts.

- Meals in Greece are social. It is almost unthinkable to eat alone. The atmosphere is very relaxed with close friends sharing common plates of food.

  - You may have to be assertive with some waiters to get the service you desire.

BREAKFAST (*To Proinó*): 7 to 9 a.m.
- Roll or bread, cheese, butter and jam or honey, (Greek) coffee/tea.

LUNCH (*Toh Gevma*): 1:30 to 3 p.m.
- Could be the main meal.

- Light meal: Sandwich, cheese, fruits.

DINNER (*Toh Deepno*): 8 to 10 p.m.
- *Ouzo* is served with the appetizer.

- Light supper—yogurt and bread.

- Main meal—appetizers, meat or fish, salad, fruit, coffee and dessert.

- Beer or wine and water are served with the meal.

## MENU TERMS

| | |
|---|---|
| *Orektiká* | Appetizer |
| *Kyro piato* | Main course |
| *Epidorpio* | Dessert |
| *Psomí* | Bread |
| *Soúpa* | Soup |
| *Lachaniká* | Vegetables |
| *Moshari* | Beef |
| *Chirinó* | Pork |
| *Arnáki* | Lamb |
| *Kotópoulo* | Chicken |
| *Psáari* | Fish |
| *Avgá* | Eggs |

## TYPICAL FOODS

- Olive oil is used for much of the cooking.

- *Moussaka*: Eggplant with meat sauce and cheese.

- *Tiropeta*: Cheese pie.

- *Spanakopeta*: Spinach pie.

- *Dolmathes*: Grape leaves stuffed with ground meat and rice.

- *Souvlaki*: Small pieces of meat and vegetables on a skewer. A shish kebab (usually lamb).

- *Gyros*: Ground meat mixed with spices grilled on a vertical spit.

- *Arnáki* (lamb), *kotópoulo* (chicken), *psária* (seafood), *elies* (olives), *tyri* (cheese), *ryzi* (rice).

### DRINKING

- *Krasi* (wine) or *bíra* (beer) is served with meals.

- *Ouzo*: An anise liquor often mixed with water; served with appetizers.

- *Retsina*: Wine with resin added.

- *Ellenikó kafé* (coffee): Greek style, thick and very strong. You request bitter (without sugar), medium or sweet.

### TOASTS

- *Stinygiasou* (stee-nee-GEE-ah-su), "To your health" (singular). Informal.

- *Eis igían sas* (ees i-GEE-an sas), "To your health" (plural). Formal.

- *Kali epitihia* (kahl-EE eh-pee-tee-HEE-ah) is a toast to good luck and success in business.

- The host would normally propose the first toast.

- It is acceptable for a woman to propose a toast.

## TIPPING

- Restaurants: A service charge of 10 percent is included in the bill; small change can be left for both the waiter and the busboy as an additional gratuity for good service. In a *taverna*, leave the tip on the table. In a restaurant, put the tip on the plate brought by the waiter on which the bill is presented.

- Taxis: Not expected. Ten percent if the trip was exceptionally long or driver gave extra help. Get an approximation of the fare before you get into a cab.

- Hotel bellboys: DR235 per bag.

- Cloakroom attendants: Dr225 to 250.

- Washroom attendants: Dr125.

- Ushers: Dr300.

---

- Seat yourself in most restaurants.

# MANNERS

- In a *taverna* (casual establishment), a group generally orders several different dishes to be shared with everyone.

- In a restaurant each person orders his own dish.

- A guest may go to the kitchen and choose dinner by looking into several different pots (in smaller, less formal establishments).

- Greeks may share the bill with the host, but a foreigner should not try to do so. Generally, the person who invites pays the bill.

- When dining in a home, you will be offered several helpings of each dish. Eat all you like—it's a compliment to your host.

- The oldest guests will be served first. The male guest of honor is seated next to the hostess. The female guest of honor is next to the host.

- The dessert spoon is above your plate.

- In continental restaurants bread is served at every meal, but there is no bread plate. Bread is put directly on the table.

- When entertaining at home, the hostess prepares everything. For small groups the plate comes from the kitchen prepared. For large groups, the food is served buffet style.

*Some foods, such as appetizers, are eaten with fingers. Watch your host.*

- Keep your hands on the table at all times during a meal—not in your lap. However, keep your elbows off the table.

- When finished eating, place knife and fork side by side on the plate at the 5:25 position.

- Eat everything on your plate.

- If you cannot eat everything on your plate, you must tell the hostess that it is too much food the moment you are given your plate. At that time, your plate will either be brought back to the kitchen and some food taken off or the hostess will insist that you try to eat what you can. In this case, you need not eat everything.

- Put your napkin next to your plate when you finish eating.

- Dinners usually end about 11 p.m.

- Greeks will not offer to give you a tour of their home. Wait until you have established a relationship with your Greek colleague until you ask to see his/her home.

## DRESS

- Dress is more informal than in most European countries.

- Dress does not determine status.

- You can wear jeans as long as they are clean and neat.

- Women most often wear dresses.

- Women never wear pants or shorts in churches or monasteries.

BUSINESS

- Men: Suits, sport coats and ties.

- Women: Suits and dresses.

RESTAURANT

- Men: Jackets and ties in winter, usually more casual in summer.

- Women: Dresses or dress pants and blouses.

FORMAL

- Men: Dark suits or tuxedos.

- Women: Evening dresses.

## GIFTS

HOSTESS

- Always bring a gift for the hostess when invited to someone's home.

- Gifts will be opened immediately upon receipt.

- Presents should be wrapped.

- Give: Expensive wine, brandy, pastries, whiskey or cut flowers, or have a flower arrangement sent in advance of dinner.

- Bring a box of candy for the kids.

- Do not give: Inexpensive wine, knives or any sharp objects.

## BUSINESS
- Gifts are commonly exchanged among business colleagues.

- Inexpensive or expensive gifts can be given depending on the relationship.

- Give: Expensive wine, something for the home, handicrafts or a gift with your company logo.

- Do not give: Inexpensive wine, sharp objects.

---

## TOILET TIPS

| | |
|---|---|
| *Toaléta* | Restrooms |
| *Ginekón* | Ladies |
| *Andrón* | Men |
| *Zesto nero* | Hot water |
| *Kryo nero* | Cold water |

---

DO:

- Praise the children in the family.

- Eat more, stay longer or do whatever a host insists upon several times. The offer will be very sincere.

- Treat the elderly with respect.

- Respect the Greek flag and national emblem.

- Compliment the food and home of your hosts.

- In villages, avoid praising a specific item excessively, especially a handmade item, or your host may insist on giving it to you.

- Try to join in Greek dances. It is greatly appreciated.

- Bargain in shops or at the market anywhere in Greece, but not in department stores.

- Expect Greeks to ask personal questions such as, "Are you married?" or "Do you have children?" This is not rude, but an attempt to get to know you personally.

- Expect pushing and shoving in lines. Push back or you will never get anywhere.

# HELPFUL HINTS

*Greek hospitality is exceptional. Ancient Greeks believed a stranger might be a god in disguise and, therefore, were especially kind to strangers.*

**DO NOT:**

- Do not appear to exploit or dominate a relationship.

- Do not join in political discussions. The loyalty of Greek to Greek will win.

- Women should not pay attention to annoying men in the city.

## PUNCTUALITY

- Punctuality is not important in Greece. Greeks are generally casual about time—more so socially than in business.

- A foreigner is expected to be on time for business meetings, even though his Greek counterpart may be late.

- The Greeks believe that setting a specific length of time for a meeting is irrational.

- Dinner party—Arrive at least 30 minutes late. An 8 p.m. invitation means "after 8."

## STRICTLY BUSINESS

### BUSINESS CARDS

- Business cards in English are acceptable.

- Give a business card to everyone involved in your business dealings.

- There are no rituals involved.

### CORPORATE CULTURE

STRUCTURE: Company structure is narrow and vertical. The boss is the owner or the owner's trusted employee; the boss gives directives and takes complete responsibility. Subordinates are delegated specific tasks with little responsibility.

MEETINGS:  Meetings are a forum to express opinions or to inform the group and seldom have a formal agenda.  Business meetings usually begin with a general discussion and evolve into spirited exchanges in which everyone may speak or argue; consensus is important, and meetings will last (or be reconvened) until there is agreement.

COMMUNICATION:  English is commonly used in business, but it's best to inquire in advance whether an interpreter is needed. Greeks distrust written communications; letters and memos are often stiff and formal.

Don't telephone in lieu of a meeting; face-to-face contact is vital.  Trust is the major qualification for acceptance; Greeks want to know you before doing business with you, and there is no substitute for personal contact.  It is acceptable for a foreigner to call a Greek businessperson at home.

BE AWARE:

- Courteous and patient persistence is required for success.

- Be meticulous in your documentation.  Put everything on paper and get the appropriate signatures.

- Contracts should be kept simple.

- Being connected to the right people is critical.

- Pretentiousness and aloofness are not appreciated in business relationships.

## ENTERTAINMENT

- You will be offered coffee, ice water, *ouzo* or whiskey during a meeting.

- Business entertaining is usually done in a restaurant.

- Business breakfasts are rare.

- Lunch entertaining is generally only for business guests.

- Socializing is based on compatibility, not business.

- Business dinners are more of a social occasion and business discussions are usually limited; follow your host's lead in this matter.

- Greeks entertain friends in their homes quite often.

- Be extremely careful of your wine intake. Greeks can handle their drinking and may take advantage of your inability to do so.

- Spouses are commonly invited to dinner.

APPOINTMENTS

**Office Hours:**     Monday through Saturday
                     8 a.m. to 2:30 p.m.

**Bank Hours:**      Monday through Friday
                     8 a.m. to 2 p.m.

- The official work day starts early and ends at lunch; it may start again at 5 p.m.

- Many businesses are closed Wednesday afternoon.

- Avoid business appointments in July and August, the week before and after Christmas, and at Greek Orthodox Easter (changes every year).

- Prior appointments are advised.

---

- Greece is a good place for a foreign woman to do business, despite some discrimination against women in companies, clubs or groups.

- Women's opportunities in business depend on their connections, the same as for men.

- Many women continue to work after they have children. Greece has excellent maternity leave but lacks day-care facilities. Grandparents usually assist in taking care of the kids.

- Women are well-represented in politics and professions.

# ESPECIALLY
# FOR
# WOMEN

- It could be a problem for a foreign woman to invite a Greek man to lunch or dinner. Invite others along as well or, if for dinner, invite his wife. A Greek man will always try to pay, but if you make arrangements beforehand and are insistent, he probably will give in.

- If you are dining alone, choose a good restaurant to avoid being harassed by men.

- Verbal harassment from men is not uncommon and is considered by Greeks to be a sign of admiration.

- Be careful to watch your purse at all times.

## HOLIDAYS AND FESTIVALS

- Do not plan to make a business visit or schedule any appointments during the following holidays or festivals. Be sure to check for the numerous regional and local holidays and festivals.

| | |
|---|---|
| January | New Year's Day (1), Epiphany (6). |
| March | Shrove Tuesday (the day before the first day of Lent), Independence Day (25). |
| March/April | Easter (Friday - Monday). |
| April/May | Ascension Thursday (40 days after Easter). |
| May | Flower Festival (1). |
| May/June | Whitsunday (Pentecost) and Whitmonday (49 and 50 days after Easter). |
| August | Feast of the Virgin Mary (15). |
| October | National Day. |
| December | Christmas (25), Boxing Day (26). |

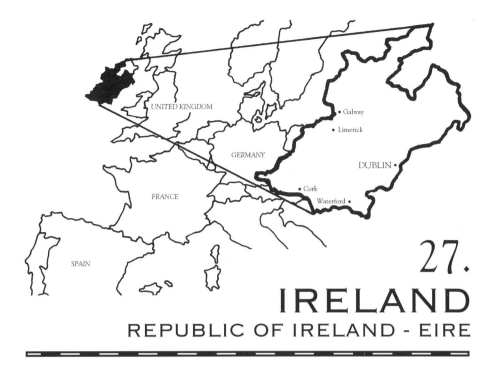

# 27.
# IRELAND
## REPUBLIC OF IRELAND - EIRE

## VITAL STATISTICS

POPULATION:   3.5 million (1992).

CAPITAL:   Dublin, with a population of 1 million (1992).

LAND SIZE:   27,136 square miles, slightly larger than West Virginia.

GOVERNMENT:   Republic since 1949. The chief executive, the *Taoiseach* (prime minister), is the leader of the majority party in power; the *Taoiseach* appoints the cabinet. The head of state is a president elected by direct vote every seven years. The legislature has two chambers. The upper house, the Senate, which has no power of veto, has 60 members, 11 nominated by the prime minister, the others indirectly elected. The lower house, the *Dail*, has 166 members elected through an electoral system every five years.

NATURAL
RESOURCES:      Zinc, lead, natural gas, crude oil, barite, copper, gypsum, limestone, dolomite, peat, silver.

LIVING
STANDARD:       GDP = US$14,400 per capita (1992).

AGRICULTURE:    Accounts for 11 percent of GDP and 15 percent of the labor force; principal crops include turnips, barley, potatoes, sugar beets, wheat, meat and dairy products; 85 percent self-sufficient in food; food shortages include bread grains, fruits and vegetables.

INDUSTRIES:     Food products, brewing, textiles, clothing, chemicals, pharmaceuticals, machinery, transportation equipment, glass and crystal.

CLIMATE:        A stable maritime climate greatly influenced by the Gulf Stream. Mild winters with average of 40°F (5°C). Cool summers with average of 60°F (16°C).

CURRENCY:       Irish punt (£Ir) = 100 pence. The Irish pound is officially called the punt. British pounds can be used in many hotels, restaurants and shops. Punt notes are in denominations of £Ir100, 50, 20, 10, 5 and 1. Coins are in denominations of £Ir1 and 50, 20, 10, 5, 2 and 1 pence.

# THE PEOPLE

CORRECT
NAME:             Irish, Irishmen.

ETHNIC
MAKEUP:           96 percent Irish, 2 percent English and Welsh,
                  1 percent Northern Irish.

VALUE
SYSTEM:           The Catholic faith has been a major influence on
                  Irish life. Material goods are less important than
                  family, friends and enjoying life. The Irish have a
                  quick wit and are easygoing and cheerful. They are
                  interested in people and place great value on the
                  individual.

FAMILY:           Families are close and very important. Extended
                  families like to live close to one another. Although
                  many young people are forced to emigrate to the
                  U.S. or England to find work, a great effort is made
                  to bring them back home.

RELIGION:         94 percent Roman Catholic, 3 percent Church of
                  Ireland, 1 percent Presbyterian. The hope for an
                  egalitarian society after British rule has been
                  unfulfilled. The British left behind an elaborate
                  class system based on education, wealth and
                  professional status. The major unifying force is the
                  Catholic Church. Beliefs and attitudes are more
                  akin to Southern Europe than England and
                  Northern Europe.

| | |
|---|---|
| **MEETING AND GREETING** | • Shake hands with everyone present—men, women and children—at a business or social gathering. Shake hands again when leaving. |
| | • A firm handshake with eye contact is expected. |
| | • The Irish are warm, hospitable people. |
| | • *Céad mile fáilte* (kayd MEE-la FALL-chah), "A hundred thousand welcomes," is a common greeting. |
| | • "Cheerio" or "God bless" are common farewells. |
| **NAMES AND TITLES** | • Use last names and appropriate titles until specifically invited by your Irish hosts or colleagues to use their first names. |
| | **Example: Mr. McCormick.** |
| | • The Irish usually shift to first names shortly after meeting. |
| | • Titles are used. Dr. and Professor are commonly used. Medical doctors are addressed as Dr. and surgeons as Mr. |
| **LANGUAGE** | • English is used everywhere by everyone. Irish (Gaelic) is the official language, but it is spoken on a daily basis only in small areas of Ireland, such as the islands off the west coast. |
| | • The Irish language has both sentimental and nationalistic importance. |

- Road signs are in English and Gaelic.

- Official documents use both English and Gaelic.

- English is used in business, not Irish.

- Gaelic is taught in schools and a proficiency test is required for graduation. Government employees and teachers must pass a Gaelic proficiency exam as a condition of employment.

- Be aware that the Irish don't like to say "No" to a request. They often say "Maybe" or "We'll see," instead of "No."

*Conversation is Ireland's national pastime.*

- The Irish are not physically very demonstrative and are not comfortable with public displays of affection.

- The Irish are uncomfortable with loud, aggressive and arrogant behavior.

- The "V for victory" gesture, if made with your palm facing you, is obscene.

## BODY LANGUAGE

• Many Irish/English words are unique to Ireland, with different meanings than in North America.

| Irish English | American English |
|---|---|
| boreen | country lane |
| jar | a couple of drinks |
| dither | slow |
| knocked up | awakened |
| homely | pleasant |
| boot | trunk of car |
| bonnet | hood of car |
| press | cupboard |
| runners | tennis shoes |
| footpath | sidewalk |
| bill | check |
| frock | dress |
| queue | line |
| ladies/gents | restroom |

*Don't be surprised if someone invites you over for crack! This means fun and jokes in Ireland.*

- Most larger cities in Ireland have several restaurants, hotels and castles that specialize in excellent continental cuisine.

- Irish food is best when unpretentious.

- Fresh vegetables and high-quality meat abound.

BREAKFAST: 8 to 10 a.m.
- The best-known Irish meal.

- It can include cereal (hot or cold), juice, and a *fry up* (eggs, grilled sausage, bacon, tomatoes, black pudding, brown bread and butter). Toast with marmalade is eaten after the *fry up*.

LUNCH: 1 to 2 p.m.
- May be a hot dish or a cold meal.

DINNER/TEA: 5 to 8 p.m.
- Dinner: Meat, potatoes, vegetables, dessert.

- Tea (supper): A light dinner of cold cuts and salad or a *fry up*. May also be a meal of just biscuits or cakes.

*Irish food is traditional, simple, hearty and delicious.*

## TYPICAL FOODS

*The potato is king! How can you not enjoy a country where two and sometimes three different styles of potatoes are served at the same meal?*

- *Colcannon*: A mix of potatoes, cabbage and onion usually served with sausage and bacon.

- *Mixed Coddle*: Boiled bacon and sausages.

- *Fish and Chips*: usually eaten with vinegar and salt.

- Oysters, trout, salmon and bay prawns.

- Boiled bacon and cabbage.

- Soda bread and wheaten (brown) bread .

## DRINKING

- *Guinness Stout* is the Irish national drink.

- Enjoy a beer, whiskey or wine with your Irish host or guest unless you don't drink for health reasons. Always buy your round of drinks.

- Refusing a drink is a major insult in Ireland.

- Ask for lager if you want American-style beer.

- Irish beer is served at room temperature.

- The Irish drink tea, tea and more tea.

## TYPICAL DRINKS

- *Black Velvet*: *Guinness* and champagne mixed together.

- *Irish Mist*: Whiskey-based liqueur.

- *Irish whiskey*.

- *Irish Coffee*: Coffee with whiskey and cream.

- *Pocheen*: Extremely strong liquor (moonshine) sold illegally. Irish use it to cure all; drink it with caution. They also rub it on stiff joints to cure arthritis.

*Shandy: Beer and lemonade (sounds awful but tastes good).*

## TOASTS

- Slainte (SLAHN-chah), "Good luck." More formal than "Cheers," another common toast.

- It is acceptable for a woman to give a toast.

## TIPPING

- Restaurants: A service charge of 10 percent is usually included in the bill. No extra is expected. If the service charge is not included in the bill, leave a 10 percent tip.

- Pubs: A tip is not necessary. If you have table service, you may leave a small tip.

- Theaters: Do not tip.

- Taxis: 10 percent of total.

- Porters: 1 punt per bag.

- Cloakroom attendants: 1 punt.

- Hotel chambermaids: 1 punt per day.

- Hairdressers/barbers: 10 percent of bill.

## MANNERS

- Irish manners are less reserved than those of the English and more gregarious.

- Table manners are close to those of England, only a bit more relaxed.

- Do not ask for a tour of an Irish home; wait to be invited.

- The small plate next to your dinner plate is for the peelings removed from boiled potatoes.

- It is polite to eat everything served to you in a private home.

## DRESS

- Dress modestly and conservatively.

- Avoid loud colors, especially the kelly green worn only by tourists.

- Avoid white pants, nylon running suits and other apparel that will not blend with Irish style.

- Tweeds, wools and subdued colors are recommended.

- A raincoat and umbrella are needed year-round.

- Dress for non-business occasions is generally casual. Few restaurants require a coat and tie except in Dublin. Check in advance.

- Weather is rarely warm enough for shorts. Wear shorts only at the beach.

BUSINESS/THEATER

- Men: Suits, sport coats and ties.

- Women: Suits, dresses and blazers (women wear pants less than in North America).

---

## HOSTESS

# GIFTS

- Always bring a small gift for the hostess when invited to someone's home.

- Gifts will be opened immediately upon receipt.

- Give: Flowers, chocolates, a bottle of wine or continental cheeses.

- Do not give: Expensive or ostentatious gifts; red or white flowers (symbols of death); lilies (for religious occasions only).

## BUSINESS

- Gift giving and receiving is unusual in a business setting.

- Small gifts may be exchanged, but are not expected, at the successful conclusion of negotiations.

- Small business gifts are commonly given at Christmas.

- Give: Pens, books, desk accessories, ties, paperweights.

## HELPFUL
## HINTS

──────────

*A driver offers you a seat or a lift, not a ride. To ask for a ride has an obscene connotation.*

──────────

DO:

- The Irish respect reserved behavior. Initial meetings should be low-key.

- Assume children will be included in family entertaining.

- Write a thank-you note for a gift or dinner.

- Always be sincere. The Irish dislike pretentious behavior.

DO NOT:

- Do not be surprised to meet a member of the clergy at a family function.

- Don't rush the Irish; they enjoy a slower pace.

- Never push ahead. Take your proper place in "queues" (lines).

- Do not comment on how small or quaint everything is compared to home.

- Do not eat at an American fast food chain. It shows a lack of appreciation for the local culture.

- Do not refer to the Irish prime minister as Mr. Major (or any other British prime minister).

- The Irish are tolerant of tinkers (gypsies). However, they can be dangerous; don't attempt to make friends with them.

- The Irish have a relaxed sense of time and may be a little late for business or social meetings. However, a foreigner should be on time for business meetings.

## PUNCTUALITY

## BUSINESS CARDS

- Cards are exchanged, but not necessarily immediately upon meeting.

## STRICTLY BUSINESS

## CORPORATE CULTURE

STRUCTURE: The structure of Irish companies is similar to that of British companies, but the Irish have a more flexible approach. The boss is the managing director or general manager, who is elected by the board.

Planning and strategy are relatively short-term; the Irish prefer to improvise rather than follow a rigid plan. Systems and rules with a practical (rather than intellectual) approach to problem-solving are favored. The Irish dislike bureaucracy and, while outwardly accepting authority, rebel against it inwardly.

MEETINGS: The golf course is the social and business hub of Ireland; business relationships are developed and business decisions made (or at least influenced) on the links. Don't be misled by their easygoing demeanor; the Irish are astute and tenacious negotiators.

COMMUNICATION: English is spoken in business; you won't need an interpreter.

BE AWARE:

- The European Community ranks the Irish the hardest workers in Europe. The work force is well-educated and, increasingly, technically skilled.

- Remember, the Irish want to do it their way. The British tried unsuccessfully to change Irish ways; you won't succeed if you insist on doing it your way.

- Who you know is vital to success; business contacts are best initiated through a well-connected third party.

### ENTERTAINMENT

- Business entertainment is most common in a restaurant.

- Business breakfasts are appropriate.

- Business dinners are usually more of a social occasion and a good way to develop relationships.

- Spouses may or may not be invited to a business dinner.

*Be genuine, buy your round in the pub, slow down— and you'll have no problem with the Irish.*

APPOINTMENTS

**Office Hours:** Monday through Friday
9 a.m. to 5 p.m.

**Bank Hours:** Monday through Friday
8:30 a.m. to 12:30 p.m.
1:30 to 3 p.m.

- Don't schedule business trips during July and August, the Christmas and New Year's season, or the first week in May (trade fairs for many businesses).

## ESPECIALLY FOR WOMEN

- Traditional and conservative attitudes remain toward Irish women in the workplace. However, the younger generation is more open to women in business.

- The "Old Boys Club" still exists. Who you know is vital to getting the job done.

- It is acceptable for a foreign woman to invite an Irishman to dinner. However, because of the small chance that such an offer could be misconstrued, it's probably best to stick with lunch.

- If a woman would like to pay for a meal, she should state this at the outset.

- It is considered more proper for a woman to order a glass of beer or stout rather than a pint. (One glass = 1/2 pint).

*The President of Ireland is a woman, Mary Robinson.*

- Women are allowed to buy a round of drinks.

- Ireland is one of the safest countries in Europe. Hitchhiking is common—you may see women hitchhiking alone. It's wise, however, to take greater caution in Dublin. Pickpockets and purse snatchers are a problem. Watch purses carefully on buses, streetcars and trains.

---

## HOLIDAYS AND FESTIVALS

- Do not plan to make a business visit or schedule any appointments during the following holidays or festivals. Be sure to check for the numerous regional and local holidays and festivals.

| | |
|---|---|
| January | New Year's Day (1). |
| March | St. Patrick's Day (17). |
| March/April | Easter (Friday - Monday). |
| June | Bank Holiday (first Monday). |
| August | Bank Holiday (first Monday). |
| October | Halloween (31). |
| December | Christmas Day (25), St. Stephen's Day (26). |

# 28.
# ITALY
## ITALIAN REPUBLIC

## VITAL STATISTICS

POPULATION:     58 million people (1992).

CAPITAL:        Rome, with a population of 2.8 million (1990).

LAND SIZE:      116,500 square miles, slightly larger than Arizona.

GOVERNMENT:     Republic since 1946. Italy has 20 regions, with
                varying degrees of autonomy.  The head of state,
                the president of the republic, is elected for seven
                years by a college of parliament and regional
                representatives.  Parliament has two chambers,
                the 630-member Chamber of Deputies and the
                315-member regional Senate, with equal powers.
                Executive power is vested in a Council of
                Ministers, whose leader is known as president of
                the council.

| | |
|---|---|
| LIVING STANDARD: | GDP = $20,200 per capita (1992). |
| NATURAL RESOURCES: | Mercury, potash, marble, sulfur, dwindling natural gas and crude oil reserves, fish, coal. |
| AGRICULTURE: | Accounts for about 4 percent of GDP and 10 percent of the work force; self-sufficient in foods other than meat and dairy products; principal crops—fruits, vegetables, grapes, potatoes, sugar beets, soybeans, grain, olives. |
| INDUSTRIES: | Machinery, iron and steel, chemicals, food processing, textiles, motor vehicles, clothing, footwear, ceramics. |
| CLIMATE: | Temperate in the north, Mediterranean in the center and south. Mild winters and long, dry summers. Average temperatures around 77°F (25°C) in summer, 46°F (8°C) in winter, with local variations according to altitude. |
| CURRENCY: | Italian lira (L), plural lire. Notes are in denominations of L100,000, 50,000, 10,000, 5,000, 2,000 and 1,000. Coins are in denominations of L500, 200, 100 and 50. |

# THE PEOPLE

CORRECT
NAME: Italians.

ETHNIC
MAKEUP: 98 percent Italian.
Minorities: Germans,
Slovenes, Albanians,
French.

VALUE
SYSTEM: Cultural achievement is
Italy's greatest source of pride. Being cultivated is
not a nicety but a social necessity. Inventiveness,
imagination, intelligence and education are
prized. Personal relations are scrupulously
maintained with loyalty highly valued, especially
in families. Modest and retiring behavior is not
valued, but a comfortable dignity is admired.
Italians are receptive to new ideas and fresh
solutions.

FAMILY: The family is the most important affiliation in
Italy. Strong, traditional ties bind families
together. Northern families live in a nuclear
unit. In the south, many generations live in the
same town or even the same home.

RELIGION: Predominantly Roman Catholic.

## MEETING AND GREETING

- Shake hands with everyone present—men, women and children—at a business or social meeting. Shake hands again when leaving.

- Handshake is firm with eye contact.

- Friends may greet each other with a kiss on both cheeks.

- Women should extend their hand first to men.

- *Buon giorno* (bwone JOR-noh) means "Good morning" or "Good day" and is used until 1 p.m.

- *Buona sera* (BWONE-ah SAY-rah) means "Good afternoon" or "Good evening" and is used after 1 p.m.

- *Ciao* (chow) means "Hi" or "Goodbye" (an informal greeting) and is used between friends only. Never greet a stranger with *Ciao*.

## NAMES AND TITLES

- Use last names and appropriate titles until specifically invited by your Italian hosts or colleagues to use their first names.

- Younger people go quickly to first names and *tu*, the familiar "you."

- Address Italians by *Signor/Signora/Signorina* unless a professional or academic title is used.

| | | |
|---|---|---|
| **Sir, Mr.** | *Signor* | see-NYOR |
| **Madame, Mrs.** | *Signora* | see-NYOR-a |
| **Miss** | *Signorina* | see-nyor-EE-na (women under 18) |

**Example:** *Signor Mangini.*

- Professional and academic titles are often used for university graduates:

  | | |
  |---|---|
  | *Professore* | Professor (medical doctor) |
  | *Dottore* | Liberal arts degree |
  | *Avvocato* | Law degree |
  | *Ingegnere* | Technical degree |

  **Example: *Dottore Mangini* not *Signor Mangini***

- Women almost always use their maiden name in business and on legal documents. They generally use their married name or both family names outside of business.

- *Lei* (lay): Formal "you" is used for anyone on a professional level.

- *Tu* (too): Informal "you" is used only for friends and family.

*Use* dottore *if you are unsure of a person's proper title.*

---

# LANGUAGE

- Italian is the official language.

- There are French- and German-speaking minorities.

- Many Italians are bilingual.

- English is spoken frequently in business, fairly commonly in hotels, occasionally in restaurants, and almost never in taxis.

- In Italy there are numerous "linguistic islands," where languages other than Italian are still spoken. Three million people belong to linguistic minorities.

## BODY LANGUAGE

- Men who are friends may embrace.

- Persons of the same sex may walk arm-in-arm when in public.

- Acquaintances may kiss cheeks.

- Maintain eye contact while talking—otherwise Italians might think you are hiding something.

- People push and shove in crowded places. This is not considered rude.

- Italians are known for using the most body language of all Europeans, but its use is declining.

- The fingertip kiss means beautiful; used to show appreciation for food, art, a woman, etc.

- The "hand purse" (finger tips held together) means a question, something good, fear, etc. It is considered almost the Italian national gesture. Do not ever mimic these gestures!

- The more refined Italians do not use hand gestures and many even consider them rude.

# PHRASES

| English | Italian | Pronunciation |
|---|---|---|
| Good morning/ day | *Buon giorno* | bwone JOHR-noh |
| Good afternoon/ evening | *Buona sera* | BWONE-ah SAY-rah |
| Good night | *Buona notte* | BWONE-ah NOH-tay |
| Please | *Per favore* | pair fah-VOH-ray |
| Thank you | *Grazie* | GRAAT-see |
| You're welcome | *Prego* | PRAY-goh |
| Yes | *Si* | see |
| No | *No* | noh |
| Excuse me | *Mi scusi* | mee SKOO-zee |
| Goodbye | *Arrivederci* | ah-ree-va-DARE-chee |
| How are you? | *Come sta?* | KOH-may stah? |
| Pleased to meet you | *Molto lieto* | MOAL-toh LEE-ay-toh |

# DINING
# AND
# DRINKING

*To beckon a waiter or waitress, raise your index finger and make eye contact. You can also say* Mi scusi *when making eye contact.*

BREAKFAST (*La Prima Colazione*): 7 to 8 a.m.

- Very light meal: Coffee, *biscotti* (cookies) or a roll.

LUNCH (*La Colazione* or *Il Pranzo*): 1 p.m. in the north; later hours in the south.

- Light and casual unless this is a formal business lunch.

- Lunch may even be a sandwich ordered in.

- In southern Italy, especially for foreign guests, lunch may be more formal.

DINNER (*La Cena*): 8 to 9:30 p.m.; later hours in southern Italy and during summer.

- Main meal.

- May include soup, pasta, main dish, salad, fruit and cheese or dessert.

- The main meal may last two to four hours.

- Dinner in a restaurant is typical entertainment.

## MENU TERMS

| | |
|---|---|
| *Antipasti* | Appetizers |
| *Primi piatti* | Pasta dishes |
| *Secondi piatti* | Meat or fish dishes |
| *Dolce* | Dessert |
| *Pane* | Bread |
| *Minestre, zuppe* | Soup |
| *Verdure* | Vegetables |
| *Manzo* | Beef |
| *Maiale* | Pork |
| *Agnello* | Lamb |
| *Pollo* | Chicken |
| *Pesce* | Fish |
| *Uova* | Egg |

## TYPICAL FOODS

- *Mortadella:* Bologna with peppercorns.

- *Prosciutto:* Dried, salted ham.

- *Tortellini:* Ring-shaped pasta with filling.

- *Gnocchi:* Potato-flour dumpling.

- *Pesto:* Sauce made of basil, garlic, olive oil, parmesan cheese and pine nuts.

- *Cannelloni:* Tube-shaped pasta filled with meat or cheese and covered with tomato sauce.

- *Pizza:* Various regional styles, many unlike what we're familiar with in the U.S.

- *Polenta:* Cornmeal porridge.

- *Panzanella:* Crust bread mixed with herbs, tomatoes, onions, garlic, olive oil, vinegar and spices.

### DRINKING

- Cocktails are not common in Italy. Cocktail hours are short or nonexistent.

- Drinking without eating is rare.

- Hard drinking is rare and not appreciated. Even mild intoxication is considered very ill-mannered.

- Women drink very little in Italy.

- *Vino* (wine) is generally served with every course of a meal.

- Beer, scotch, *grappa*, mineral water and soft drinks are available.

### TOASTS

- *Salute* or *Alla salute* (ah-lah sa-LOO-tay), "To your health." Formal or informal.

- *Cin-cin* (chin-chin), "To your health." Formal or informal.

- At formal occasions, women generally do not propose a toast.

## TIPPING

- Tip anyone who provides a service for you.

- Restaurants: Most have a cover charge. In addition, a service charge of 10 to 15 percent is always included in the bill; small change (minimum of L1,000—never coins) can be left as an additional gratuity for good service. An extra tip is expected.

- Waiters in Europe are professionals—not students or people between other jobs. Respect them as such and tip accordingly.

- When you have a coffee at a bar, pay at the register and get receipt. Leave a tip of L1,000 lire on the bar with the receipt.

- Taxis: 15 percent of fare.

- Hairdressers and barbers: 15 percent.

- Cloakroom attendants: L500-1,000. An amount generally is posted.

- Washroom attendants: L100.

- Doormen: L1,000 if they call a taxi for you.

- Ushers: L1,000.

- Porters: L1,000 to 1,500 per bag.

---

# MANNERS

- The female guest of honor is seated next to the host; the male guest of honor is seated next to the hostess.

- Allow the hostess to begin eating before guests begin.

- Italians do not use bread plates. Break bread and place it next to your plate on the table.

- Butter is not served with bread.

- Roll pasta with your fork against the sides of your pasta plate. *Never use your spoon to help roll pasta.*

- Use only a fork to eat salad; never cut salad with a knife.

- Keep your hands on the table at all times during a meal—not in your lap. However, keep your elbows off the table.

- Use your knife (not your fingers) to pick up pieces of cheese and put it on your bread or cracker.

- Grated cheese is never served with a fish dish or with pasta that has fish as an ingredient.

- Take a small amount of food when being served; your hostess will always offer a second helping, and it's impolite to refuse.

- Keep your wine glass almost full if you don't want a refill.

- The knife and fork above your plate are for dessert.

- Eat fruit with a knife and fork, except for grapes and cherries.

- Try to eat everything on your plate, but if you are full, it's not considered rude to leave some food on your plate.

- When finished eating, place your knife and fork side-by-side on the plate at the 5:25 position. The fork should be on the left and the knife on the right with the blade facing the fork.

- Do not leave the table until everyone is finished eating.

- Ask for your check when you are finished eating. It may not be brought until you ask.

- If you invite someone to a restaurant, you pay for the meal.

- Never ask for a tour of anyone's home. It is considered impolite.

---

- Italy is a major center of European fashion.

- Italians dress elegantly but conservatively.

- Dress formally in the cities.

- Don't wear shorts in the city unless they are smart, stylish and Bermuda length.

- Don't wear sweatsuits or warmup suits except for athletic activities.

- Old, torn or dirty clothing is seldom seen and not appreciated.

- Making a good impression matters deeply to Italians.

BUSINESS/ RESTAURANT

- Men and women dress conservatively and formally for business and entertaining.

- Men: Suits, sport coats, ties.

- Women: Dresses or suits. Do not dress like a man. Wear feminine clothing.

- Most women do not wear hose in the summer.

# DRESS

*Italians are chic. Even people in small towns spend a great deal of money on their wardrobes and dress well at all times.*

- Men: Dark suits and ties.

- Women: Dresses and heels.

Casual
- Wear smart, stylish casual clothes.

- Men: Pants and shirts, sweaters, sport coats.

- Women: Pants or skirts. Pants are not worn as often as in the U.S.

- Italians are elegant even when casual.

- Jeans are acceptable if they are neat, clean and stylish.

## GIFTS

- Italians are very generous gift givers. You will be embarrassed if you give a "cheap" gift.

- Gifts are wrapped beautifully.

- Do not wrap a gift in black with a gold ribbon—a sign of mourning.

- Gifts are opened in front of the giver when received.

### HOSTESS
- Always bring a gift for the hostess when invited to someone's home.

- Give a high-quality, significant gift.

- Send flowers or a gift to the host's home on the day after a party.

- Pink or yellow roses and mixed bouquets are favorites.

- Give: A box of chocolates, flowers (uneven number), pastries, a vase.

- Do not give: Cheap or practical gifts, an even number of flowers, chrysanthemums (a symbol of death), knives or scissors (bad luck) or red roses (symbols of love or passion).

## BUSINESS

- Gifts are generally not exchanged at initial meetings, but taking a gift in your briefcase is recommended in case your Italian hosts give you one. You'll be in a position to reciprocate. Gift-giving is common in business.

- Gifts may be exchanged at negotiations, but not necessarily.

- Give: Desk accessories, recorded music, books, whiskey, cognac, high-quality liquor.

- Gifts with your company logo are acceptable if the logos aren't large or gaudy.

- Do not give: Cheap or practical gifts, knives or scissors (bad luck), money, personal items.

---

## TOILET TIPS

| | |
|---|---|
| *Toilette/WC* | Restrooms |
| *Signore* | Ladies |
| *Signori* | Men |
| *Acqua calda (C)* | Hot water |
| *Acqua fredda (F)* | Cold water |

---

## HELPFUL HINTS

**DO:**

- Send a thank-you note after being entertained or given a gift.

- Compliment your hosts.

- Give attention to or bring a small gift for children.

- Cover your mouth if you must yawn, but try hard not to.

- Remove your hat (men) when entering a building.

- Bargain in stores or markets. Shopkeepers may say no, but they won't be insulted if you ask politely.

- Park your car in a reputable, attended lot or garage. Car thieves are common in larger cities.

- Leave most valuables in a secure place and take common-sense precautions with those you carry. Pickpockets are a problem, especially in major cities.

**DO NOT:**

- Do not make impolite bodily noises—belching, etc.

- Never remove your shoes in public.

- Do not be nosy or ask people where they live or what they do for a living.

- When being entertained in a home, guests arrive 15 to 30 minutes after the time specified on the invitation.

- Punctuality for business meetings is very important.  Deliberate lateness in business is viewed as sloppy.

- Foreigners are expected to be on time, but you may be kept waiting by your Italian colleagues.  Call with an explanation if you are delayed.

- It is extremely impolite to break an appointment.

## BUSINESS CARDS

- Business cards are used only in business—not socially, unless requested.

- Do not give a business card to the same person twice.  They are exchanged only the first time you meet.  You must remember to whom you have given a business card.

- Present a business card to each person in a meeting.

- When receiving a business card, look at the name and title carefully, then set it on the table in front of you or put it in your briefcase.

- Never throw a business card across the table like you are dealing playing cards to someone.

## CORPORATE CULTURE

STRUCTURE: There is a wide diversity of organizational styles. Reporting lines often are not clear, and organizations are built mostly on personal alliances.

*Italians love to make money, but with panache.*

The boss in a company is generally the owner, chairman or managing director. The boss is respected for charisma, creativeness, empathy, consistency and reliability.

Nothing of importance is done by a textbook plan. Pragmatism and improvisation are the keys to success—protocol, rules and organization charts are generally ignored.

Development and execution of a plan or project requires a respected leader capable of establishing personal relationships in order to achieve commitment and cooperation.

MEETINGS: Generally, business discussions begin after a few minutes of small talk. Meeting style is unstructured and informal. Formal presentations are not common, but when made are usually a forum for displaying the leader's status, personality and charisma.

Decisions are generally made and agreed to privately before meetings; the purpose of the meeting is to evaluate the mood or test the support of colleagues, not to make a decision. New ideas are generally cleared with everyone before being presented in meetings. Decisions that are made and agreed to may never be implemented.

COMMUNICATION: English is quite common in business, but check ahead of time to see if an interpreter is necessary. Establish a personal relationship with Italians; they like to deal with people they know and trust. Do not call an Italian businessperson at home except in an emergency.

BE AWARE:

- Although Italians generally believe in enjoying life and work, there are distinctly different approaches to work in the northern and southern parts of the country. In the south, people take time to enjoy life and do business in a leisurely way. In the north, people believe in getting business done without wasting time. Pace yourself accordingly.

- Italians keep their work and private lives very separate.

- Italians enjoy a lot of humor and can be self-deprecating at times.

## ENTERTAINMENT

- Business may be done at a breakfast meeting, but it is not recommended.

- Business entertainment is generally done at lunch or dinner in a restaurant.

- Dinner entertainment is more of a social occasion to get to know people. Business discussions are usually very limited.

- Only discuss business at social events if requested to do so.

- Spouses are often involved in entertaining.

---

## APPOINTMENTS

| | |
|---|---|
| **Office Hours:** | **Monday through Friday 8:30 a.m. to 1 p.m. 4 to 8 p.m.** |
| **Bank Hours:** | **Monday though Friday 8:30 a.m. to 1:30 p.m.** |

- Make business appointments well in advance.

- Some Italians work six days a week.

- Do not schedule meetings in August or during the Christmas or Easter holidays.

---

# ESPECIALLY FOR WOMEN

- The business community is male-dominated. Few Italian women are in managerial positions or the professions—exceptions are in family companies. No women are in the higher echelons of banking. Only 38 percent of Italian women under 65 are in the labor market—one of the lowest percentages in Western Europe.

- Very little feminism exists. However, it is becoming more common in the north.

- Italians are generally not inhibited when interacting with the opposite sex. Enjoy the fun and flirtation that are part of the spirit of life in Italy.

- Do not pour wine if you are a guest. This is considered unfeminine by Italians. Also, women generally do not propose a toast.

- Do not expect Italian men to pull out your chair or help you with your coat.

- Do not walk alone at night. Stay in a first-class hotel when traveling alone.

- Don't be afraid to eat alone in northern Italy. However, depending on your dress and actions, men may approach a woman eating alone in southern Italy.

- It is better for a woman to invite an Italian man to lunch—but if you invite him to dinner, ask if he would like to bring his wife. Drawing on the centuries-old tradition of gallantry, the Italian man usually will make a strong attempt to pay for lunch or dinner.

## HOLIDAYS AND FESTIVALS

- Do not plan to make a business visit or schedule any appointments during the following holidays or festivals. Be sure to check for the numerous regional and local holidays and festivals.

| | |
|---|---|
| January | New Year's Day (1), Epiphany (6). |
| March/April | Easter (Sunday-Monday). |
| April | Liberation Day (25). |
| May | Labor Day (1). |
| August | Assumption of the Virgin (15). |
| November | All Saints' Day (1). |
| December | Immaculate Conception (8), Christmas (25), St. Stephen's Day (26). |

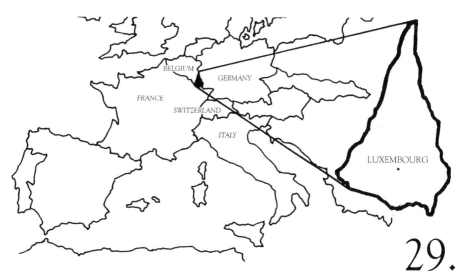

# 29.

# LUXEMBOURG

## GRAND DUCHY OF LUXEMBOURG

## VITAL STATISTICS

POPULATION:     400,000 (1992).

CAPITAL:        Luxembourg, with a population of 76,000 (1991).

LAND SIZE:      999 square miles,  two-thirds the size of
                Rhode Island.

GOVERNMENT:     Parliamentary monarchy.  The grand duke
                appoints a prime minister who forms a
                government responsible to a single 60-member
                Chamber of Deputies elected through an
                electoral system for five years.

LIVING
STANDARD:       GDP = $27,700 per capita (1992).

| NATURAL RESOURCES: | Iron ore (no longer exploited). |
|---|---|
| AGRICULTURE: | Accounts for less than 3 percent of GDP (including forestry); principal products include barley, oats, potatoes, wheat, fruits, wine grapes; cattle-raising is widespread. |
| INDUSTRIES: | Banking, iron and steel, food processing, chemicals, metal products, engineering, tires, glass, aluminum. |
| CLIMATE: | Temperate. Humid and damp in the fall and early spring. Occasionally cold in the winter. |
| CURRENCY: | Luxembourg franc (LF). LF1 = 100 centimes. Notes are in denominations of LF5,000, 1,000 and 100. Coins are in denominations of LF50, 20, 10, 5 and 1, and 50 and 25 centimes. The Luxembourg franc is on par with the Belgian franc. However, Luxembourg francs are not always legal tender in Belgium. Belgian francs are always accepted in Luxembourg. |

# THE PEOPLE

CORRECT
NAME:              Luxembourgers.

ETHNIC
MAKEUP:            Descendants of several different nationalities.
                   Ethnic mixture of French and German, 75
                   percent.  Guest workers from Portugal, Italy,
                   France, etc., 25 percent.

VALUE
SYSTEM:            Modesty, friendship and a strong national pride
                   are valued.  The people cherish their
                   independence and separate identity in Europe.
                   They enjoy a slower pace of life than most of
                   northern Europe.

FAMILY:            Family is very important.  Parents influence every
                   aspect of children's lives.  This is weakening as
                   more young people leave to study/work abroad.

RELIGION:          97 percent Roman Catholic,  3 percent
                   Protestant and Jewish.

| | |
|---|---|
| **MEETING AND GREETING** | • Shake hands with everyone present—men, women, and children—at a business or social meeting. Shake hands again when leaving.<br><br>• Handshake is gentle.<br><br>• Good friends kiss cheeks—one kiss on each side.<br><br>• English greetings are acceptable. |
| **NAMES AND TITLES** | • Use last names and appropriate titles until specifically invited by your hosts or colleagues to use their first names.<br><br>• First names are used for close friends and family only.<br><br>• Use professional titles.<br><br>• Mr., Mrs. or Miss are appropriate.<br><br>• Women often keep their maiden name or hyphenate their name and their husband's name. |
| **LANGUAGE** | • *Luxembourgish* is the national language. It is used more in spoken language than written. Eighty percent speak the language, which is a Frankish-Germanic dialect mixed with German and French words.<br><br>• French and German are the official languages.<br><br>• All levels of people speak French and German fluently. |

- Nearly half the people speak at least two foreign languages and 40 percent speak three or more.

- There is a sense of identity and pride based on knowing and speaking Luxembourgish, which is done mainly at home and on social occasions.

- French, German and English are spoken and written in most companies.

- English is spoken and understood widely, especially since it is compulsory in secondary schools.

- French is the language of civil service, law and parliament. Newspapers are written both in German and French.

- Attempts to use the local dialect are greatly appreciated. Conversely, locals resent foreigners who have lived and worked in their country many years without learning at least some Luxembourgish.

---

- Luxembourgers are friendly but reserved.

- Do not put your hands in your pockets while speaking to anyone.

- Cover your mouth when yawning or sneezing.

## BODY LANGUAGE

## PHRASES

See French and German phrases. The following are
Luxembourgish phrases:

| English | Luxembourgish | Pronunciation |
|---|---|---|
| Good morning | *Gudden Muergen* | GOOD-en MOY-en |
| Good evening | *Scheinen gudden Metteg* | SHEEN-en GOOD-en MET-egg |
| Please | *Wannechgelift* | van-EESH-ge-leeft |
| Thank you | *Merci* | MARE-see |
| You're welcome | *Ech bieden ierch* | eesh BEE-den eersh |
| Yes | *Yo* | yo |
| No | *Nee* | nay |
| Excuse me | *Entschoellecht* | ent-SHOUL-lecht |
| Goodbye | *Awuër or Aeddi* | AH-vwar or ED-ee |
| How are you? | *Wie get et?* | VAY get et |
| Pleased to meet you | *Et freet mech Enchanteiert* | et freet mech ahn-shan-TAY-eert |

- International cuisine.

- Most restaurants have German and French style food, and most menus are written in both French and German.

- No country has more Michelin star restaurants per capita than Luxembourg.

BREAKFAST (*Ze Muergen*): 7:30 a.m.
- Continental style.

- Rolls or croissants with jam.

- Coffee or tea.

LUNCH (*Ze Metteg*): 12:30 p.m.
- Most often the main meal of the day.

- Soup, fish, meat, potatoes, salad, vegetables, dessert.

DINNER (*Oweud Iesseu*): 7 p.m.
- Usually a smaller meal.

- Home: Open-faced sandwiches, soup and salad.

- Restaurant or home with guests: Regular three-course meal.

- Wine, beer and sparkling water are most often served with lunch and dinner.

## TYPICAL FOODS

- Freshwater fish (trout, pike and crayfish).

- Sauerkraut—served only with sausages or smoked pork.

- Multiple stews of meat and vegetables.

- Cooked cheese—to spread on dark bread with mild mustard.

- Chocolates—some of the best in the world.

- *Letzeburger Ham:* Ardennes smoked ham.

- *Treipen:* Pork gut filled with meat, blood and cabbage, cooked until black.

- *Judd mat Gardebounen:* Smoked pork with fava beans or broad beans.

- *Quenelles:* Fish dumplings, most often pike.


## DRINKING

- *Wein* (wine) and *Bier* (beer) are the most popular drinks.

- Order Luxembourg white wines, which are generally very good.

- Coffee is never served with a meal—only with or after dessert.

## TOASTS

- *Prost* (prewst), "Cheers." Informal.

- *Op är Gesondheet* (ahp air ge-SAHND-heat), "To your health." Formal.

- Toasts can also be in French or German.

- The host gives the first toast.

- A woman can propose a toast.

---

## TIPPING

- Restaurants: A service charge of 15 percent is always included in the bill. Leave a small additional tip.

- Taxis: 10 to 20 percent of fare.

- Cloakroom attendants: Usually charge a fixed price.

- Porters: LF50 to 100, depending on the number of bags.

- Bathroom attendants: LF20.

---

## MANNERS

- Manners are similar to those in Belgium and France.

- Keep your hands on the table at all times during a meal—not in your lap. However, keep your elbows off the table.

- Compliment the food.

- To quietly signify that you are not finished or that you would like more food, cross your knife and fork in the middle of your plate.

- When finished eating, place your knife and fork side by side on the plate at the 5:25 position.

- Leaving food on your plate is impolite.

- Do not ask for a tour of your host's home; it is considered impolite.

**DRESS**

- Same as in Belgium.

- Cleanliness and neatness are very important.

- Casual means sweaters, sport coats, shirts without a tie.

**GIFTS**

### HOSTESS

- Always bring a gift for the hostess when invited to someone's home.

- A gift for the hostess will probably not be unwrapped immediately (unless no other guests are present or expected).

- Give: Bouquet of flowers (not chrysanthemums), high quality bottle of liqueur (ask the retailer to recommend one), chocolates.

### BUSINESS

- Small business gifts may be exchanged but usually not at the first meeting.

- It is acceptable but not expected to give a Christmas gift to a Luxembourger colleague, but never send it to a Luxembourger's home.

- Give: Books, recorded music, good quality liquor.

## TOILET TIPS

| | |
|---|---|
| *Toilettes/WC* | Restrooms |
| *Dames* | Ladies |
| *Messieurs* | Men |
| *C (Chaud)* | Hot water (red dot) |
| *F (Froid)* | Cold water (blue dot) |

## HELPFUL HINTS

DO:

- Respect people's privacy.

- Recognize Luxembourg's uniqueness and its nationality.

- Blow your nose in private, if possible.

- Expect the pace of life to be less hurried than in most of Europe.

DO NOT:

- Never chew gum in public.

- Do not lump the Luxembourgers together with the French or Belgians, and especially not with the Germans.

## PUNCTUALITY

- Luxembourgers insist on punctuality for most social occasions.

- For dinners in a private home, arrive 15 minutes later than what is stated on the invitation. Be on time for dinner in a restaurant.

- Luxembourgers take punctuality for business meetings very seriously and expect that you will do likewise; call with an explanation if you will be delayed.

# STRICTLY BUSINESS

## BUSINESS CARDS

- Business cards are commonly exchanged.

- Business cards in English are acceptable.

## CORPORATE CULTURE

STRUCTURE: Newer and younger companies are developing a participative management style. Older, more established companies traditionally have had a rigid hierarchy, but union representation on the board has become more common and a consensus-oriented management style is evolving.

MEETINGS: Meetings are brief. Major decisions are made privately among executives and managers, not in meetings. Luxembourgers skip the small talk and get right down to business.

COMMUNICATION: French, German, English and Luxembourgish are all commonly used in business. Chances are you won't need an interpreter, but it's a good idea to check in advance. Never be assertive, critical, aggressive or rude in dealing with Luxembourgers. Don't call a Luxembourger at home unless you've arranged to do so in advance.

BE AWARE:

- Many international banks and multinational companies use Luxembourg as their European headquarters or distribution center.

- There have been no major strikes since 1922. Absenteeism is low. One-third of the work force is from Belgium, France and Germany.


## ENTERTAINMENT

- Most business entertainment is done in restaurants.

- Business breakfasts are acceptable.

- Dinner is more of a social occasion and a time to enjoy good food, wine and discussion.

- Spouses are sometimes invited to dinners with business colleagues.

APPOINTMENTS

| | |
|---|---|
| **Office Hours:** | Monday through Friday<br>8 a.m. to noon<br>1 to 3 p.m. |
| **Bank Hours:** | Monday through Friday<br>8:30 a.m. to 4:30 p.m. |

## ESPECIALLY FOR WOMEN

- The business community is male-dominated, but many women work.

- The women of Luxembourg have excellent maternity leave and usually return to work after having children.

- Local women have a prominent role in politics. For more than 20 years, the mayor of Luxembourg City has been a woman.

- A foreign woman does not have to think twice to invite a Luxembourg man to dinner. Make arrangements in advance with the waiter to pay for business dinners.

- Do not plan to make a business visit or schedule any appointments during the following holidays or festivals. Be sure to check for the numerous regional and local holidays and festivals.

| | |
|---|---|
| January | New Year's Day (1). |
| February | Shrove Tuesday. |
| March/April | Easter (Friday-Monday). |
| April/May | Ascension Thursday (40 days after Easter). |
| May | Labor Day (1). |
| May/June | Whitsunday and Whitmonday (49 and 50 days after Easter). |
| June | Grand Duke's Birthday—National Holiday (23). |
| August | Assumption (15). |
| September | *Schueberfouer* (Fair Monday—first Monday). |
| November | All Saints' Day (1), All Souls' Day (2). |
| December | Christmas (24-26). |

# 30.

# NETHERLANDS

## KINGDOM OF THE NETHERLANDS

## VITAL STATISTICS

POPULATION:    15.1 million (1992).

CAPITAL:    Amsterdam (population 700,000 in 1991) is the capital, but The Hague is the seat of the government.

LAND SIZE:    16,041 square miles, almost twice the size of New Jersey.

GOVERNMENT:    Parliamentary monarchy. The queen is the head of state, but the prime minister is the head of government. Executive power lies with a council of ministers headed by the prime minister. The two-chamber legislature, the States-General, has a 75-member upper chamber elected for six years by 12 provincial councils and a 150-member lower chamber directly elected through the electoral system for four years.

LIVING
STANDARDS:    GDP = US$20,869 per capita (1992).

NATURAL
RESOURCES:    Natural gas, crude oil, fertile soil.

AGRICULTURE:  Accounts for 4 percent of GDP; animal production predominates; crops include grains, potatoes, sugar beets, fruits, vegetables; shortages of grain, fats and oils.

INDUSTRIES:   Agroindustries, metal and engineering products, electrical machinery and equipment, chemicals, petroleum, fishing, construction, microelectronics, finance.

CLIMATE:      Generally temperate, though winter temperatures can fall to 1.5°F (-17°C). Summers warm but unsettled and windy. Driest in spring.

CURRENCY:     Netherland Dutch guilder (NDG). NDG1=100 cents. Notes are in denominations of NDG1,000, 250, 100, 25 and 10. Coins are in denominations of NDG5, 2.5 and 1, and 25, 10 and 5 cents.

# THE PEOPLE

CORRECT
NAME:                Dutch, Dutchmen, Dutchwomen, Netherlanders.

ETHNIC
MAKEUP:              95 percent Dutch, approximately 5 percent foreign
                     nationals.

VALUE
SYSTEM:              Dutch society is egalitarian. The people are modest
                     and tolerant, independent, self-reliant, outward-
                     looking and entrepreneurial. The Dutch have an
                     aversion to the nonessential. They value
                     education, hard work, ambition and ability.
                     Ostentatious behavior is to be avoided.
                     Accumulating money is good but spending money
                     is a vice. A high style is considered wasteful and
                     suspect. People take pride in their cultural heritage
                     but also in being modern and nontraditional.

FAMILY:              Dutch families are strong, with children taught to
                     respect parents. Families are of moderate size. The
                     social welfare system allows family members to be
                     quite independent from one another. Parents
                     receive money to help them raise children and
                     need not save for their children's education;
                     adequate pensions are provided for the elderly.

RELIGION:            36 percent Roman Catholic, 27 percent Protestant,
                     6 percent other, 31 percent unaffiliated.

## MEETING AND GREETING

- Shake hands with everyone present—men, women, and children—at a business or social meeting. Shake hands again when leaving.

- Handshake is warm and friendly with eye contact.

- People only hug or embrace when they are close friends.

- Dutch will shake hands and say their last name, not "Hello."

- Dutch answer the phone with their last name, i.e., *"Janssen."*

- Introduce yourself and shake hands at a business and social meeting if no one is present to introduce you. Dutch consider it rude not to identify yourself.

- Good friends may kiss on one cheek, then the other, and then back to the first.

## NAMES AND TITLES

- Use last names and appropriate titles until specifically invited by your Dutch hosts or colleagues to use their first names.

- Younger colleagues at all levels will go rapidly to first names and *jij*, the informal "you."

- Professional titles are important to some people and should be used correctly at all times. Lawyer, Engineer, Doctor and Professor are sometimes used. It is generally clear when introduced if titles are important to a person. Otherwise use general titles.

| Mr. | *Mijnheer* | muh-NAYR |
| Mrs. | *Mevrouw* | muhv-ROW |
| Miss | *Juffrouw* | yuf-ROW |
| Ms. | *Mejuffrouw* | muh-yuf-ROW |

**Example:** *Mijnheer Korthuis.*

- Most Dutch will give you their first initial and their last name. If they give you their first name, they are granting you permission to address them by their first name.

- In business it is better to be formal and stay with last names until specifically invited to use first names.

- In formal communications a letter requires correct titles, especially for foreign service or business letters.

---

## LANGUAGE

- The official language is Dutch.

- People in the northeastern province of Friesland speak Frisian.

- English, German and French are widely spoken and understood.

- 73 percent of the people speak at least one other language (often English).

- The Dutch avoid superlatives and do tend to be negative.

- Compliments are offered sparingly, and to say that something is "not bad" is to praise it.

- A person who never offers criticism is seen as either being simple-minded or failing to tell the truth.

- The Dutch will argue but seldom take offense.

- A foreigner need not worry too much about saying something that will hurt people's feelings.

## BODY LANGUAGE

- The Dutch are basically reserved and don't touch in public.

- The Dutch respect a person's privacy and seldom speak to strangers. It is more likely that they will wait for you to make the first move. Don't be afraid to do so.

- Eye contact and facial expressions are important. The Dutch expect eye contact while speaking with someone.

- Hugging and embracing is more common in southern areas. People in the northern area are more reserved.

- Moving your index finger around your ear means you have a telephone call, not "you're crazy." The crazy sign is to tap the center of your forehead with your index finger. This gesture is very rude.

*The Dutch rarely display anger or extreme exuberance.*

# PHRASES

| English | Dutch | Pronunciation |
| --- | --- | --- |
| Good morning | *Goeden morgen* | GHOO-duh MOR-ghen |
| Good afternoon | *Goeden middag* | GHOO-duh MIH-dag |
| Good evening | *Goeden avond* | GHOO-duh avnt |
| Please | *Alstublieft* | AHLS-too-bleeft |
| Thank you | *Dank u* | dahnk ew |
| You're welcome | *Geen dank* | ghain dahnk |
| Yes | *Ja* | yah |
| No | *Nee* | nay |
| Excuse me | *Pardon* | pahr-DAWN |
| Goodbye | *Tot ziens* | tawt seenss |
| Pleased to meet you | *Aangenaam* | AAHN-ghe-naam |
| How are you? | *Hoe gaat het met u?* | who ghaat het met ueh |

## DINING AND DRINKING

- To beckon a waiter or waitress, raise your hand, make eye contact, and say *ober* (waiter) or *mevrouw* (waitress).

- Cuisine is not a source of special pride to the Dutch. Food is not an important part of the social culture.

- Socializing is often over coffee, not meals.

- Meals are plain and private—their place is generally within the family.

- Dutch may have coffee with cookies or pastries at 10 a.m. and tea with cookies at 4 p.m.

BREAKFAST (*Het Ontbijt*): 7 to 8 a.m.
- Bread, toast with jam, cornflakes and milk, cheese or meat, *krentebollen* (raisin rolls) and coffee/tea.

LUNCH (*De Lunch or Middageten*): noon to 1 p.m.
- Generally a light meal.

- Open-faced sandwiches and *kroket* (deep-fried sausages) are popular for lunch.

- Restaurant business lunches are becoming more common.

DINNER (*Het Avondeten or Dinev*): 5:30 to 6:30 p.m.
- Main meal of the day (in the cities).

- Soup, meat/fish, potatoes and gravy, vegetables, salad, fruit, ice cream or pudding, and coffee.

- Dutch invite guests for drinks, wine, cheeses

- Dutch invite guests for drinks, wine, cheeses and hot savories (about 8 or 9 p.m.). Do not expect a meal unless the invitation says dinner.

## MENU TERMS

| | |
|---|---|
| Voorgerecht | Appetizer |
| Hoofdgerecht | Main course |
| Nagerecht | Dessert |
| Brood | Bread |
| Soep | Soup |
| Groenten | Vegetables |
| Vlees | Meat |
| Rundvlees | Beef |
| Varken | Pork |
| Lam | Lamb |
| Kip | Chicken |
| Vis | Fish |
| Ei | Egg |

*Indonesian restaurants are popular in the Netherlands.*

## TYPICAL FOODS

- *Rijsttafel* (rice table): Spicy Indonesian specialties with various meats, vegetables, sauces and rice.

- *Nieuwe haring*: First herring of the year served with raw onions.

- *Verse oesters*: Fresh oysters.

- *Broodjes*: Buttered rolls with anything from cheese to crabmeat.

- *Frieten:* French fries eaten with mayonnaise.

- *Stroopwafels:* Syrup waffles.

- *Bitterballen:* Deep fried, spicy meatballs.

- *Erwtensoep:* Thick, hearty, meaty pea soup usually eaten with thick slabs of rye bread.

- *Flensjes* or *Pannekoeken:* Large Dutch pancakes, served with a great variety of toppings from bananas to bacon.

- *Ontbijtkoek:* Spice cake, usually served for breakfast.

- *Edam, Gouda* and *Kernhem* cheeses.

### DRINKING

- *Jenever:* Very strong gin-type liquor. Often followed by a beer chaser. A man's drink.

- Dry sherry: A lady's drink in the afternoon.

- Sherry, *bier* (beer) and *jenever* are pre-dinner drinks in a home.

- *Wijn* (wine) is served with the meal.

- *Advokaat:* Thick, yellow, pungent concoction made from eggs, served with whipped cream and eaten with a spoon.

### TOASTS

- *Proost* (prohst), "Cheers." Formal or informal.

- Say *Proost*, take a sip of your drink, and say *Proost* again. Then acknowledge each guest with your eyes or clink their glasses and put your glass down.

- *Eet smakelijk* (ate smaahk-AY-lick), "Eat deliciously," is said by the host and hostess before eating. It is a sign for the guests to start eating.

- A woman can propose a toast.

---

## TIPPING

- The Netherlands is a self-service country. You are expected to handle your own luggage, weigh your own vegetables in a supermarket and pump your own gasoline.

- Restaurants: A service charge of 15 percent is always included in the bill. As an additional gratuity, round the bill up to the nearest guilder when paying.

- Taxis: Round up to nearest guilder.

- Washroom attendants: 25 Dutch cents in the saucer on the counter.

- Porters: 50 Dutch cents per piece of luggage. A total of NDG1 or 2 is usual.

- Hairdressers and barbers: Round up to the nearest NDG5 or 10.

- Hotel doormen: 50 Dutch cents-NDG1 for obtaining a cab.

- Chambermaids: NDG1 per night.

- Ushers in theaters: NDG1 or nothing.

- Cloakroom attendants: NDG1.

*The Dutch call themselves stingy when it comes to tipping.*

# MANNERS

- Dutch manners are frank, no-nonsense informality combined with strict adherence to basic etiquette.

- Food does not play the major role in hospitality that it does in many other cultures. It is not considered essential for making someone feel welcome.

- Do not expect to be offered a meal unless the invitation specifically mentions "dinner." Only in the last 10 years or so has it become customary for Dutch people to invite each other to their homes for dinner.

- Men should not sit down until all women have been seated.

- The female guest of honor is seated next to the host. The male guest of honor is seated next to the hostess.

- Allow the hostess to start eating and drinking before you begin.

- Take a small quantity of food to start. A second helping will be offered, and it is polite to accept.

- It is impolite not to taste every dish served.

- Keep your hands on the table at all times during a meal—not in your lap. However, keep your elbows off the table.

- There is no salad plate.

- The dessert spoon is above the dinner plate.

- Use your knife and fork to eat all food, including sandwiches, fruit and pizza.

*There is no smoking in many areas. Always ask permission before smoking.*

- Bread usually isn't served at dinner.

- It is considered very rude to get up and leave the table during dinner (even to go to the restroom).

- You may leave a small amount of food on your plate when you are finished eating.

- To signify that you would like more food or that you are not finished, cross your knife and fork in the middle of your plate.

- When finished eating, place your knife and fork side by side at the 5:25 position on your plate.

- Parties may go very late. Plan to stay at least one and a half hours after dinner.

- Sometimes the hostess serves wine and cheese at midnight.

- Compliment someone's home or furniture sincerely.

- Do not ask for a tour of your host's home; it is considered impolite.

- The Dutch will make it clear that you are their guest if they intend to pay the bill in a restaurant, otherwise expect to "go Dutch" and pay your fair share. No one will be embarrassed at splitting the bill.

# DRESS

- Dress is informal and subdued.

- When the occasion calls for proper dress, the Dutch carefully adhere to it.

## BUSINESS

- Men: Suits and ties. Sport coats are usually acceptable.

- A traditional suit and tie is required only in certain circles of business and government.

- Taking off your jacket in the office is acceptable. It means getting down to business. Whenever leaving your office, put your jacket back on.

- In a meeting, the chairperson sets the tone whether jackets should be on or off.

- Women: Suits and dresses.

## RESTAURANT

- Men: Better restaurants will require suits and ties.

- Women: Dresses or skirts and blouses.

## THEATER/CONCERTS

- Except for opening night, either formal (dark suits) or informal attire is appropriate.

- Women: Dresses or skirts and blouses.

## CASUAL

- Blue jeans are acceptable but it depends on the occasion and the circumstances.

- Halter tops and shorts are for the beach only.

*Do not make any assumptions or judgments about a Dutch person's status or wealth on the basis of their outward appearance—you will not see much glamour.*

## HOSTESS

- Always bring a small, wrapped gift for the hostess when invited to someone's home.

- Present your gift upon arrival; it will be opened upon receipt.

- Sending flowers on the morning of or the day after a party is also appropriate.

- Bring children a small gift or candy.

- Give: Flowers, chocolates, books, wine, candy.

- Do not give: Knives, practical gifts, expensive gifts (could be embarrassing).

## BUSINESS

- Gifts are exchanged in business only once a close, personal relationship has developed.

- It is acceptable but not expected to give a Christmas gift to a colleague in the Netherlands.

- Give: Books, art objects, wine, liquor.

# GIFTS

*The Dutch find any form of ostentation a bit embarrassing. A grand gesture of generosity will only make them uncomfortable.*

## TOILET TIPS

| | |
|---|---|
| *Toilet/WC* | Restrooms |
| *Dames* | Ladies |
| *Heren* | Men |
| *Warm* | Hot water |
| *Koud* | Cold water |

**DO:**

- Learn about Dutch politics.

- Respect people's privacy by not asking personal questions.

- A gentleman stands when a woman enters the room.

**DO NOT:**

- Do not call the Netherlands "Holland." Holland is a region within the Netherlands.

- Do not give personal compliments until you know someone well.

- Never chew gum in public.

- Do not discuss money or prices.

- Do not make a joke or derogatory comment about the royal family.

- Do not put your hands in your pockets while speaking to or greeting someone.

- Do not interrupt.

*Holland is a region within the Netherlands.*

## PUNCTUALITY

- The Dutch insist on punctuality for social occasions.

- The Dutch take punctuality for business meetings very seriously and expect that you will do likewise; call with an explanation if you are delayed.

- Lateness, missed appointments and postponements are viewed as indicators of untrustworthiness and will damage a relationship.

## BUSINESS CARDS

- Exchange business cards during or after conversation. No set ritual exists.

- Business cards in English are acceptable.

## CORPORATE CULTURE

STRUCTURE: Autocratic management still exists in many companies, while others have moved toward a more horizontal structure and more participative management style. The difference depends on age: the age of top executives, the age of the company, and the age of the industry. The younger all three, the greater the tendency toward participative management.

MEETINGS: Meetings are regular and frequent; basic protocol is observed, but with informal manners. Meetings are held primarily for discussion of issues followed by decisionmaking. The Dutch tend to get right down to business.

Presentations should be practical and factual, with ideas researched, well thought-out and clearly presented.

COMMUNICATION: English is widely used in business; an interpreter will not be needed. Communications between functions or departments are open and tolerant; strategy is clear and communicated to all levels. Managers take work home and don't mind being called there.

BE AWARE:

- Negotiations may be fast-paced, but the decisionmaking process in many companies is ponderous. After the decision is made, implementation is fast and efficient.

- Dutch companies are frugal and profit-oriented, without being obsessed with numbers.

- Success is attributed to the team, rather than to individuals, but individuals are held accountable for decisions.

- Commitments are honored. Do not promise anything or make any offer you can't deliver on.

### ENTERTAINMENT

- Most business entertaining is done in a restaurant, but the Dutch do a fair share of home entertaining as well.

- Business breakfasts are not very common.

- Business people like to entertain and be entertained.

- If you wish to treat your Dutch colleagues to fine dining, take them to a French restaurant.

*Dutch are hard-working and pragmatic. They are open to new ideas.*

- It is appropriate to discuss business during a business lunch.

- Spouses are often included in a business dinner. Ask if your host expects your spouse to be included in a business function. Business can be discussed at any time during the meal, except if the spouse is present.

- People generally go home promptly after work and eat dinner with their families.

---

## APPOINTMENTS

**Office Hours:**    **Monday - Friday**
**8:30 a.m. - 4:30 p.m.**

**Bank Hours:**    **Monday - Friday**
**9 a.m. - 4 p.m.**

- Every region has a different vacation period. Check June through August or July through September and Christmas. Do not plan business trips during these times.

- Make appointments well in advance.

- Schedules, routine and appointment dates are carefully structured and adhered to. Rescheduling an appointment at the last minute is considered rude.

---

## ESPECIALLY FOR WOMEN

- A foreign businesswoman will not have difficulty being accepted in the Netherlands.

- The percentage of women who are employed outside the home is one of the lowest in Europe, and those who do work are generally in lower paying jobs. Not many day-care centers or other facilities exist for the benefit of working mothers.

- Women make up 30 percent of the work force. In the Netherlands, married women in a career are a rarity with few presently in managerial positions. Women usually still give up work when they have children.

- Equality of women has become a policy priority in the Netherlands. Many Dutch-women see the struggle for equal opportunities as only just beginning, even though small strides have already been made.

- It is acceptable for a businesswoman to invite a man to dinner. Businesswomen will have no problem paying for a meal in a restaurant.

- Allow a gentleman to walk on the sidewalk nearest the street.

- Women can dine alone in a bar or restaurant without being disturbed.

- Ask at your hotel which areas should be avoided for safety reasons.

- Use taxis if you are out alone at night.

- Watch purses carefully on buses and streetcars.

- Do not plan to make a business visit or schedule any appointments during the following holidays or festivals. Be sure to check for the numerous regional and local holidays and festivals.

| | |
|---|---|
| January | New Year's Day (1). |
| March/April | Easter (Friday-Monday). |
| April | The Queen's Birthday (30). |
| April/May | Ascension Thursday (40 days after Easter). |
| May | Liberation Day (5). |
| May/June | Whitsunday and Whitmonday (49 and 50 days after Easter). |
| June | Corpus Christi (60 days after Easter). |
| December | Feast of St. Nicholas (5–most businesses open until noon), Christmas (25-26). |

# 31.
# NORWAY
## KINGDOM OF NORWAY

## VITAL STATISTICS

POPULATION:    4.3 million (1992).

CAPITAL:       Oslo, with a population of 467,000 (1992).

LAND SIZE:     125,181 square miles, slightly larger than
               New Mexico.

GOVERNMENT:    Constitutional monarchy.  Executive power lies
               with the prime minister and state council.  The
               165-member *Storting* is elected for four years
               through an electoral system.  The *Storting* divides
               into the *Lagting* and *Odelsting*.

LIVING
STANDARD:      GNP = US$23,000 per capita (1992).

NATURAL
RESOURCES:     Crude oil, copper, natural gas, pyrites, nickel,
               iron ore, zinc, lead, fish, timber, hydropower.

AGRICULTURE:   Accounts for 2.8 percent of GDP and 6.4 percent
               of labor force; among world's top 10 fishing
               nations; livestock output exceeds value in crops;
               over half of food needs imported.

INDUSTRIES:    Petroleum and gas, food processing, shipbuilding,
               pulp and paper products, metals, chemicals,
               timber, mining, textiles, fishing.

CLIMATE:       West coast has marine climate with cool summers
               and mild, rarely freezing winters, moderated by the
               Gulf Stream; coastal rainfall can be as much as
               2,000mm (80 inches) a year. Inland summers are
               warmer, winters are colder and there is less rain.

CURRENCY:      Norwegian krone (NOK). NOK1=100 øre.
               Notes are in denominations of NOK1,000, 500,
               100 and 50. Coins are in denominations of
               NOK10, 5 and 1, and 50 øre.

# THE PEOPLE

CORRECT
NAME:                  Norwegians.

ETHNIC
MAKEUP:                Germanic (Nordic, Alpine, Baltic), Lapps.

VALUE
SYSTEM:                Tolerance, kindness to each other and
                       independence are highly valued. Personal and
                       national independence are a great source of
                       pride. Sincerity, modesty and equality are
                       important values. Peace and progress are mottos
                       in the country that sponsors the Nobel Prizes.
                       Simplicity and nature are at the core of the
                       Norwegian lifestyle. Norwegians treasure their
                       landscape, outdoor activity, sailing, cross-country
                       skiing, etc. In fact, many Norwegians have a
                       modest second home (*hutte*) in the mountains.

FAMILY:                Families are very important. Husbands and wives
                       share authority equally. Family size is small—
                       typically parents and two children. Many young
                       people live together before or instead of
                       marrying. Families with children receive
                       financial support from the government. The
                       majority of homes are single-family houses built
                       of wood.

RELIGION:              94 percent belong to the Church of Norway,
                       which is Evangelical Lutheran.

| | | |
|---|---|---|
| **MEETING** | • | Shake hands with everyone present—men, women, and children—at a business or social meeting.  Shake hands again when leaving. |
| **AND** | | |
| **GREETING** | | |
| | • | Handshake is brief and firm. |
| | • | When introduced for the first time, address the other person by both first and last name, i.e., *Mr. John Lund.* |
| | • | *Morn* (morn), "Good morning," is said regardless of time of day. |
| | • | *Hei* (hey), "Hi," is an informal greeting among good friends. |
| | • | *God dag* (goo dahg), "Good day." |

| | | |
|---|---|---|
| **NAMES** | • | Names that end in *-en* are most likely Norwegian or Danish.  Names that end in *-on* are most likely Swedish. |
| **AND** | | |
| **TITLES** | • | Use last names and appropriate titles until specifically invited by your Norwegian hosts or colleagues to use their first names. |
| | • | For formal occasions and with first introductions address people with *Herr, Fru* or *Frøken* + first name + last name. Thereafter, skip the first name and use only *Herr, Fru* or *Frøken* + last name. |

| Mr. | *Herr* | har |
|---|---|---|
| Mrs. | *Fru* | fruh |
| Miss | *Frøken* | FROO-ken |

**Example:  *Fru Inga Bjørnsen.***
**After initial introduction:  *Fru Bjørnsen.***

- Norwegians are quite casual. They most often address one another with *God dag* + last name. They will most likely ask you to do the same.

  **Example: *God dag, Bjørnsen.***

- It is becoming more common for Norwegian women to keep their own last name after marrying (unless their husband's name is of a higher status).

- The traditional way to address a Norwegian couple would be to use *Herr* and *Fru* with the first and last name of the husband or just the last name of the husband.

  **Example: *Herr* and *Fru Nils Johansen* or just *Herr* and *Fru Johansen.***

- A contemporary way to address a Norwegian couple would be to use *Herr* and *Fru* together with the first names of both the husband and wife and the husband's last name.

  **Example: *Herr* and *Fru Nils* and *Inger Johansen.***

- Occupational titles are not normally used. As a foreigner, you may want to use Professor, Doctor, Engineer, etc. when first meeting, but the more informal Norwegians will ask you to call them by their last name alone.

- Don't address a lawyer with an occupational title.

- Clergyman are addressed by their last name alone. Reverend is not used.

  **Example: *Morn, Hassell.***

*The informal way to address Norwegians is by their last name alone: "Morn, Bjørnsen."*

## LANGUAGE

- The official Norwegian language has two forms with subtle differences:

  *Bokmål* -Language used mostly in urban areas.
  -"Book language" (influenced by Danish).
  -Uses: Written words, instructions and broadcasting.
  -Spoken by 75 percent of the people.

  *Nynorsk* -Language used mostly in rural areas.
  -Law requires it to be used in a certain percentage of schools and broadcast media.

- English is widely spoken and understood.

- Norwegian children study Norwegian, English and French in school.

*Overanimated behavior is not appreciated.*

## BODY LANGUAGE

- There is little personal touching except between relatives and close friends.

- Do not back-slap.

- Do not put your arm around anyone.

  - Cover your mouth when yawning.

# PHRASES

| English | Norwegian | Pronunciation |
|---|---|---|
| Good morning | *God morgen* | goo MORE-en |
| Good day | *God dag* | goo dahg |
| | *Morn* (informal) | morn |
| Good evening | *God kveld* | goo kuehld |
| Please | *Vaer så snill* | vahr so snil |
| Thank you | *Takk* | takh |
| You're welcome | *Vaer så god* | vahr so goo |
| Yes | *Ja* | yah |
| No | *Nei* | nay |
| Excuse me | *Omforlatelse* | ohm-fah-LAHT-el-seh |
| Goodbye | *Adjø* (formal) | ahd-YER |
| | *Ha det* (informal) | hahl duh |

## DINING
## AND
## DRINKING

- To beckon a waiter or waitress, raise your hand with your index finger up.

BREAKFAST (*Frokost*): 8 to 9 a.m.
- Bread, cheese, cold cuts, eggs, jam, juice, coffee or tea.

LUNCH (*Lunsj*): Noon.
- Open-faced sandwich, fruit.

DINNER (*Middag*): 5 to 6 p.m. main meal, 7 to 8 p.m. dinner party.

- Soup, meat or fish, potato/vegetable, dessert.

- Appetizer, soup, main course (salad served with meal).

### MENU TERMS

| | |
|---|---|
| *Forret(er)* | Appetizer |
| *Hovedretter* | Main course |
| *Dessert* | Dessert |
| *Brød* | Bread |
| *Supper* | Soup |
| *Grønnsaker* | Vegetable |
| *Biff* | Beef |
| *Svin/Gris* | Pork |
| *Lam* | Lamb |
| *Kylling* | Chicken |
| *Fisk* | Fish |
| *Egg* | Egg |

## TYPICAL FOODS

- Fish and cheese are staples of the Norwegian diet.

- *Reinsdyr:* Reindeer steak with lingonberries.

- *Røkelaks:* Smoked salmon.

- *Flatbrød:* Crisp thin rye bread.

- *Gravlaks:* Salmon cured with dill.

- *Sild:* Herring.

- *Fiskepudding:* Fish pudding with bread crumbs and cream.

- *Smørbrød* or *Snitter:* Bread with a topping, such as shrimp, salad, salmon, roast beef.

- *Smørgåsbord:* Buffet-style eating.

## DRINKING

- *Aquavit:* A very potent hard liquor similar to a spiced vodka. Often served with food that has a high fat content—used to calm the stomach. Does not go well with wine; usually served with a beer chaser.

- Sherry, scotch and champagne may be served as cocktails.

- Wine is served with dinner.

- Port and madeira are served with dessert.

- Cognac is served after dinner.

- Many Norwegians drink *øl* (beer) with their dinner. *Lett øl* (light beer) refers to low alcohol content rather than low calorie content.

*Lett øl has a lower alcohol content than regular beer.*

- Do not drink and drive. Norway has very strict laws for intoxicated drivers and the legal limit for blood alcohol content is only 0.05. One beer can put you over the limit.

## TOASTS

- *Skål* (skohl), "Cheers." Formal or informal.

- The host makes a small speech and offers the first toast.

- For a formal toast, look into the eyes of the person being toasted and give a slight nod, then say *Skål*.

- You can drink *aquavit* in one gulp, but be careful since it is very strong.

- Before putting your glass down, meet the other person's eyes again and nod.

- Toast the hostess with *Takk* ("Thank you.")

- In a formal setting, the meal ends with the male guest of honor tapping his glass with a knife and thanking the hostess on behalf of all the guests. A little story or joke may accompany the toast.

- It's acceptable for women to propose a toast.

## TIPPING

- Tipping is not common outside the principal cities.

- Restaurants: A service charge of 15 percent is always included in the bill; small change is customarily left (don't exceed 5 percent) as an additional gratuity for good service.

- Taxis: Round fare up. Tip is included.

- Porters: NOK10-20.

- Gas station attendants, hairdressers, hotel maids and doormen are all paid a good salary. No tip is necessary.

---

- Be punctual for dinner; 7 p.m. means 7 p.m.

- Cocktail period is generally short (30 to 45 minutes).

- Host and hostess sit at opposite ends of the table.

- The female guest of honor is seated next to the host. The male guest of honor is seated next to the hostess.

- Don't start eating until your hostess starts.

- Keep your hands on the table at all times during a meal—not in your lap. However, keep your elbows off the table.

- Do not pick up an open-faced sandwich— cut with knife and fork if provided.

- It is not uncommon to smoke between courses, but ask first.

- It is polite to finish everything on your plate. Norwegians do not like to waste food, but you are not expected to overstuff yourself.

- When finished eating, place your knife and fork side by side on the plate at the 5:25 position.

*Dinners are generally long, with three courses and much conversation.*

- Thank your hostess at the end of the meal.

- It is impolite to leave immediately after dinner.

- Do not ask for a tour of your host's home; it would be considered impolite.

---

## DRESS

- European style, conservative.

- Warm clothing advised—climate is cool much of the year.

BUSINESS
- Men: Sport jackets, ties or suits.

- Women: Suits, dresses or dress pants.

RESTAURANT
- Men: Suits (better restaurants require ties).

- Women: Dresses, dress pants, skirts/blouses.

OPERA, BALLET OR THEATER
- Men: Dark suits. Tuxedos are not common.

- Women: Cocktail dresses.

- Some people do wear casual clothes.

CASUAL
- Clean jeans and T-shirts are appropriate (not torn or faded).

## HOSTESS

- Always bring a small gift for the hostess when invited to someone's home.

- Gifts are opened upon receipt.

- If invited to a dinner party, it would be a good idea to send flowers to the hostess the morning of the dinner.

- Do give: Flowers, chocolates, wine, pastries, liquor (very expensive in Norway).

- Do not give: Carnations, bouquet of only white flowers such as lilies (funeral only), wreath (even at Christmas—for funerals only).

## BUSINESS

- Gifts are normally not exchanged at business meetings, but small gifts may be appropriate at the successful conclusion of negotiations.

- It's acceptable but not expected to give a Christmas gift to a Norwegian colleague.

- Give: Brandy or whiskey that is good quality but not too expensive.

*Liquor is a good gift. It is very expensive in Norway.*

## TOILET TIPS

| | |
|---|---|
| *Toalett/WC* | Restrooms |
| *Damer* | Women |
| *Herrer* | Men |
| V | Hot water (red dot) |
| K | Cold water (blue dot) |

# HELPFUL HINTS

DO:

- Be sincere. Norwegians consider Americans too glib and too casual.

- Recognize the adventurous spirit of the Norwegian people.

- Be reserved in expression of personal feelings.

- Speak in a quiet voice.

- Respect Norwegians' pride in their history and culture.

- Norwegians are very proud of their landscape. Take the time to notice it, appreciate it and comment on it.

- When entering a home, wait to be invited to sit down.

- Respect personal privacy. Do not discuss income, social status, age, etc.

- Offer your seat to a woman or elderly person on a bus, train, etc.

## DO NOT:

- Do not use "Pleased to meet you" or "How are you?" Norwegians believe that the Americans use these phrases without being sincere. If a Norwegian were to say, "How are you?" a long, detailed answer would be expected.

- Do not compare things in Norway to things in America, or suggest that America is better.

- Never be too casual.

- Never invite someone to dinner or suggest "getting together" unless you are willing and able to follow through.

*Never lump Norwegians together with Swedes or Danes.*

## PUNCTUALITY

- Norwegians insist on punctuality for social occasions.

- Norwegians take punctuality for business meetings very seriously and expect that you will do likewise; call if you will be delayed.

## STRICTLY BUSINESS

### BUSINESS CARDS

- Business cards in English are acceptable and are generally exchanged without much ceremony.

### CORPORATE CULTURE

STRUCTURE: Participative management is the norm in Norwegian companies. Consensus is a priority, but the boss makes the final decisions. Norwegians are very familiar with U.S. business practices.

MEETINGS: Informality is the rule in meetings; casual conversation and jokes are mixed with serious business.

COMMUNICATION: Most Norwegian businesspeople are fluent in English, and you're unlikely to need an interpreter. It is acceptable to call a Norwegian businessperson at home before 10 p.m.

> Norwegians have both a strong work ethic and a strong interest in leisure activities.

BE AWARE:

- Most office workers finish their work at 4 or 5 p.m. on the dot, but it's not unusual for managers to stay at their desk into the evening.

- Norwegians do not flaunt their success, wealth or material possessions and do not appreciate people who do.

### ENTERTAINMENT

- Breakfast meetings are not typical.

- Business lunches are to discuss business.

- Business dinners are mostly social, but business can also be discussed. Allow the host to open the discussion. Spouses are generally not included in business dinners at a restaurant.

- Business entertaining is generally done first in restaurants. Home entertaining of business colleagues is common once you get to know someone.

- First-class restaurants are very expensive. It is probably best to ask your Norwegian colleague to recommend a restaurant.

APPOINTMENTS

| Office Hours: | Monday through Friday |
|---|---|
| | 9 a.m. to 5:30 p.m. |
| | 8 a.m. to 3 p.m. (summer) |

| Bank Hours: | Monday through Friday |
|---|---|
| | 8:15 a.m. to 2:30 p.m. |

- Avoid July, August, one week before and one week after Christmas, the week before Easter, and May 17/18.

- Arrange appointments in advance.

---

- A foreign woman will find Norway a good place to do business. Equality of women is very advanced, and there are women at all levels in corporate and public life.

- It is acceptable for a foreign woman to invite a Norwegian man to dinner. She should have no problem paying the bill.

- Women can go alone to a bar or restaurant.

- It is safe to walk alone at night in most areas.

## ESPECIALLY FOR WOMEN

## HOLIDAYS AND FESTIVALS

- Do not plan to make a business visit or schedule any appointments during the following holidays or festivals. Be sure to check for the numerous regional and local holidays and festivals.

| | |
|---|---|
| January | New Year's Day (1). |
| March/April | Easter (Friday - Monday). |
| April/May | Ascension Thursday (40 days after Easter). |
| May | Labor Day (1), National Day (17). |
| May/June | Whitsunday (Pentecost) and Whitmonday (49 and 50 days after Easter). |
| June | Midsummer Fest (23). |
| December | Christmas (25), Boxing Day (26). |

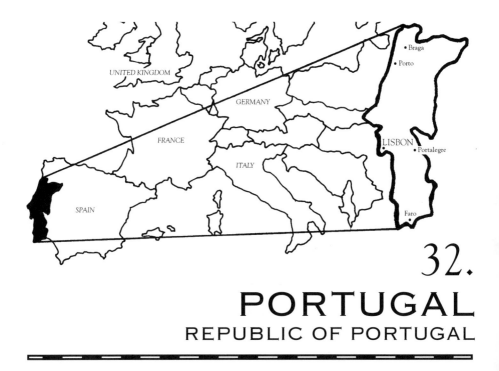

# 32.

# PORTUGAL
## REPUBLIC OF PORTUGAL

## VITAL STATISTICS

POPULATION: 10.4 million people (1992).

CAPITAL: Lisbon, with a population of 2.06 million (1991).

LAND SIZE: 35,550 square miles, slightly smaller than Indiana.

GOVERNMENT: Republic. The head of state is the president, elected for a five-year term. The president appoints the leader of the majority party as prime minister. The 230-member unicameral legislative *Assembléa da Republica* is elected for a four-year term. Madeira and the Azores have been autonomous units within the republic since 1976.

LIVING
STANDARD:    GDP = US$7,903 per capita (1992).

NATURAL
RESOURCES:   Fish, forests (cork), tungsten, iron ore, uranium
             ore, marble.

AGRICULTURE: Accounts for 6.1 percent of GDP and about 20
             percent of the labor force;  small, inefficient
             farms;  imports more than half of food needs;
             major crops include grain, potatoes, olives,
             grapes;  the livestock sector provides sheep,
             cattle, goats, poultry, meat, dairy products.

INDUSTRIES:  Textiles and footwear; wood pulp, paper and
             cork; metalworking; oil refining; fish canning;
             wine; tourism.

CLIMATE:     Mild and wet in winter, warm and dry in summer,
             with droughts in the south.  Temperatures
             average from 45°F (7°C) in the north in January
             to around 68°F (20°C) in the south in August.

CURRENCY:    Escudo (EsC).  EsC1 = 100 centavos.  Notes are
             in denominations of EsC10,000, 5,000, 1,000 and
             500.  Another term for 1,000 escudos is 1 conto.
             Coins are in denominations of EsC200, 100, 50,
             20, 10, 5, 2.50 and 1.

# THE PEOPLE

CORRECT
NAME:          Portuguese.

ETHNIC
MAKEUP:        99 percent Portuguese.

VALUE
SYSTEM:        Portuguese are traditional and conservative and
               do not quickly embrace change.  Portugal is a
               self-styled country with generally reserved and
               modest people. The Catholic Church has a
               strong influence. The car is the ultimate status
               symbol.

FAMILY:        The family is the basis of Portuguese life. Aunts,
               uncles, cousins and others play an important part
               in each others' lives. Life is simple, especially in
               rural areas.  The Portuguese go home after work
               and generally entertain only on weekends.

RELIGION:      97 percent Roman Catholic, 1 percent
               Protestant.

## MEETING AND GREETING

- Shake hands with everyone present—men, women, and children—at a business or social meeting. Shake hands again when leaving.

- Handshake is firm and warm with eye contact.

- When meeting friends, men embrace and pat one another on the back, women kiss both cheeks.

- Greetings:
  *Bom dia* (bong DEE-uh), "Good day."
  *Boa tarde* (BOH-uh tard), "Good afternoon."
  *Boa noite* (BOH-uh noyt), "Good evening."

## NAMES AND TITLES

- Use last names and appropriate titles until specifically invited by your Portuguese hosts or colleagues to use their first names.

| Mr. | *Senhor* | **seeyn-YOHR** |
|-----|----------|----------------|
| Mrs. | *Senhora* | **seeyn-YOHR-a** |
| Miss | *Menina* | **mee-NEE-nah** |
| | | (used for girls under 18) |

- Use first names with close friends only.

- *Doutor/Doutora* (Doctor) is used for anyone even suspected of having a degree.

- *Engenheiro/a* and *Arquitecto/a* (engineer and architect) are also used.

- *O Senhor/A Senhora* (to give deference) are often used.

- For a very formal occasion, use *Senhor/Senhora* + professional title + last name or last two names.

  **Examples:** *Senhora Doutora Varela Brito, Senhora Engenheira Varela Brito.*

- You can drop the *Senhor/Senhora* to initially address a new acquaintance in a generally formal manner.

  **Example:** *Doutora Varela Brito.*

- After initially addressing someone, you can drop any reference to their name.

  **Example:** *Senhora Doutora.*

---

## LANGUAGE

- Portuguese is the official language in Portugal, but French and English are common second languages.

- Spanish is understood; however, replies are in Portuguese.

---

## BODY LANGUAGE

- Portuguese do not use a lot of body gestures and do not appreciate overly demonstrative gestures or body language.

- Beckon someone with the palm of your hand down and fingers or whole hand waving (as if patting someone on the head).

# PHRASES

| English | Portuguese | Pronunciation |
|---|---|---|
| Good morning/day | *Bom dia* | bong DEE-uh |
| Good afternoon | *Boa tarde* | BOH-uh tard |
| Good evening | *Boa noite* | BOH-uh noyt |
| Please | *Por favor* | por fa-VOR |
| Thank you (by man) | *Obrigado* | o-bree-GAH-doo |
| Thank you (by woman) | *Obrigada* | o-bree-GAH-duh |
| You're welcome | *De nada* | day NAH-dah |
| Yes | *Sim* | seeng |
| No | *Não* | NAH-oo |
| Excuse me | *Com licença* | com lee-SEN-sa |
| Goodbye | *Adeus* | a-DAY-oosh |
| Pleased to meet you | *Muito prazer* | MUY-tu pra-ZERR |
| How are you? | *Como está?* | KOH-moo shta |

- A waiter is summoned by raising a hand.

- The older generation of Portuguese men do not like to eat chicken because they fear the female hormones fed to chickens could make them become feminine.

- Meals can be long with much conversation.

- Food is generally grilled or boiled.

BREAKFAST *(Pequeno Almoço)*: 7:30 to 8 a.m.
- Bread, butter, jam, coffee/tea, cereals, pastries.

LUNCH *(Almoço)*: noon to 2 p.m.
- Soup, fish or meat with rice or potato and vegetable or a light snack, dessert and coffee.

- Salad is served with the main course.

- Wine and bread are served with the meal.

COFFEE/TEA BREAK *(Lanche)*: 4 to 5 p.m.
- Appetizers, sandwich, pastries, tea, espresso or milk.

DINNER *(Jantar)*: 7:30 to 8 p.m.
- Generally the same food as lunch but larger portions.

## MENU TERMS

| | |
|---|---|
| *Appertivos/Entradas* | Appetizers |
| *Menu* | Main course |
| *Sobremesa* | Dessert |
| *Pào* | Bread |
| *Sopa* | Soup |
| *Vegetal* | Vegetable |
| *Carne* | Meat |
| *Vaca* | Beef |
| *Porco* | Pork |
| *Cordeiro* | Lamb |
| *Frango* | Chicken |
| *Peixe* | Fish |
| *Ovo* | Egg |

## TYPICAL FOODS

- Portuguese are the biggest consumers of fish per capita in Europe.

- *Açorda:* Minced bread, egg, olive oil and aromatic seasoning (i.e., cilantro, coriander, pepper).

- *Bacalhau:* Dried, salted cod, cooked more than 1,000 different ways.

- *Pasteis de Bacalhau:* Deep-fried mixture of cod, potatoes, onion and parsley.

- *Frango na Pucara:* Chicken in a pot.

- *Cozido à Portuguesa:* Boiled beef, pork, chicken, various types of smoked sausages, accompanied with cabbage, carrots, potatoes, turnips and rice made with the stock used to boil all the ingredients.

- *Caldeirada:* Seafood stew of several types of fish, sliced potatoes, tomatoes, onions, garlic and several seasonings.

- *Caldo Verde:* Soup made with puree of potatoes and onions, shredded dark green cabbage and some slices of smoked sausage.

- *Pudim Flan:* Creme caramel pudding.

- *Figos Recheados:* Dried figs stuffed with chocolate and almonds and served with port.

- Expect an egg somewhere in most meals.


## DRINKING

- *Bica:* Espresso coffee.

- White port, scotch, gin and tonic, *Cinzano* (women), mineral water, *vinho* (wine—with lunch and dinner), *cerveja* (beer—summer).

- After dinner, *aguardente* (a very strong local brandy) or port may be served.


## TOASTS

- Á *sua Saúde* (a sua sa-OOD), "To your health." Formal and informal.

- The guest of honor is always toasted and should reciprocate by giving a toast of thanks.

- It is acceptable for women to offer a toast.

## TIPPING

- Restaurant: A service charge of 15 percent is usually included in the bill (bill will read *serviço*); small change can be left as an additional gratuity for good service. If the service charge is not included, leave a 15 percent tip.

- Give small change (EsC150-200) to ushers, porters, taxi drivers, cloakroom attendants, washroom attendants and gas station attendants.

## MANNERS

- Don't stretch at the table.

- Do not eat until everyone has been served and your hostess begins to eat.

- Keep your hands on the table at all times during the meal—not in your lap. However, keep your elbows off the table.

- Dinners are generally family style—the guest of honor serves himself first and passes dishes around the table.

- Fish is eaten with a special knife and fork.

*Portugal is not Spain. Portuguese are not Spanish!*

- Don't soak up gravy with bread in your hands; use a piece of bread on your fork.

- To signify that you would like more food, place your fork diagonally from the left and your knife straight down to form a triangular position.

- It is polite to leave some food on your plate.

- When finished eating, place your knife and fork side by side on the plate at the 5:25 position.

- Fold your napkin and place it back on the table beside your plate after a meal.

- Don't ask for a tour of your host's home; it would be considered impolite.

- A return invitation to the hostess is appreciated.

---

## DRESS

- Conservative.

- Male dressing is based primarily around a jacket and tie.

- Women most often wear dresses.

- There is little difference in dress between work and social life.

### BUSINESS
- Men: Suits and ties or sport coats and ties.

- Women: Dresses, suits or pant suits.

### RESTAURANT
- Check in advance if coat and tie are required.

- Men: Suits and ties.

- Women: Dresses.

### OPERA/THEATER
- Men: Suits and ties.

- Women: Cocktail dresses.

## GIFTS

### HOSTESS

- Always bring a small gift for the hostess when invited to someone's house.

- A gift is opened immediately upon presentation.

- Flowers for the hostess and table wine for the host are recommended gifts.

- Give: Expensive chocolate, expensive flowers (not chrysanthemums).

### BUSINESS

- Gifts are normally not exchanged at business meetings, but small gifts may be appropriate at the successful conclusion of negotiations, or more commonly at Christmas.

- Give: Pens, crystal, ashtrays, diaries or any gift that might be related to the business itself.

### TOILET TIPS

| | |
|---|---|
| *Casa de Banho* | Restrooms |
| *Senhoras* | Ladies |
| *Homens* | Men |
| *Água quente* | Hot water |
| *Água fria* | Cold water |

**DO:**

- Compliment sincerely.

- Defer to older people.

- Allow host to open the door when it is time to leave.

- Keep a relaxed attitude about time.

- Bargain only in craft shops—not in department stores, other shops or food markets.

**DO NOT:**

- Do not be "nosy" or overly inquisitive.

- Do not eat while walking in public places—except ice cream cones.

- Never point with your finger.

- Don't join the hostess in the kitchen unless invited.

- Do not interrupt conversations.

*In Portuguese bullfights, unlike those of other countries, the bull is not killed.*

## PUNCTUALITY

- Punctuality is not important to Portuguese for social or business meetings.

- Punctuality by foreign visitors is expected and appreciated.

- Portuguese do not take punctuality for business meetings seriously and are often 15 to 30 minutes late, but they expect that you will be on time; call with an explanation if you are delayed.

## STRICTLY BUSINESS

### BUSINESS CARDS

- Business cards are exchanged frequently.

- Business cards in English are acceptable.

### CORPORATE CULTURE

STRUCTURE: The organization of most Portuguese companies is hierarchical, with subordinates having limited power and responsibility.

There is extensive government involvement in larger companies, but privatization has been underway since 1989. Small and medium-sized companies have been and remain in the private sector. Heavy industry has traditionally been dominated by a dozen powerful families, but a new breed of entrepreneurs—many educated in the U.S.—is emerging.

MEETINGS: Meetings are chiefly for briefing or discussion. Decisions may require several meetings, or one that lasts into the evening. Don't expect clear, decisive results.

Agendas exist, but are not always adhered to. Everyone is encouraged to contribute. Portuguese are flexible and collaborative in private, but view meetings as a place for competitive self-assertion; they strongly express their point of view before seeking common ground. If agreement or support is required at a meeting, you must lobby participants privately beforehand.

Allow your Portuguese host to initiate business discussions. He or she may offer refreshments and friendly conversation before getting down to business.

COMMUNICATION: While many younger managers know English, it will be appreciated if you have documents translated into Portuguese before sending them. Plan on hiring an interpreter for business meetings. It is acceptable and common to call a Portuguese businessperson at home.

BE AWARE:

- Trust and personal loyalty are important.

- Business relationships are personal and informal.

- Organizational procedures are often complex but can be negotiated.

- Delivery dates must be carefully negotiated and clearly understood if you expect them to be met.

### ENTERTAINMENT

- Business entertainment is most common in a restaurant.

- Business breakfasts are acceptable.

- People often have long lunches and relaxed dinners in restaurants.

- Dinner with business colleagues is a social event. Do not discuss business at dinner unless the host raises the subject.

- Business colleagues may eat together at a restaurant, but they seldom socialize other than that.

- Spouses may be included in a dinner invitation, but not always.

*Accept coffee, soda or an alcoholic beverage when offered by a business colleague, even if you don't drink it.*

### APPOINTMENTS

**Office Hours:** **Monday to Friday**
**9:30 a.m. to 12:30 p.m.**
**2:30 to 6 p.m.**

**Saturday**
**9:30 a.m. to 12:30 p.m.**

**Bank Hours:**    Monday to Friday
9:30 a.m. to noon.
2 to 4 p.m.

Saturday
9:30 a.m. to 11:30 a.m.

- Prior appointments are necessary. Confirm the appointment near the date.

- Do not plan a business trip in August.

- Unique festivals and holidays are celebrated in specific regions and cities. Check for local holidays before planning a business trip.

---

- Foreign businesswomen are treated fairly and with respect. However, traditionally, conservative attitudes toward women have prevailed. Currently, there is a strong movement towards Portuguese women being involved in business. Many women work outside the home in the urban areas.

- Portuguese men are still macho, especially in the country. It is better for a foreign woman to invite a Portuguese man to a business lunch rather than dinner. If you invite a man to dinner, it is better to ask if he would like to bring his wife.

- Going to a bar or nightclub alone is frowned upon. It may bring unwelcome attention.

- Take a taxi after dark or when there aren't many people around.

- The charm of Portuguese men will not allow a woman to pay for a lunch or dinner. It is acceptable to try.

## ESPECIALLY
## FOR
## WOMEN

# HOLIDAYS AND FESTIVALS

- Do not plan to make a business visit or schedule any appointments during the following holidays or festivals. Be sure to check for the numerous regional and local holidays and festivals.

| | |
|---|---|
| January | New Year's Day (1). |
| February | Pancake Tuesday (Carnival-day before Ash Wednesday). |
| March/April | Easter (Friday-Monday). |
| April | Anniversary of the Revolution (25). |
| April/May | Ascension Thursday (40 days after Easter). |
| May | Labor Day (1). |
| May/June | Whitsunday and Whitmonday (49 and 50 days after Easter). |
| June | Corpus Christi (60 days after Easter), St. Anthony's Day (3), National Day of Portugal (10). |
| August | Assumption (15). |
| October | Proclamation of the Republic (5). |
| November | All Saints' Day (1). |
| December | Independence Day (1), Day of the Immaculate Conception (8), Christmas (25). |

33.
# SPAIN
## KINGDOM OF SPAIN

## VITAL STATISTICS

POPULATION:     39.1 million (1992).

CAPITAL:        Madrid, with a population of 3.2 million (1990).

LAND SIZE:      194,884 square miles, slightly more than twice
                the size of Oregon.

GOVERNMENT:     Parliamentary monarchy. The king is the head of
                state, but the president is the chief executive. The
                president is elected by popular vote but approved
                by the monarch. The bicameral legislature, the
                *Cortes*, has a 350-member Congress of Deputies
                elected through the electoral system for a four-year
                term, and a Senate with 208 members. There are
                17 autonomous communities, each with its own
                flag, legislature, power and responsibility.

LIVING
STANDARD:      GDP = US$12,719 per capita (1992).

NATURAL
RESOURCES:     Coal, lignite, iron ore, uranium, mercury, pyrites,
               fluorspar, gypsum, zinc, lead, tungsten, copper,
               kaolin, potash, hydropower.

AGRICULTURE:   Accounts for about 5 percent of GDP and 14
               percent of labor force; major products include
               grain, vegetables, olives, wine grapes, sugar beets,
               citrus fruit, beef, pork, poultry, dairy; largely self-
               sufficient in food; fish catch of 1.4 million metric
               tons is among top 20 nations.

INDUSTRIES:    Textiles and apparel (including footwear), food
               and beverages, metals and metal products,
               chemicals, shipbuilding, automobiles, machine
               tools, tourism.

CLIMATE:       Temperate in the north, 48°F to 64°F (9°C to
               18°C). More extreme in the center, with hot,
               dry summers and cold winters; average
               temperatures 75°F (24°C) in July, 41°F (5°C) in
               January. Mediterranean in south.

CURRENCY:      Peseta (Pta). Notes are in denominations of
               Pta25,000, 10,000, 5,000, 2,000, 1,000, 500 and
               200. Coins are in denominations of Pta500, 200,
               100, 50, 25, 10, 5 and 1.

# THE PEOPLE

CORRECT
NAME:            Spaniards, Spanish.

ETHNIC
MAKEUP:          73 percent Spanish, 16 percent Catalan, 8
                 percent Galician, 2 percent Basque.

VALUE
SYSTEM:          Personal pride and individualism are highly
                 valued.  People strive to project affluence and
                 social position.  Personal appearance and image is
                 very important.  Character and breeding are
                 highly valued.  Modesty is valued over
                 assertiveness.  Human relationships are very
                 important.  The flaunting of superiority,
                 intelligence or ability is not appreciated.

FAMILY:          The family is the basic economic and social unit in
                 Spain and a source of personal security.
                 Traditionally, men were expected to be strong and
                 masculine while women were expected to be
                 feminine and tolerant.  However, this is changing as
                 the younger, post-Franco generation stresses greater
                 equality between men and women.  Potential
                 spouses must usually gain parental approval.
                 Collapse of traditional authority systems has family,
                 church and state in a striking state of change.

RELIGION:        97 percent Roman Catholic.

## MEETING AND GREETING

- Shake hands with everyone present—men, women, and children—at a business or social meeting. Shake hands again when leaving.

- Handshake is firm with eye contact.

- Hugs and kisses are reserved for friends.

## NAMES AND TITLES

- Use last names and appropriate titles until specifically invited by your Spanish hosts or colleagues to use their first names.

| Mr. | *Señor* | sen-YOHR |
|-----|---------|----------|
| Mrs. | *Señora* | sen-YOHR-a |
| Miss | *Señorita* | sen-yohr-EET-a |
| | | (girls under 18 years old) |

- The last name is a combination of the father's family name followed by the mother's maiden name.

  **Example: Father**    Juan *Sastre*
             Mother    Andrea *Segovia*
             Son    Jose Luis *Sastre Segovia*

- In conversation and correspondence use only the family name.

  **Example: Jose Luis Sastre Segovia would be addressed as *Señor Sastre*.**

- Women keep their maiden name after marriage.

- The titles *Don* and *Doña* are used to address an older person or to show respect. The titles are also used for high-level executives and in more formal relationships.

- *Don/Doña* are used with the first name only.

  **Example: *Francisco Garcia-Mancha would be addressed as Don Francisco.***

- Never use *Don/Doña* with your own name.

---

- There are four official languages in Spain: Castilian (Spanish, the language spoken and understood by everyone), Catalan (17 percent, mostly northeast), Galician (7 percent, mostly northwest), and Basque (2 percent, mostly north).

- Spaniards appreciate any attempt foreigners make to speak their language.

- English is spoken mostly only in tourist centers.

*Spaniards say, "Don't talk while I am interrupting."*

---

- Generally, Spaniards stand very close.

- Spaniards show affection publicly to their friends and family.

- Men may embrace each other when meeting (friends and family only).

- Never touch, hug, or back-slap a Spaniard you do not know well.

- Women may kiss each other on the cheek and embrace.

- Eye contact from a Spanish woman to a Spanish man may be interpreted as an expression of interest, but staring at foreigners is common and should not be interpreted as such.

- Spaniards speak a lot with their hands. Never mimic them.

## PHRASES

| English | Spanish | Pronunciation |
|---|---|---|
| Good morning/day | *Buenos días* | bway-nohs DEE-ahs |
| Good afternoon | *Buenas tardes*<br>(until 8 p.m.) | bway-nahs TAHR-dehs |
| Good evening | *Buenas noches*<br>(after dark) | bway-nahs NOH-chehs |
| Please | *Por favor* | pohr fah-BOHR |
| Thank you | *Gracias* | GRAH-see-ahs |
| You're welcome | *De nada* | day NAH-dah |
| Yes | *Sí* | see |
| No | *No* | noh |
| Excuse me | *Perdóneme* | perh-DOHN-nay-may |
| Goodbye | *Adiós* | as-DYOHS |
| Pleased to<br>meet you | *Encantado*<br>(said by man)<br>*Encantada*<br>(said by woman) | en-ken-TAH-doe<br><br>en-ken-TAH-dah |
| How are you? | *¿Cómo está usted?* | KOH-moh ehs-TAH oos-TEHD |

- Spanish food is not hot and spicy.

- Staples include meat, eggs, chicken, fish, vegetables and fruit.

- Olive oil is used to fry food.

BREAKFAST (*Desayuno*): 7 to 8 a.m.
- Generally a light meal of coffee or hot chocolate, bread and jam, or *churros* (a batter made of flour and butter, deep-fried and sprinkled with sugar).

LUNCH (*Almuerzo*): 2 to 3 p.m.
- The main meal of the day, often including an appetizer, a main dish accompanied by a salad, bread (served without butter) and fresh fruit/dessert.

- Some businessmen grab a quick sandwich but most stop for a traditional three-course lunch.

DINNER (*Cena*): 9 to 10 p.m.  Later on weekends.
- A light meal, usually a sandwich (*bocadillo*) or sweet bread or crackers with tea or hot milk.

- Supper can be another three courses, sometimes with lighter food served for the main course.

*To summon a waiter hold up an index finger, make eye contact and say, "Por favor, señor." There are few waitresses in Spain.*

## MENU TERMS

| | |
|---|---|
| *Aperitivo, Entradas* | Appetizers |
| *Plato principal,* | |
| *Plato fuerte* | Main course |
| *Postre* | Dessert |
| *Pan* | Bread |
| *Sopa* | Soup |
| *Verduras* | Vegetables |
| *Carne de res* | Beef |
| *Pollo* | Chicken |
| *Cerdo* | Pork |
| *Cordero* | Lamb |
| *Pescado* | Fish |
| *Huevo* | Egg |

## TYPICAL FOODS

- Don't be surprised to see a lot of egg dishes for the main course.

- *Paella*: Rice with clams, mussels, squid.

- *Carne al Horno*: Roast meats.

- *Langosta del Pobre*: Monkfish.

- *Tapas*: Wide variety of appetizers (chorizo sausage, chicken, pork, ham).

- *Gazpacho*: Cold vegetable soup.

- *Huevos Fritos*: Fried eggs.

- *Empanadas*: Meat filled turnovers.

- *Merluza en Salsa Verde*: Hake (the country's most popular fish) in green sauce.

- *Tortilla*: Spanish potato omelette.

- *Flan*: Caramel custard.

## DRINKING

- *Jérez* (sherry): The national drink. 90 percent of the people in southern Spain drink sherry.

- *Sangría*: Popular drink for Spaniards.

- *Vino* (wine): Red, white and rosé, served with both lunch and dinner.

- Most people in northern Spain drink wine and *cerveza* (beer).

- Spaniards are not insulted if their guests do not drink alcoholic beverages when they are hosting.

## TOASTS

- *Salud* (sa-LOOD), "Health." Formal and informal. (Also said after someone sneezes.)

- Toasts can be made at any time—be brief.

- After host stands, says a few personal thoughts and raises glass, everyone stands and says *Salud*. In a small group it may not be necessary to stand.

- It is acceptable for women to give toasts.

## TIPPING

- It is common to round the bill up to the nearest hundred pesetas for any service rendered.

- Restaurants: A service charge of 10-15 percent is usually included in the bill (bill will read *propina incluida*); small change (Pta100-200) can be left as an additional tip for good service. If the service charge is not included, leave a 10-15 percent tip.

- Bars: Leave a Pta50-100 tip whenever you order a drink.

- Taxis: 10 percent. More for long trips or help with luggage. Official surcharge for airport runs and baggage.

- Porters: Pta150 per bag. At a five-star hotel, Pta100 depending on the service.

- Ushers: Pta50-100.

- Cloakroom attendants: Pta100.

- Gas station attendants: Pta50.

- Washroom attendants: Pta100.

- Hairdressers: Pta200.

- Barbers: Pta100.

- Maids: Pta100 per night.

- Room service: Pta100.

- Doormen: Pta100. Not necessary to give every time.

- Ladies and older people are seated first.

- The female guest of honor is seated next to the host. The male guest of honor is seated next to the hostess.

- Fruit knife and fork or dessert utensils may be placed above the dinner plate.

- No bread and butter plate is used. Bread is set directly on the table.

- Butter is served with bread at breakfast only.

- Restaurants generally charge for bread by the piece.

- Keep your hands on the table at all times during the meal—not in your lap. However, keep your elbows off the table.

- Compliments and friendliness to waiters are appreciated.

- Compliment hostess, waiter, etc. on the food.

- Spaniards don't waste food. It is better to decline food rather than leave food on your plate.

- Do not ask for a doggy bag or to take food home.

- When finished eating, place your knife and fork side by side on the plate at the 5:25 position.

- Stay until the guest of honor leaves.

- A Spaniard's home is considered private. Do not ask for a tour of someone's home. Allow them to offer.

*Manners are based on easy, relaxed formality.*

# DRESS

- Appearance is extremely important to a Spaniard.

- Dress conservatively. Avoid bright or flashy colors.

- Shoes are the most important element of dress. Shabby-looking shoes can ruin a very nice outfit.

  - Spaniards dress elegantly, even for casual occasions.

    - Dressier outfits are required for cities, especially fine restaurants.

      - If you want to blend in, don't wear sneakers.

### BUSINESS

- Men: Jackets and ties—even in warm weather. If the senior person takes his jacket off during a meeting, you may do so too.

- Women: Dresses, blouses and skirts.

### RESTAURANT

- Better restaurants require coats and ties. Check if a tie and jacket are required.

- Men: Jackets and ties.

- Women: Dresses, dressy pants, suits.

## CASUAL/BEACH

- Dress "smart casual" and never sloppy.

- Swimsuits, beach attire or shorts are worn only in resort or beach areas.

- Topless beaches are common. Nude beaches are in remote areas.

- Wear a cover-up on streets and in restaurants.

---

# GIFTS

## HOSTESS

- Always bring a small, wrapped gift for the hostess when invited to someone's home.

- Bring a gift for children. Treat them as very special.

- Gifts are opened immediately.

- Give: Pastries, cakes, chocolates, flowers (but red roses connote passion, yellow roses infidelity). Give an odd number of flowers.

- Do not give: Chrysanthemums, dahlias or 13 flowers (unlucky number).

## BUSINESS

- Gifts are normally not exchanged at business meetings, but small gifts may be appropriate at the successful conclusion of negotiations. It's acceptable, but not expected, to give a Christmas gift to a Spanish colleague.

- Give: Desk items, books, art, music.

- Do not give: An expensive gift, which might imply a bribe.

## TOILET TIPS

| | |
|---|---|
| *Servicios* | Restrooms |
| *Damas* | Ladies |
| *Caballeros* | Men |
| C | Hot water |
| F | Cold water |

## HELPFUL HINTS

DO:

- Adjust to the Spanish concept of space. Spanish people stand very close when speaking.

- When speaking, expect to be interrupted.

- Be patient. Nothing is done in a hurry.

- Bullfights are serious business. Bullfighting is considered more an art than a sport in Spain. Follow bullfight protocol.

- Understand that all Spaniards are not bullfighters and some don't even like to go to bullfights.

- Consider it a compliment to be invited to someone's home. This is seldom done.

- Expect taxis to charge for each piece of luggage in addition to the fare.

- Allow Spaniards to talk about their families.

- Beware of gypsies. Gypsies often approach with a flower or a gift and hand it to unsuspecting tourists. A demand for payment will follow.

*Bullfighting is considered more an art than a sport in Spain.*

DO NOT:

- Do not mistake the Spaniards' sense of self-reliance and personal worth as intolerance. Spaniards are very proud people.

- Avoid the use of your car horn in the city—use it only when necessary.

- Do not leave items visible in your car.

- Do not carry packages and handbags on the arm that is next to the street.

---

## PUNCTUALITY

- Spaniards have a casual attitude about arriving on time for social occasions/business appointments.

- Punctuality by foreign visitors is expected and appreciated.

- It is acceptable and common, for social meetings, to be late by 30 minutes in southern and 15 minutes in northern Spain.

- Never be late for a bullfight.

# STRICTLY
# BUSINESS

## BUSINESS CARDS

- Use business cards printed in Spanish and English.

- Present business cards at the end of the meeting.

## CORPORATE CULTURE

STRUCTURE: Companies are run from the top, with orders passed down the chain of command. The boss is in charge, asserts authority and solves problems. He is expected to be strong and consistent. Shared decisionmaking is viewed as a weakness.

Spaniards are used to criticism from the boss, but are likely to resent criticism from colleagues or outsiders. Often, a person reprimanded will not admit doing wrong.

The organizational chart is social, not functional. People on the third or fourth level may have more real power than those at the top.

MEETINGS: Spain is not a meeting culture; meetings are held when necessary to communicate instructions or save time. In negotiations, leave room for concessions, but don't haggle.

COMMUNICATION:  Most large companies
conduct business in English and Spanish, but
Spanish is the dominant language of business
and you cannot expect that English will be
spoken.  Check ahead to see if an interpreter is
needed.  Most Spaniards won't mind being
called at home on important business.

BE AWARE:

- Never embarrass anyone.  Pride and honor
  are very serious matters.

- Expect to encounter delay and
  procrastination.

- Loyalty is to people, not institutions.

- Bankers are the business elite, but in recent
  years entrepreneurs have become highly
  admired.

- Spaniards' lack of trust in rules and
  regulations produces a constant crisis
  atmosphere.

## ENTERTAINMENT

- Breakfast meetings are acceptable but not
  favored.

- Lunches/dinners are a vital part of business
  used to establish a relationship.

- Business can be discussed at any time during
  the meal, but follow the lead of your host.

*Conflict and stress
exist in business
between the old
management style
(bureaucratic and
authoritarian
managers over 50)
and the new, more
participative
management style
employed by
younger managers.*

- Business entertaining is most common in a restaurant. You may be invited to a home during the last days of meetings.

- Social life outside of work is generally with people of the same level from different companies.

- Spouses can be invited to dinner, but this is not always the case.

---

## APPOINTMENTS

| | |
|---|---|
| **Office Hours:** | **Monday to Friday** |
| | **9:30 a.m. to 2:30 p.m.** |
| | **4:30 to 7:30 p.m.** |
| **Bank Hours:** | **Monday to Saturday** |
| | **9 a.m. to 2 p.m.** |

- Vacations are typically between July 15 and Sept. 15.

- No business is done from 1:30/2:30 to 4:30 p.m. (lunch break).

- Book appointments at least two weeks in advance.

---

## ESPECIALLY FOR WOMEN

- Foreign women are accepted in the business community. However, it is important to establish credentials and ability immediately.

- Traditionally, a macho and chauvinistic behavior toward women, known as *machismo,* has persisted. Professional progress for women has been slow, but this is changing and professional women are being more widely accepted in the business community.

- Traditionally, young women have married and left the job market permanently in their 30s. Today, most working women return to work after a maternity leave. Day care, nanny services, grandparents or other relatives are all commonly used.

- Currently, though many women work, it is uncommon to find women on the "fast track." Women lawyers and doctors are extremely rare. Educationally qualified women (a recent phenomenon) are gradually making some gains.

- Be aware of eye contact. Returning a man's gaze may be interpreted as flirting or a show of interest.

- Do not dine alone in a restaurant or bar at night. For lunch it is acceptable.

- It is acceptable for a visiting businesswoman to invite a businessman to dinner. Realize it is very difficult for women to pay for a man's meal. Spanish men expect to pay. Speak to the maitre d' or waiter in advance if you wish to pay.

## HOLIDAYS AND FESTIVALS

- Do not plan to make a business visit or schedule any appointments during the following holidays or festivals. Be sure to check for the numerous regional and local holidays and festivals.

| | |
|---|---|
| January | New Year's Day (1), Three Kings' Day/ Epiphany (6). |
| February | Carnival (not a work holiday, but there are several local festivals). |
| March | St. Joseph's Day (19), Father's Day (19). |
| March/April | Easter (Thursday-Monday). |
| April/May | Ascension Thursday (40 days after Easter). |
| May | May/Labor Day (1). |
| May/June | Whitsunday and Whitmonday (49 and 50 days after Easter). |
| June | Corpus Christi (60 days after Easter). |
| July | Feast of Santiago (25) - the Patron Saint of Spain. |
| August | Feast of the Assumption (15). |
| October | National Day *El Pilar* (12). |
| November | All Saints' Day (1). |
| December | Constitution Day (6), Feast of the Immaculate Conception (8), Christmas (25). |

# 34.
# SWEDEN
## KINGDOM OF SWEDEN

## VITAL STATISTICS

POPULATION: 8.6 million (1992).

CAPITAL: Stockholm, with a population of 1.5 million (1992).

LAND SIZE: 173,800 square miles, slightly smaller than California.

GOVERNMENT: Constitutional monarchy. King's duties are mostly ceremonial. The head of government is the prime minister. Members of the 349-person *Riksdag* (parliament) are elected for three-year terms. Municipal councils handle local affairs.

LIVING
STANDARD: GDP = US$30,482 per capita (1992).

NATURAL
RESOURCES:    Zinc, iron ore, lead, copper, silver, timber,
              uranium, hydropower potential.

AGRICULTURE:  Animal husbandry predominates, with milk and
              dairy products accounting for 37 percent of farm
              income; main crops include grains, sugar beets,
              potatoes.

INDUSTRIES:   Iron and steel, precision equipment (bearings,
              radio and telephone parts, armaments), wood
              pulp and paper products, processed foods, motor
              vehicles.

CLIMATE:      Monthly average temperature ranges vary
              according to latitude: in south, from 27°F (-3°C)
              to 64°F (18°C); in far north, from 7°F (-14°C) to
              57°F (14°C).

CURRENCY:     Swedish krona (SEK). SEK1 = 100 öre. Notes
              are in denominations of SEK1,000, 500, 100, 50
              and 20. Coins are in denominations of SEK10, 5
              and 1, and 50 öre.

# THE PEOPLE

CORRECT
NAME:          Swedes.

ETHNIC
MAKEUP:        91 percent homogeneous Swedish, 3 percent
               Finnish, small SAMI (formerly Lappish) and
               European immigrant minority.

VALUE
SYSTEMS:       Swedes are very proud of their nation, towns and
               regions. They are primarily middle class, which
               most people find just. Patriotism is important.
               Sweden has one of the most far-reaching social
               security systems in the world.

FAMILY:        Family life has changed in Sweden, but families
               are still very important. Most women work
               outside the home. Many men and women live
               together before or instead of marriage. After
               living together for six months, a Swedish couple
               is granted the same legal rights as a married
               couple. Average family size is less than two
               children.

RELIGION:      95 percent Lutheran.

## MEETING AND GREETING

- Shake hands with everyone present—men, women, and children—at a business or social meeting. Shake hands again when leaving.

- Younger people generally do not shake hands when meeting friends.

- Older people expect a handshake when being greeted or when leaving.

- If no one is available to introduce you, it is polite to shake each person's hand and introduce yourself.

- Formal greetings:

  *God dag* (goo dog), "Good day."
  *God morgon* (goo MOHR-ahn), "Good morning."

- Casual greetings (used by most people):

  *Hej* (hey), "Hi."
  *Hallå* (hall-LOW), which gets someone's attention—not a greeting.

- Use last names and appropriate titles until specifically invited by your Swedish hosts or colleagues to use their first names.

- Swedes are quick to go to first names with their fellow countrymen.

- Titles are used but generally only for very formal occasions.

- Use *Herr, Fru,* or *Fröken* + last name.

| | | |
|---|---|---|
| **Mr.** | *Herr* | hair |
| **Mrs.** | *Fru* | frew |
| **Miss** | *Fröken* | FRUH-ken |

- Swedish is the official language.

- Most people speak English. English is a required second language in school.

- Swedes appreciate people speaking a few words of Swedish.

- Generally, Swedes are reserved in body language.

- Keep eye contact at all times while talking with someone.

- People do not often embrace or touch in public. However, it is becoming increasingly common to see friendship displayed publicly.

# PHRASES

| English | Swedish | Pronunciation |
| --- | --- | --- |
| Good morning | *God morgon* | goo MOHR-ahn |
| Good afternoon/day | *God dag* | goo dog |
| Good evening | *God afton* | goo AHF-tohn |
| Please | *Var vänlig* | vahr VAHN-leeg |
| Thank you | *Tack så mycket* | tahk so MICK-et |
| You're welcome | *Var så god* | vahr so goood |
| Yes | *Ja* | yah |
| No | *Nej* | nay |
| Excuse me | *Ursäkta mig* | OOR-SECT-uh may |
| Goodbye | *Adjö or Hejdå* | ahd-YOU or HAY-doh |
| Pleased to meet you | *Det var trevligt* | det vahr TREV-lickt |
| How are you? | *Hur mår du?* | hur more do |

BREAKFAST (*Frukost*): 7 to 8 a.m.
- Coffee, tea, bread (hard rolls), cheese.

LUNCH (*Lunch*): noon to 1 p.m.
- Hot dish, open-faced sandwich, dessert, coffee.

DINNER (*Iddag*): 5 to 7 p.m.
- Three courses (casual dinner):
  - Meat or fish, potatoes, vegetables.
  - Salad.
  - Dessert followed by coffee.

- Four courses (business or formal dinners):
  - Smoked salmon, caviar, marinated herring or soup.
  - Meat or fish, potatoes, vegetables.
  - Salad.
  - Dessert followed by coffee.

# DINING AND DRINKING

*To beckon a waiter, wave your hand and make eye contact.*

## MENU TERMS

| | |
|---|---|
| *Förrätt* | Appetizer |
| *Huvudrätt* | Main course |
| *Efterrätt* | Dessert |
| *Bröd* | Bread |
| *Soppa* | Soups |
| *Grönsaker* | Vegetables |
| *Kött* | Meat |
| *Oxkött* | Beef |
| *Fläsk* | Pork |
| *Lamm* | Lamb |
| *Kyckling* | Chicken |
| *Fisk* | Fish |
| *Ägg* | Egg |

- Swedes do not eat a lot of fat or meat.

- Swedes eat a lot of fish, cheese, vegetables and fruit.

- Sweden is famous for its *smörgåsbord* (large buffet) for parties and special occasions. Hot and cold foods are placed on a large table for self-service.

- Swedes eat food in a prescribed order: Cold fish dishes, cold meats and vegetable salads, small hot dishes (meatballs, sausages), desserts (cheese, fruit, pastry).

## TYPICAL FOODS

- *Gravlax:* Salmon cured with dill.

- *Lutefisk:* Lye-treated dried codfish.

- *Renkött:* Reindeer meat.

## DRINKING

- *Vin* (wine) or *öl* (beer).

- *Renat*: A popular brand of *brännvin* (vodka).

- Cocktails: Vodka, scotch, brandy, wine, gin, Campari.

- *Aquavit*: Distilled from grain or potatoes and sometimes flavored with caraway seeds and other spices.

## TOASTS

- *Skål* (skohl), "Cheers." Formal or informal.

- Allow your host and seniors in rank and age to toast first.

- Before anyone drinks, the host makes a small speech and offers the first toast.

- Don't take a drink until the host has given a toast.

- When toasting, meet the other person's eyes, nod and say *Skål* before putting your glass down.

*Toasts are often quite formal.*

- After making a toast, the men must wait for the women to put their glasses down first. Do this immediately. It can be very annoying for men to wait too long for the women to put their glasses down.

- Traditionally, when toasting with *aquavit*, you drink it in one gulp. But be careful since these drinks are very strong. A foreigner would not be expected to drink in one gulp.

- The meal ends with the male guest of honor tapping his glass with a knife or spoon and thanking the hostess on behalf of all the guests. The female guest of honor thanks the host.

- It is acceptable for a woman to propose a toast.

## TIPPING

- Restaurants: A service charge of 15-20 percent is always included in the bill; it is a common practice to round up the bill to the nearest krona when paying the waiter/waitress. In five-star restaurants you would leave a 5 percent additional gratuity on the table.

- Taxis: A 10 percent tip is usually included in the fare; it is a common practice to round up the fare to the nearest krona.

- Gas station attendants, hairdressers, barbers, hotel maids and doormen are all paid good salaries. No tip is necessary.

## MANNERS

- Behavior may be very formal.

- There may be no cocktail hour.

- Often dinner is served immediately at dinner parties.

- The female guest of honor is seated next to the host. The male guest of honor is seated next to the hostess.

- A butter knife is usually provided. Do not use a dinner knife for butter.

- Keep your hands on the table at all times during a meal—not in your lap. However, keep your elbows off the table.

- The main course is usually passed a second time when dining in a home.

- Try to eat everything on your plate, but if you must leave food because you are too full, your hosts should not be offended.

- When finished eating, place knife and fork side by side on the plate at the 5:25 position.

- Usually leave dinner no later than 11 p.m.

- Call or preferably write the next day to thank your host and hostess.

- Do not ask for a tour of your host's home unless you have a well-established relationship.

---

- European style, warm clothing.

## DRESS

- Be well dressed in public at all times.

- Swedes wear fashionable but casual clothing, which nevertheless is often elegant.

- Traditionally, furs have been worn both in daytime and in the evening, but increasing demonstrations against fur wearers have caused a decline in the number of furs being seen in Sweden.

- Men: Conservative. Suits and ties.

- Women: Dresses, suits, and pant suits.

RESTAURANT
- Men: Suits and ties, unless casual attire has been indicated.

- Women: Dresses or elegant pants, unless casual attire has been indicated.

OPERA, BALLET OR THEATER
- Men: Suits. Tuxedos (called "smoking jackets") are worn for formal occasions.

- Women: Dresses or "dressy" pant suits. Cocktail dresses are worn for formal occasions.

---

## GIFTS

### HOSTESS
- Always bring a small gift for the hostess when invited to someone's home.

- Gifts are opened immediately.

- A small gift of candy for the children is appreciated.

- Give: Flowers (unwrap before giving), wine (liquor is special because it is very expensive in Sweden), chocolates, books, records, cassettes.

- Do not give: Crystal or any items made in Sweden.

## BUSINESS

- Gifts are generally not exchanged in business, but it is common to give small gifts for Christmas to a Swedish colleague.

- Give: Gifts representative of your business or home area.

- Do not give: Items made in Sweden.

## TOILET TIPS

| *Toalett/WC* | Restrooms |
| *Damer* | Ladies |
| *Herrar* | Men |
| *Varmvatten* | Hot water |
| *Kallvatten* | Cold water |

DO:

# HELPFUL HINTS

- Embrace, touch or kiss only close friends.

- Be patient in lines for buses, trains, etc.

- Know, appreciate and compliment Sweden's accomplishments—its economy, high standard of living, sports, architecture, history, etc.

- Remember to thank someone for dinner or a gift upon next meeting.

- Use "like," not "love," when describing an event, object, etc.

- A man should tip his hat to women and remove his hat while talking to a woman.

## DO NOT:

- Do not eat fast, or you'll confirm Swedes' view of Americans as people who shovel food into their mouths.

- Do not praise another city or area in Sweden over the one you are visiting. Swedes are very proud of their own town or region.

- Do not criticize Swedish lifestyle, sexual habits, suicide rate, prices, etc.

- Do not compliment lightly. Insincere comments are considered rude.

- Do not be surprised to see people changing clothes on the beach—with or without a towel as cover.

---

## PUNCTUALITY

- Swedes insist on punctuality for social occasions. Meals may be served immediately upon arrival.

- It is better to wait around the corner of the house to ensure arriving on time than risk being a few minutes late.

- Swedes take punctuality for business meetings very seriously and expect that you will do likewise; call with an explanation if you are delayed.

## BUSINESS CARDS

- Business cards are exchanged. No ritual is followed.

- Business cards in English are acceptable.

## CORPORATE CULTURE

STRUCTURE: The structure of most Swedish companies is horizontal and functional, with most decisions made by middle- and lower-level managers in an organization. Authority is earned by competence, and senior managers regularly delegate key decisions.

The decisionmaking process is time-consuming, but the implementation of decisions is rapid.

MEETINGS: Meetings begin and end punctually, and agendas are clearly set. Meetings can be for briefing, discussion or decisionmaking. Swedes usually get right down to business after very brief cordialities. They will be factual, practical and precise and will get to the point quickly; they expect the same of you. Swedes are tough negotiators.

Presentations are important. They should be clear, to the point and detailed, and they should be backed up by numerous facts, figures, tables and charts.

COMMUNICATION: English is commonly used in business, and an interpreter will rarely be needed. When communicating with Swedes, be clear and concise in detailing what you expect from them; they will be equally clear with you. Don't call a Swedish businessperson at home unless the matter is urgent and you have a well-established relationship.

BE AWARE:

- The pace of business is slow and relatively relaxed—don't rush people.

- Personal relationships are important but are clearly separated from doing business.

- Swedes may appear stiff or aloof when you first meet them, but strong personal relationships can develop when they get to know you.

ENTERTAINMENT
- Business entertaining is most often done in a restaurant.

- Business breakfasts are acceptable, but not as common as in the U.S.

- Business can be discussed at any time during a meal.

- Business lunches are common and business is discussed.

- Spouses may be included in business dinners.

- Coffee breaks and lunches are long.

APPOINTMENTS

**Office Hours:**    Monday to Friday
                     8 a.m. to 5 p.m.

**Bank Hours:**      Monday to Friday
                     9:30 a.m. to 3 p.m.
                     Thursday
                     4 to 5:30 p.m.

- In summer many businesses close by 3 or 4 p.m.

- Avoid July and August, Feb. 20 and March 1 (school holidays), and the Christmas and Easter seasons.

## ESPECIALLY FOR WOMEN

- Sweden is a good place for women to do business. Foreign women are widely accepted. However, Swedes are more conservative in their views toward professional women than their reputation might indicate.

- In Sweden women make up 48 percent of the work force—one of the highest percentages in the world.

- It is not a problem for a foreign woman to invite a Swedish man to dinner. A businesswoman may pay the check in a restaurant without any embarrassment.

- A woman can eat alone in the better restaurants, as well as in the bars and restaurants of major hotels.

- Women are usually safe walking alone at night.

# HOLIDAYS AND FESTIVALS

- Do not plan to make a business visit or schedule any appointments during the following holidays or festivals. Be sure to check for the numerous regional and local holidays and festivals.

| | |
|---|---|
| January | New Year's Day (1), Epiphany (6). |
| March/April | Easter (Friday-Monday). |
| April/May | Ascension Thursday (40 days after Easter). |
| May | Labor Day (1). |
| May/June | Whitsunday and Whitmonday (49 and 50 days after Easter). |
| June | Swedish Flag Day (6), Corpus Christi (60 days after Easter). Midsummer Day (*Midsommar*) —celebrations commence on Midsummer Eve and can last for a week (24). |
| November | All Saints' Day (1). |
| December | Christmas (24-25), Boxing Day (26), New Year's Eve (31). |

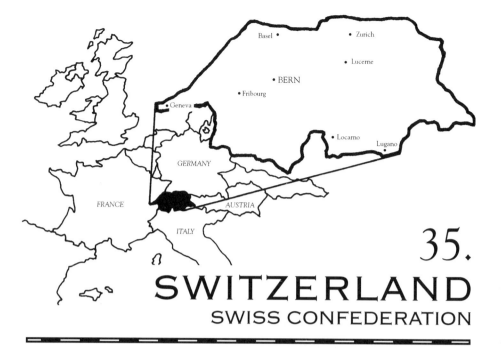

# 35.

# SWITZERLAND
## SWISS CONFEDERATION

## VITAL STATISTICS

POPULATION:     6.9 million (1992).

CAPITAL:        Bern, with a population of 304,000 (1992).

LAND SIZE:      15,941 square miles, as large as Massachusetts,
                Connecticut and Rhode Island combined.

GOVERNMENT:     Federal republic. Switzerland is a decentralized
                federal state with each of the 20 cantons and six
                half-cantons having their own system of
                government. Each community has it own
                constitution and laws, but under the supervision of
                the canton. At the federal level, democracy
                becomes representative. The Federal Assembly
                consists of two houses: the National Council with

representatives of the people and the Council of States with representatives of the cantons. The members are directly elected. The president of the National Council serves for one year and is technically the president of Switzerland. The president presides over the Federal Council.

| | |
|---|---|
| LIVING STANDARD: | GDP = US$34,780 per capita (1992). |
| NATURAL RESOURCES: | Hydropower potential, timber, salt. |
| AGRICULTURE: | Dairy farming predominates; less than 50 percent self-sufficient; food shortages include fish, refined sugar, fats and oils (other than butter), grains, eggs, fruits, vegetables, meat. |
| INDUSTRIES: | Machinery, chemicals, watches, textiles, precision instruments. |
| CLIMATE: | Wide variations: Atlantic in the west, Mediterranean in the south, continental in the east. Temperature varies with altitude. The climate is generally very moderate—never very hot or cold. |
| CURRENCY: | Swiss franc (SFr or SwF). SwF1 = 100 centimes. Notes are in denominations of SwF1,000, 500, 100, 50, 20 and 10. Coins are in denominations of SwF5, 2 and 1, and 50, 20, 10 and 5 centimes. The Swiss franc, with hardly any fluctuations in its value, is the world's hardest currency. |

# THE PEOPLE

CORRECT
NAME:           Swiss.

ETHNIC
MAKEUP:         Mixed European stock.  65 percent German, 18
                percent French, 10 percent Italian, 1 percent
                Romansch, 6 percent others.

VALUE
SYSTEM:         Swiss value cleanliness, honesty, hard work and
                material possessions.  Motto: "Unity, yes;
                Uniformity, no."  They are very proud of their
                environment and have a long tradition of
                freedom.  They value sobriety, thrift, tolerance,
                punctuality and a sense of responsibility.  They
                are very proud of their neutrality and promotion
                of worldwide peace.  The Swiss have a deep-
                rooted respect for saving and the material wealth
                it brings.

FAMILY:         Family life has changed, but the family is still the
                most important unit in Swiss society.  Families
                are small with one or two children.  Many
                women work outside the home.  Premarital sex is
                acceptable to most people and many couples
                choose to live together instead of or before
                marrying.

RELIGION:       48 percent Roman Catholic, 44 percent Protestant.

## MEETING AND GREETING

- Shake hands with everyone present—men, women, and children—at a business or social meeting. Shake hands again when leaving.

- Handshake is firm with eye contact.

- Allow the hosts to introduce you at parties.

- Switzerland is a multilingual society—verbal greetings vary according to region.

- A greeting in English is acceptable if you do not know any German, French or Italian greetings.

## NAMES AND TITLES

- Use last names and appropriate titles until specifically invited by your Swiss hosts or colleagues to use their first names.

- First names are reserved for very close friends and family.

- Address people by their correct titles according to the section of Switzerland you are in:

  | | |
  |---|---|
  | German section | *Herr* and *Frau* |
  | French section | *Monsieur* and *Madame* |
  | Italian section | *Signor* and *Signora* |

- Academic and professional titles are used frequently.

- German, French, Italian and Romansch are the national languages.

- French and German are used most often.

- Each canton (province) chooses the language it will use.

- Territoriality of language is valued. For example, in Parliament each member speaks in his or her mother tongue.

- Many Swiss speak and understand English.

- German Swiss, *Schweizerdeutsch*, is different from standard German. The dialect is difficult for other German-speaking people to understand.

- Swiss appreciate any effort made to speak the language of the region.

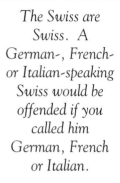

*The Swiss are Swiss. A German-, French- or Italian-speaking Swiss would be offended if you called him German, French or Italian.*

## BODY LANGUAGE

- Do not point your index finger to your head. This is an insult.

- Much of the body language depends upon the region— German, French or Italian.

- Poor posture is frowned upon.

- Do not stretch or slouch in public.

# PHRASES

- See German, French and Italian phrases.

## DINING AND DRINKING

- Dining habits and food vary according to the region. See Germany, France and Italy for more regional information.

BREAKFAST (French, *Petit Déjeuner*; German, *Frühstück*; Italian, *Prima Colazione*): 7 to 9 a.m.
- Continental breakfast.

- Cheese, bread with butter and jam, fresh fruit, yogurt, *Birchermuesli* and coffee.

LUNCH (French, *Déjeuner*; German, *Mittagessen*; Italian, *La Colazione* or *Pranzo*): noon to 1:30 p.m.
- Traditionally the main meal of the day.

- Could be a light meal if you have a dinner party that evening.

- Soup, meat, potatoes, rice, vegetable, salad and fruit.

DINNER (French, *Dîner*; German, *Nachtessen*; Italian, *Cena*):  6 to 8 p.m.; dinner party, 7 to 8 p.m.
- Light meal—soup, bread with cheese, cold cuts, salad.

*In the German section of Switzerland beckon a waiter by saying, "Herr Ober," and a waitress by saying, "Fräulein." It is rude to wave your hand.*

- The main meal of the day will be served at dinner parties.

- Cocktails, a full four-course meal and after-dinner drinks.

## TYPICAL FOODS

- Sausages, leek soup, cheese and fish.

- *Fondue:* Cheese fondue—Cheese melted in a pot, bread dipped in melted cheese (accompanied by white wine). Meat fondue—Pieces of meat dipped in a pot of hot oil or broth, served with sauces (accompanied by red wine).

- *Raclette:* Cheese melted in front of a fire and served with onions and baked or boiled potatoes, accompanied by white wine.

- *Roesti:* Sliced, roasted potatoes.

- Italian Swiss
    - *Polenta:* Cornmeal porridge.
    - *Ossobucco:* Braised veal shank.

- French Swiss—similar to French food.

- German Swiss
    - *Geschnetzeltes:* Veal (minced) with thick cream sauce.
    - *Bernerplatte:* Sauerkraut and/or string beans with smoked pork chops, bacon, ham and pork sausages.
    - *Birchermuesli:* Oat flakes soaked in milk with fresh fruit and berries and nuts (as breakfast, light lunch or light dinner).

## DRINKING

- *Campari*, *Cynar* (artichoke extract), *blanc-cassis* (blackberry liquor and white wine), *pastis* (anise liquor), vermouth, sherry or white wine are served before the meal.

- Swiss seldom drink cocktails before meals, but instead may drink white wine or champagne.

- Beer, hard cider, white and red wine are served during the meal.

- Hard liquor and cordials are served after the meal.

- Coffee is served only after the meal.

- Swiss specialties: *Grappa* (Swiss Italian brandy), *marc* (Swiss French brandy), *pflümliwasser* (plum brandy), *kirsch* (cherry brandy), *apricot* (apricot brandy), *poire Guillaume* (pear brandy).

- Although water is of excellent quality, nobody drinks tap water, only mineral water. Generally, the Swiss believe that tap water is for external use only.

## TOASTS

- The host proposes the first toast—don't drink until after the toast is proposed.

- Clink glasses when invited by others. Lift your glass, but wait for the host to start drinking before you do.

- Look at the host, raise your glass and say one of these four toasts:

| | | |
|---|---|---|
| German: | *Prost* | "Cheers" |
| French: | *A Votre Santé* | "To your health" |
| Italian: | *Salute* | "To your health" |
| English: | To your health | |

- It is polite to propose a toast to thank your host for dinner.

- It is acceptable for a woman to propose a toast.

---

- Tipping is not common in Switzerland. An automatic service charge of 15 percent is included in all hotel, restaurant, café, bar, taxi and hairdressing services by law.

- Restaurants: A service charge of 15 percent is always included in the bill; small change can be left as an additional gratuity for good service.

- Porters: SFr1-2 per bag.

- Taxis: An automatic service charge of 15 percent is included.

- Cloakroom attendants: SFr1.

- Washroom attendants: 50 centimes - SFr1.

- Gas station attendants: 10 percent of gas bill if tip is not included.

- Ushers: No tip.

- Beauty salons/barbers: An automatic service charge of 15 percent is included.

# TIPPING

## MANNERS

- Seldom will you be invited to a Swiss home. It is an honor if you are entertained in someone's home.

- Keep your hands on the table at all times during a meal—not in your lap. However, keep your elbows off the table.

- Cut potatoes, soft foods and salads with a fork, not a knife.

- Use your eating utensils to eat almost all foods, even fruit and sandwiches.

- White asparagus is eaten with your hands.

- Break bread with your hands if possible. Do not use a knife.

- It is polite to try a little of everything offered to you.

- The hostess appreciates guests who take a second helping.

- If salt and pepper are not on the table, don't ask for them.

- Don't smoke at the dinner table. Wait, watch and ask permission before smoking at the table.

- Try to finish everything on your plate when dining in someone's home. It is impolite to leave food on your plate.

- When you are finished eating, place your knife and fork side by side on the plate at the 5:25 position.

- Leave a party no later than midnight.

- It is correct to seat yourself in most pubs and inexpensive restaurants. Ask the waiter if you are uncertain.

- It is considered impolite to ask for a tour of your hosts' home.

---

## DRESS

- Attire should always be clean and neat! The Swiss are known for conservative and neat attire.

- Never wear shorts (or any clothes exposing your knees or shoulders) when visiting a church.

*The Swiss are conservative in dress and manner.*

BUSINESS

- Men: Suits and ties.

- Women: Suits or dresses; pants are acceptable if they are part of a suit.

RESTAURANT

- Check in advance if a coat and tie are required.

- Casual attire for a restaurant means "smart casual."

- Better restaurants prefer elegant attire.

FORMAL

- Invitation will specify formal, if required.

- Men: Dark suits, unless black tie is indicated on the invitation.

- Women: Cocktail dresses.

- Men: Trousers, shirts, sweaters.

- Women: Skirts or dress pants, sweaters.

- Jeans are worn (clean and neat).

---

# GIFTS

## HOSTESS

- Always bring a small, attractively wrapped gift for the hostess when invited to someone's home.

- Do not give a personal gift.

- It is polite to send flowers to the hostess the morning of a large party or the next day with a thank-you note.

- Bring a small gift for children.

- Give: Candy (good quality), pralines, flowers (odd number, unwrap before presenting), pastries (cake).

- Do not give: A large, expensive gift (considered vulgar and could make the recipient uncomfortable), red roses or carnations (for romance only), white chrysanthemums or white asters (for funerals only).

*Red roses or carnations are for romantic relationships only.*

## BUSINESS

- Gifts are normally not exchanged at business meetings, but small gifts may be appropriate at the successful conclusion of negotiations. It's acceptable but not expected to give a Christmas gift to a Swiss colleague.

- Be prepared to give a gift in case you are given one. A gift with your company logo tastefully imprinted is acceptable.

- Give: Whiskey, cognac, a good pictoral book, desk accessories, a good bourbon, a bottle of very good wine.

- Do not give: Anything with a sharp point.

## TOILET TIPS

See French, German and Italian Helpful Hints.

DO:

- Show courtesy—it's highly valued.

- Expect pushing and shoving in lines, especially in ski lift lines.

- Show great respect for elderly.

- Expect strangers to be seated at your table in a pub or inexpensive restaurant. You do not need to talk with them.

- Greet clerks when entering and leaving shops.

DO NOT:

- Never litter (you will be scolded publicly).

- Never put your hands in your pockets while talking with someone.

- Never ask a person's age, job or family status.

# HELPFUL
# HINTS

- Never put your feet on a desk, chair or table.

- Do not expect quick friendships. However, when friendship is given, it is for life.

- Never bargain anywhere in Switzerland, including markets.

## PUNCTUALITY

- Swiss insist on punctuality for social occasions—they are insulted by tardiness.

- Swiss take punctuality for business meetings very seriously and expect that you will do likewise; call with an explanation if you will be delayed.

## STRICTLY BUSINESS

### BUSINESS CARDS

- Business cards are exchanged.

- Business cards in English are acceptable.

- Hand your business card to the receptionist upon arrival for a meeting.

- Give a card to each person you are meeting with.

- Bring a good supply of business cards.

*Unemployment and inflation are low and labor relations excellent. Swiss are known for excellent quality and craftsmanship.*

### CORPORATE CULTURE

STRUCTURE: The business climate is very conservative, and companies are structured in the traditional, vertical manner. The culture of companies can vary somewhat depending on whether they are in the German, French or Italian areas of Switzerland.

MEETINGS:  Brief small talk is made before doing business.  Meetings, like other activities in Swiss companies, are impersonal, brisk, orderly, well-planned and task-oriented. Presentations must be orderly, well-prepared, thorough and detailed; remember, the Swiss dot every "i" and cross every "t."

Patience is required; discussions are detailed, cautious and sometimes pessimistic. Decisionmaking is slow and methodical.  The Swiss are hard but fair bargainers, not hagglers.

COMMUNICATION:  Generally, English is spoken in business with foreigners, but it's a good idea to check in advance whether an interpreter is needed.  Information is closely held and communicated only upon request.  It is not acceptable to call a Swiss businessperson at home—do so only in an emergency.

BE AWARE:

- Swiss are formal and courteous.  They are also hard-working, thrifty and reliable.

- Personal relationships develop only after a business relationship has been established.

## ENTERTAINING

- Business breakfasts are not very common.

- Business lunches are more usual than business dinners, but this is changing.

- Business is discussed over meals.

- Business entertainment is almost always done in a restaurant.

- Spouses are generally included in business dinners.

## APPOINTMENTS

| | |
|---|---|
| **Office Hours:** | **Monday to Friday** |
| | **8 a.m. to noon** |
| | **1:30 to 5:30 p.m.** |
| **Bank Hours:** | **Monday to Friday** |
| | **9 a.m. to 4 p.m.** |

- Prior appointments are essential.

- July and August are vacation months. Don't schedule a business trip during this time.

## ESPECIALLY FOR WOMEN

- Foreign and Swiss women are treated fairly and professionally in Switzerland. However, both sexes have a conservative view of women's role in society. A relatively small number of Swiss women hold top jobs; Swiss women must have better qualifications than men to get to the top in a corporation.

- Banking and finance are dominated by men.

- Slowly, more women are becoming involved in business and public life.

- Only since 1972 have women voted on the federal level.

- Day care is easily obtained.

- Many Swiss businessmen would be embarrassed if a foreign businesswoman invited them to dinner. Swiss men are very conservative and still expect to pay for a meal. If possible, a foreign businesswoman should invite a Swiss businessman to lunch rather than dinner.

- It is generally safe for a woman to go out alone at any hour.

---

- Do not plan to make a business visit or schedule any appointments during the following holidays or festivals. Be sure to check for the numerous regional and local holidays and festivals.

## HOLIDAYS AND FESTIVALS

| | |
|---|---|
| January | New Year's Day (1-2). |
| March/April | Easter (Friday-Monday). |
| April/May | Ascension Thursday (40 days after Easter). |
| May/June | Whitsunday and Whitmonday (49 and 50 days after Easter). |
| May | Labor Day (1—not official). |
| June | Corpus Christi (60 days after Easter) . |
| August | National Day (1). |
| December | Christmas (25-26). |

# 36.
# TURKEY
## REPUBLIC OF TURKEY

## VITAL STATISTICS

POPULATION:     59.6 million (1992).

CAPITAL:     Ankara, with a population of 2.6 million (1990).

LAND SIZE:     300,947 square miles, slightly larger than Texas.

GOVERNMENT:     Republic. The 1982 constitution provides for a 450-member national assembly, elected for a five-year term through an electoral system. The executive's powers are limited by a constitutional court and a national security council, which is dominated by the military and headed by the president.

LIVING
STANDARD:     GNP= US$2,000 per capita (1992).

| NATURAL RESOURCES: | Antimony, coal, chromium, mercury, copper, borate, sulphur, iron ore and marble. |
|---|---|
| AGRICULTURE: | Accounts for 18 percent of GDP and employs about half of the work force; products include tobacco, cotton, grain, olives, sugar beets, citrus fruit, variety of animal products; self-sufficient in food most years. |
| INDUSTRIES: | Textiles, food processing, mining (coal, chromite, copper, boron minerals), steel, petroleum, construction, lumber, paper. |
| CLIMATE: | Much of the interior is semiarid, with continental extremes of temperature. Winters are cold, around 32°F (0°C) in Ankara in January, down to -40°F (-40°C) in the eastern mountains; summers are warm, around 71°F (22°C) in Ankara in July, hotter on the Mediterranean coast. |
| CURRENCY: | Turkish lira (TL). TL1 = 100 kuruş (kuruş are not currently in use). Notes are in denominations of TL50,000, 20,000, 10,000, 5,000 and 1,000. Coins are in denominations of TL1,000 and 500. |

Three precent of Turkey lies in Europe and the remaining 97 percent lies in Asia. The Bosporous Strait separates Istanbul, the only major city in the world located on two continents, into its Asian and European sections.

# THE PEOPLE

CORRECT
NAME:                Turks.

ETHNIC
MAKEUP:              85 percent Turks, 15-20 percent Kurds.

VALUE
SYSTEM:              The Turks are extremely patriotic. People are
                     proud of their ancestors, who ruled great empires,
                     and of the achievements of their modern society.

FAMILY:              The family is the most important social unit.
                     Each person is dependent upon and loyal to the
                     family. Families almost always include unmarried
                     adult children and sometimes married sons and
                     families. Rural life is still traditional, but in cities
                     women frequently work outside the home.

RELIGION:            99 percent Sunni Muslim. Islam is not the state
                     religion.

## MEETING AND GREETING

- Shake hands with everyone present—men, women, and children—at a business or social meeting. Shake hands again when leaving.

- Shake hands with elders first.

- Handshake is firm.

- Turks who are devout Muslims may avoid looking into your eyes as a display of humble behavior.

- Greetings:
  *Merhaba* (MARE-ha-ba), "Hello."
  *Nasılsınız* (NAH-sil-si-niz), "How are you?"

- Turks may kiss both cheeks when greeting a close friend.

## NAMES AND TITLES

- Use last names and appropriate titles until invited by your Turkish hosts or colleagues to use their first names. Allow the more senior person to initiate.

- Turks use first names when addressing each other. Turks are also quick to go to first names with foreigners.

- As a display of honor, address a Turkish man using his first name + *bey* (bay), which means "sir."

**Example: Dennis Alkan becomes *Dennis Bey.***

- As a display of honor, address a Turkish woman using her first name + *hanim* (HAH-num), which means "ma'am."

   **Example: Suzan Alkan becomes *Suzan Hanim*.**

- When addressing elders or superiors, always use their first names + *bey/hanim*.

- Turks who are familiar with the Western style of addressing professionals will recognize professional titles, i.e., Doctor, PhD., Professor, but the first name + *bey/hanim* is the more polite form in Turkey.

- Titles may be used with the first name or even with *bey* or *hanim* if the name isn't known. This is less common, but used between friends.

   **Example: Dennis Osman. *Avukat*, which means "lawyer," would be used as *Avukat Dennis* or simply *Avukat Bey*.**


CORRESPONDENCE

- The most popular form to address a man or woman is *sayın*.

- Use *sayın* + full name.

   **Examples:**
   **Mr. Dennis Osman. Address as *Sayın Dennis Osman*.**
   **Ms. Suzan Alkan. Address as *Sayın Suzan Alkan*.**

## LANGUAGE

- Turkish is the official language. It is based on the Latin alphabet.

- The Kurdish minority speaks Kurdish and Turkish.

- English and German are popular second languages.

- Turks appreciate any effort to speak even a few words of their language.

- Turks make every effort to converse, no matter what the linguistic barriers.

## BODY LANGUAGE

- Turks generally have a small area of personal space and may stand closer than most foreigners are used to.

- "Yes" is a slight downward nod of the head.

- "No" is a slight upward nod of the head while making a quick sound of sucking your two front teeth (like "tsk").

- *Never point the sole of your foot toward a person.* Be especially careful of this when crossing your legs.

- Do not stand with your hands on your hips or in your pockets when talking to others, especially older people or superiors.

- "Worry beads," originally religious, are often used to relieve tension or as a nervous habit.

- In Turkey, putting your thumb between your first two fingers is equivalent to raising your middle finger in the U.S.

# PHRASES

| English | Turkish | Pronunciation |
|---|---|---|
| Good morning | *Günaydın* | ghewn-EYE-duhn |
| Good day | *İyi günler* | ee-yee-GEWN-lar |
| Good evening | *İyi akşamlar* | eey-EE ak-sham-LAR |
| Please | *Lütfen* | LEWT-fahn |
| Thank you | *Teşekkür ederim* | TE-she-kewr EH-der-em |
| You're welcome | *Bir şey değil* | beer shay deel |
| Yes | *Evet* | EH-vet |
| No | *Hayır* | hire |
| Excuse me | *Affedersiniz* | ah-fed-AHR-sen-eez |
| Goodbye (said by one who's leaving) | *Allaha ısmarladık* | ah-LAHS-mahr-lah-dik |
| Goodbye (said by one who's staying) | *Güle Güle* | gew-LEH gew-LEH |
| How are you? | *Nasılsınız* | NAH-sil-si-niz |
| Pleased to meet you (shaking hands only) | *Tanıştığımıza Memnun oldum* | tan-is-TOOHR-mooz-ah MEM-nun OLD-um |

## DINING AND DRINKING

- Continental style.

- Cuisine is rich and among the finest in the world. It can be quite lavish.

- Entertaining is most commonly done in restaurants or nightclubs, but entertaining in homes is increasing in popularity.

BREAKFAST (*Kahvaltı*): 7:30 to 8:30 a.m.
- Eggs, white cheese, olives, bread, butter, marmalade or honey, and tea.

LUNCH (*Öğle Yemeği*): 1 p.m.
- Soup, salad, vegetable casserole and bread.

DINNER (*Akşam Yemeği*): 7:30 to 8:30 p.m.
- Main meal—may be several courses.

- Wine will generally be opened and shared with guests.

- Formal meal begins with soup or a large tray of appetizers.

- The main course is usually grilled, fried or stewed seafood, chicken, lamb or beef.

*To beckon a waiter, raise your hand and wave if necessary.*

## MENU TERMS

| | |
|---|---|
| *Or dövr* | Appetizers |
| *Etli yemek* | Meat course |
| *Tatlılar* | Desserts |
| *Ekmek* | Bread |
| *Çorbalar* | Soups |
| *Sebzeler* | Vegetables |
| *Biftek* | Beef |
| *Domuz* | Pork |
| *Kuzu eti* | Lamb |
| *Tavuk* | Chicken |
| *Balık* | Fish |
| *Yumurta* | Eggs |

## TYPICAL FOODS

- *Meze:* Tray of hors d'oeuvres with an astonishing variety and abundance of food. It is the first course of a meal when alcoholic beverages are served.

- *Yufka:* A thin, flaky dough that is common for many Turkish dishes.

- *Şiş Kebap:* Shish kebabs of skewered lamb.

- *Pilav:* Rice pilaf.

- *Patlıcan Salatası:* Eggplant salad—eggplant that is roasted, pureed and mixed with yogurt and lemon.

- *Kebab:* Sliced pieces of red meat roasted or skewered.

- *Börek:* Phyllo dough filled with feta cheese, spinach or meat.

- *Deniz Ürünleri:* Seafood.

- *Zeytinyağlı Fasulye:* Green beans, tomatoes and olive oil served at room temperature.

- *Baklava* (phyllo dough with honey syrup and ground nuts) or *muhallebi* (milk pudding) for dessert.

### DRINKING

- Some Muslim Turks drink alcohol, but Turks who are strict Muslims never do.

- *Rakı:* Very strong (80 proof) anise liqueur. Usually served with hors d'oeuvres.

- *Ayran:* Yogurt, water and salt drink.

- *Bira* (beer) and *şarap* (wine) are drunk occasionally.

- *Kahve:* Thick, Turkish coffee served in very small cups. It comes *totlı* (sweet), *orta* (medium), or *sade* (without sugar).

- Turkish coffee is served after lunch or dinner—not with a meal.

---

**SERIOUSLY OLD COFFEE**

*The Turks are famous for their coffee, which is thicker and stronger than espresso. The first coffeehouse opened in 1554 in Turkey. Intellectuals, artists, political dissidents and the unemployed played chess, recited poetry or denounced the government— over a nice cup of coffee.*

---

## TOASTS

- *Şerefe* (shay-ray-FAY), "To the honor."

- *Şerefinize* (shay-ray-fay-neh-zeh), "To your honor." A bit more formal.

- Hosts may say *Buyrun* (BUOY-run), which is an invitation to begin eating.

- *Ziyade olsun* (zee-YAH-day OL-suhn), "Wishing plentifulness," is said to your hostess after the meal.

- The hostess will probably respond with *Afiyet olsun* (AH-fee-yet OL-suhn), "Wishing good health."

---

## TIPPING

- Tips are listed in U.S. currency because of the high inflation rate in Turkey.

- Restaurants: A service charge is generally not included in the bill except for expensive restaurants (the bill will read *servis dahil* if the tip is included or *hizmet dahil* if it isn't); small change can be left as an additional gratuity for good service. If the service charge is not included, leave a 10-15 percent tip. You pay your bill to the waiter or waitress at the table, but leave the tip on the table.

- Taxis: Not usually tipped, but many have come to expect tips (15 percent) from foreigners.

- Cloakroom and washroom attendants: Small tip—25 to 50 cents.

- Ushers: $1.

- Porters: $1 per bag.

- Hairdressers/barbers: 10 percent.

## MANNERS

- Turks are most gracious and generous hosts.

- Hospitality is part of Turkish culture—it is generous, sincere and almost overwhelming.

- Habits vary according to region.

- At the end of a meal compliment the host/hostess with Çok lezetli (choke LEZ-et-lee), "Very tasty," or the more sophisticated Elinize sağlik (EL-in-is-eh SAH-lick), "God bless your hands."

- Do not eat with your fingers unless your host does so.

- The hostess usually serves food at the table.

- Guests are served first, followed by elderly, children, etc.

- Hosts will probably expect you to eat a great deal and may be offended if you don't. Often guests feel they are suffering from being offered food and drinks for hours and being unable to refuse without hurting the host's feelings.

- Leave no food on your plate when you are finished eating.

- When finished eating, place your knife and fork side by side on the plate.

- Do not get up from the table until everyone is finished.

- Compliments are appreciated.

- It would be considered rude to ask someone for a tour of their home. A Turkish home is a private place.

- Turks ask even casual acquaintances what Americans consider to be very personal questions (age, salary, "Why don't you have children?").

- "Dutch treat" does not exist in Turkey. If you invite someone to dine, you pay the bill.

---

## DRESS

- Western style clothing, conservative and modest, is the most common.

- Turks tend to dress up and accessorize a lot.

- A sun hat and sunglasses are necessary in the height of summer.

- Some Turks remove their shoes and put slippers on when entering a home. Guests should do the same, if slippers are offered.

- Always remove your shoes before entering a mosque.

- Women should wear head scarves, long-sleeved blouses, pants or long skirts when visiting a mosque.

- Women should avoid short skirts, low-cut blouses and shorts.

BUSINESS

- Men: Conservative suits or sport coats and ties. In very hot weather men may go without jackets, but they do wear ties.

- Women: Suits, dresses and heels.

RESTAURANT
- Men: Check if coats and ties are required.

- Women: Dresses, dressy pants.

FORMAL
- Men: Dark suits.

- Women: Evening dresses.

CASUAL
- Smart casual—not American casual.

- Men: Shirts and pants.

- Women: Pants or skirts (not denim).

---

## GIFTS

HOSTESS
- Always bring a gift for the hostess when invited to someone's home.

- Do not bring a gift that is too lavish.

- Don't expect your hostess to open a gift when it is presented.

- Bring a small gift for children if you know the family well.

- Give: Flowers (roses or carnations), candy, chocolates, wine (if your host drinks).

- Do not give: Alcohol if you are not sure whether your host drinks.

## BUSINESS

- Gifts may be exchanged in business.

- Christmas gifts are rare, but New Year's gifts are quite common.

- Give: Gifts made in America that are not expensive, i.e. crystal, desk accessories, pens, gifts with your company logo.

- Do not give: Gifts that are overly personal.

---

## TOILET TIPS

| | |
|---|---|
| *Tuvalet* | Restrooms |
| *Bayanlar* | Ladies |
| *Baylar* | Men |
| *Sıcak su* | Hot water |
| *Soğuk su* | Cold water |

---

## DO:

- Show great respect for elders. Rise and offer your seat when elders enter a room.

- Speak in a quiet voice in public.

- You should bargain when shopping in bazaars or markets. Shopkeepers expect it.

- Ask permission before taking pictures anywhere of anyone, especially in a mosque.

- Expect your host or business colleague to offer a lightly scented cologne to cleanse and refresh yourself (not as common in big cities).

# HELPFUL HINTS

**DO NOT:**

- Do not ask personal questions until you become friends.

- Do not talk about problems or bad news when you are a guest in someone's home.

- Do not show affection in public.

- Do not bargain in big, modern stores.

## PUNCTUALITY

- Turks insist on punctuality for social occasions. For a dinner party, 7 p.m. is 7 p.m.

- Being a little late for a big party (cocktail) is acceptable.

- Turks take punctuality for business meetings very seriously and expect that you will do likewise; call with an explanation if you are delayed.

## STRICTLY BUSINESS

### BUSINESS CARDS

- Business cards in English are acceptable.

- Give a business card to the person you are meeting and anyone else to whom you're introduced.

### CORPORATE CULTURE

STRUCTURE: The chairman or general manager is the boss in most companies. The organization is strictly vertical, and decisions are made at the top.

MEETINGS: When visiting an office or factory, shake hands with each person when you arrive and again when you leave; consideration, politeness, respect and courtesy are very important to Turks. Turks generally engage in brief small talk before beginning business discussions.

COMMUNICATION: Many Turkish businesspeople speak English, but you should inquire in advance whether an interpreter will be needed. Companies doing international business most likely will have someone who understands English. It is acceptable to call Turkish businesspeople at home—at a reasonable hour and if it's absolutely necessary.

## ENTERTAINMENT

- Traditionally business entertaining has been done in restaurants. Entertaining in homes is becoming increasingly popular.

- Spouses may be included in business dinners.

- Business breakfasts are rare.

- Business can be discussed anytime during the meal, but let your business counterpart give the signal.

APPOINTMENTS

**Office Hours:**     Monday to Friday
8 a.m. to 5 p.m.

**Bank Hours:**     Monday to Friday
8:30 a.m. to 12:30 p.m.
1:30 - 5 p.m.

- Schedule business appointments in advance.

- June, July or August are vacation months. Many businesspeople are not available.

- *Ramazan*: 30 days of praying and fasting during daylight hours. It is better not to schedule meetings during this time or the three days after *Ramazan*, during a festival called *Sugar Bayram*. Check the dates: In 1994 *Sugar Bayram* is March 13-15, and this festival comes 10 or 11 days earlier each year.

# ESPECIALLY FOR WOMEN

- Foreign women are very welcome and accepted in Turkey. Attitudes toward women are generally conservative, but Turkish men tend to be very respectful.

- Many Turkish women are highly educated and have a career. They have excellent maternity leave, but many choose to stay home to supervise the education of their children.

- Feel free to accept a lunch or dinner invitation from a man relative to business. It is acceptable for a foreign businesswoman to invite a Turkish businessman to dinner and it is easy for her to pay.

- Excluding the business environment, a Turkish woman generally does not converse with a man until formally introduced.

- Avoid traveling unaccompanied. Arrange to eat or travel with a friend in big cities, if possible.

- A woman should not walk alone at night. It is not even a good idea for two or three women to walk together at night. Take a taxi everywhere after dark.

- Beware of pickpockets.

# HOLIDAYS AND FESTIVALS

- Do not plan to make a business visit or schedule any appointments during the following holidays or festivals. Be sure to check for the numerous regional and local holidays and festivals.

| | |
|---|---|
| January | New Year (1). |
| Feb.-May | *Ramazan* and *Sugar Bayram* (*Şeker*, the three days following *Ramazan*). Dates of *Ramazan* and *Şeker* vary with the Islamic (lunar) calendar. In 1994 *Şeker* is March 13-15; it is celebrated 10 or 11 days earlier each year. |
| April | National Sovereignty and Children's Day (23). |
| May | Spring Day (1), Youth and Sports Day (19), Freedom and Constitution Days (27 and 28). |
| June | Sacrifice Feast (*Kurban Bayrami*)—dates vary with the Islamic (lunar) calendar. In 1994 *Kurban Bayrami* is May 21-25; it is celebrated 10 or 11 days earlier each year. |
| August | Victory Day (30). |
| October | National Day (29). |

# 37.

# UNITED KINGDOM
## GREAT BRITAIN AND NORTHERN IRELAND

## VITAL STATISTICS

The United Kingdom consists of four countries united under one government. The United Kingdom is England, Scotland, Wales and Northern Ireland. Great Britain is England, Scotland and Wales.

England does not include Scotland, Wales or Northern Ireland. Each group likes individual recognition.

POPULATION:    57.8 million (1992).

MAJOR CITIES:  London (England) 6.4 million (1991);
               Birmingham (England) 994,000; Glasgow
               (Scotland) 703,000.

| LAND SIZE: | 94,247 square miles, slightly smaller than Oregon. |
|---|---|
| GOVERNMENT: | Parliamentary monarchy. There is not a written constitution. The legislature has two chambers: The House of Commons has 650 members elected for a term of up to five years from single-member constituencies; the less important House of Lords consists of hereditary and appointed life peers. Executive power is in the hands of the prime minister, usually leader of the majority party in the Commons, and a cabinet drawn mainly from the House of Commons. |
| LIVING STANDARD: | GDP = US$18,130 per capita (1992). |
| NATURAL RESOURCES: | Coal, crude oil, natural gas, tin, limestone, iron ore, salt, clay, chalk, gypsum, lead, silica. |
| AGRICULTURE: | Accounts for only 1.5 percent of GDP and 1 percent of labor force; highly mechanized and efficient farms; wide variety of crops and livestock products produced; about 60 percent self-sufficient in food and feed needs. |
| INDUSTRIES: | Production machinery including machine tools, electric power equipment, equipment for the automation of production, railroad equipment, shipbuilding, aircraft, motor vehicles and parts, electronics and communications equipment, metals, chemicals, coal, petroleum, paper and |

paper products, food processing, textiles, clothing and other consumer goods.

CURRENCY: Pound sterling (£). £1=100 pence. Notes are in denominations of £50, 20, 10 and 5. Coins are denominations of £1, and 50, 20, 10, 5, 2 and 1 pence. There are additional bank notes issued by Scottish banks that are legal tender in all parts of the U.K.

CLIMATE: Temperate and variable. Monthly average temperatures 60°F (16°C) in summer, 40°F (4°C) in winter.

# THE PEOPLE

CORRECT
NAME: British.

ETHNIC
MAKEUP: 82 percent English, 10 percent Scottish, 3 percent Irish, 2 percent Welsh.

RELIGION: Religion is a very private matter in the United Kingdom. 86 percent of the population is Christian. Minority religions: Muslim, Jewish, Hindu, Sikh, Buddhist.

# ENGLAND

## VITAL STATISTICS

POPULATION: 46 million.

CAPITAL: London, with a population of 7 million.

LAND SIZE: 50,363 square miles, about the size of New York state.

LIVING
STANDARD: GNP=US$13,329 per person.

NATURAL
RESOURCES: Coal, iron ore, petroleum, natural gas.

AGRICULTURE: Barley, cattle, dairy products, fruits, potatoes, sheep, wheat, fishing.

INDUSTRIES: Aircraft, automobiles, chemicals, iron, steel, machinery, pottery, porcelain, silverware, woolens, cotton, yarn.

CLIMATE: Temperate and variable. Monthly average temperature 60°F (16°C) in summer, 40°F (4°C) in winter.

CURRENCY: British pound sterling (£).

# THE PEOPLE

CORRECT
NAME:        British/English.  It is better to use British.  Scots,
             Welsh and Irish live in London.  Only use
             English if you are sure of a person's heritage.

ETHNIC
MAKEUP:      94 percent Caucasian, 1 percent Indian, 1
             percent West Indian/Guyanese.

VALUE
SYSTEM:      Tradition and customs are revered.  Politeness,
             reserve and restraint are admired.  The English
             are courteous, unassuming and unabrasive.  They
             are very proud of their long and rich history.  Dry
             humor allows them to be self-critical.

FAMILY:      Average family is about three people, one of the
             smallest in the world.  Many women work outside
             the home.  Families are generally close.

RELIGION:    Church of England (Anglican Church) is the
             official church of England.  Half of the
             population are members of the Church of
             England but many do not attend services.  Other
             denominations include:  Baptist, Congregational,
             Methodist, Catholic and Jewish.

| | |
|---|---|
| **MEETING**<br>**AND**<br>**GREETING** | • Shake hands with everyone present—men, women and children—at a business or social meeting. Shake hands again when leaving.<br><br>• Handshakes are light, not firm.<br><br>• Not everyone will offer their hand to shake.<br><br>• Women should extend their hand to men first.<br><br>• People who meet regularly generally do not shake hands.<br><br>• Say "How do you do?" upon meeting.<br><br>• The British are informal but reserved, which may cause them to appear cool and indifferent or overly formal. They are very friendly and helpful to foreigners. |
| **NAMES**<br>**AND**<br>**TITLES** | • Use last names and appropriate titles until specifically invited by your English hosts or colleagues to use their first names.<br><br>• Use of first name is increasingly common among all businesspeople even during phone conversations.<br><br>• Address people as Mr., Mrs., Ms.<br><br>**Example: *Mr. Marshall.***<br><br>• Women use whichever title they prefer: Mrs., Miss, Ms. + last name.<br><br>• Academic titles are not commonly used.<br><br>• "Doctor" is used only for a medical doctor and people with a doctorate degree. |

- Superiors are sometimes called Sir. "Madam" is not used.

- Honorary titles are used (i.e. *Sir, Dame, Lord*).

  **Example: A knighted person is addressed as *Sir* with his first name. Sir George Thomas would be called *Sir George*.**

- Ask people how they prefer to be addressed.

---

## LANGUAGE

- English is the official language of the U.K. Nearly everyone speaks English.

- The English generally do not speak other languages. However, today many younger people in Britain speak French or German.

- The English are reluctant to be offensive with language. They may be less direct and more subtle in conversation, but always polite.

- The English do not speak in superlatives. "I am quite pleased," said by the English, means they are extremely happy. Adjust your understanding.

- Humor is ever-present in English life—self-deprecating, sarcastic and sexist.

*Never try to sound British or mimic the British accent.*

## BODY
## LANGUAGE

- The English are not back-slappers or touchers—they do not display affection in public and prefer a distance between themselves and others.

- Hugging, kissing or touching affectionately is usually reserved for family members and very close friends.

- Staring is considered rude.

- The British are polite and may not let on that they are offended.

# PHRASES

Do not assume understanding the language means understanding the culture. Many gaffes are made by foreigners who understand the words but not the meanings.

| British English | American English |
|---|---|
| Crisps | Potato chips |
| Chips | French fries |
| W.C. or Loo | Bathroom |
| Lift | Elevator |
| Chemist | Druggist |
| Chat | Dialogue |
| Queue | Line |
| Not at all | You are welcome |
| Bonnet | Hood of car |
| Boot | Trunk of car |
| Biscuits | Cookies |
| Telly | Television |
| Bum | Butt (rear end) |
| Vest | Undershirt |
| Pants | Underwear |
| Trousers | Pants |
| Sorry? | What? (Did not hear or understand) |
| Home counties | Counties surrounding London |
| The South | Area within a couple hours' drive from London (image of wealth, sophistication and social status). |
| The North | The rest of the country |

# DINING
# AND
# DRINKING

*Summon a waiter by raising your hand. Don't wave or shout.*

BREAKFAST: 7:30 - 9 a.m.

- Light breakfast or English breakfast is served. A light breakfast consists of cereal, toast, coffee or tea. An English breakfast consists of juice, cereal, bacon, sausage, eggs, toast, fried mushrooms, fried tomatoes.

LUNCH: noon to 2 p.m.

- Light meal: Sandwiches, salads, fruit or sweets.

HIGH TEA: 3:30 to 4:30 p.m.

- Light meal consisting of small sandwiches, biscuits, pastries, cakes, scones with jam and clotted cream.

- Mostly served in hotels to tourists.

DINNER: 7 to 8 p.m.

- Cocktails, appetizers, soup, meat or fish, potatoes, vegetables, salad, dessert, cheese and crackers.

- Tea is served from 5 to 7 p.m. This is a light supper.

- The Sunday Joint: Traditional Sunday meal is generally at noon. A roast is served with Yorkshire pudding, etc.

## TYPICAL FOODS

- The British enjoy spicy foods, including Indian and Chinese cooking.

- *Fish and Chips:* Deep fried, breaded fish and french-fried potatoes.

- *Scones with Clotted Cream:* Biscuit-like tea cakes served with a thick cream of butter-like consistency.

- *Ploughman's Platter:* Cheese, bread, meats, butter and relishes.

- *Meat Pies:* Steak and kidney pie is the best-known.

- *Cornish Pasties:* Turnovers filled with meat, potatoes and vegetables.

- *Black Pudding:* Sausage made from pig's blood.

- *Roast Beef with Yorkshire Pudding:* The pudding resembles the pastries known as popovers in the U.S.

- *Bangers and Mash:* Mashed potatoes with sausages.

- *Trifle:* Layers of cake, fruit, pudding, sherry and cream.


## DRINKING

- If you don't drink, order a shandy and nurse it just to be polite.

- Buy your "round" when in a pub.

- Children are not allowed in most pubs.

- Drinks are served without ice. You must ask for ice if so desired.

- If you order whiskey, you'll get scotch.

- Popular drinks are: Gin and tonic, vodka and tonic, vodka and Coke, Pimms Cup.

- There are a variety of beers, the most traditional called "bitter."

- *Shandy*: Beer with lemonade (a lemon-lime soda).

- *Cider* or *Scrumpy*: Made from fermented apples.

- Coffee and tea are served after meals.

### TOASTS

- *"Cheers."* An informal toast.

- *"To the Queen."* A formal toast made after the main course at formal dinners.

- The host or hostess always initiates the first toast, which is usually given only at a formal dinner.

---

## TIPPING

- Wage levels for catering staff are deliberately set low in the expectation that tips will make up the difference.

- Restaurants: A service charge of 10 to 15 percent is usually included in the bill; small change can be left as an additional gratuity for good service. If the service charge is not included, leave a 10 to 15 percent tip.

- Hairdressers and taxi drivers: 10 to 15 percent. This is not included in the bill.

- Porters: £1 per bag.

- Washroom attendants: 50 pence.

- Hotel maids: £5 (a few days); £10 (a week).

- Quiet conversation is appreciated.

- Boisterous conversation or behavior causes embarrassment and is frowned upon.

- Drinks are served before dinner.

- The male guest of honor is seated at the head of the table or next to the hostess. The female guest of honor is seated next to the host.

- Never lift a fork before the hosts do.

- Salad is generally served with the meal.

- Keep your hands on the table at all times during the meal—not in your lap. However, keep your elbows off the table.

- Leave a very small amount of food on your plate when finished eating.

- When finished eating, place your knife and fork side by side on the plate at the 5:25 position.

- When the host folds his napkin, this signals that the meal is over.

- The guest of honor should initiate leaving a party. Leave shortly after dinner ends.

- The host, the one who extends the invitation, pays the bill in a restaurant.

- A thank-you note to the hostess is very much appreciated.

- Don't ask for a tour of your host's home; it would be considered impolite.

*The British admire good manners. Proper manners are a must at a British table.*

## DRESS

- People in the larger cities, especially London, dress more formally.

- Shorts and jeans are worn in cities by tourists or young people only.

- Men and women wear wools and tweeds for casual occasions. Slacks, sweaters and jackets are appropriate for men and women.

- Only high-style jeans are worn by women, and generally only younger women.

- Women still wear slacks less than in the U.S.

- Avoid striped ties that are copies of British regimentals.

- Men's clothing often expresses affiliation rather than style. Ties are important symbols. School, army, university or club ties are worn.

- The British are expected to know what a tie means, but a foreigner is allowed to ask.

BUSINESS

- Men: Dark suits and ties. White, striped or colored shirts are appropriate.

- Women: Suits or dresses, heels. (Not tweeds, which are country or casual wear.)

- Do not wear a blazer to work. A blazer is country or weekend wear.

## RESTAURANT

- Men: Jackets; some restaurants require ties. Dark suits are recommended for better restaurants.

- Women: Dresses and skirts, blouses or dressy pant suits.

- Pubs: Casual attire.

## THEATER/CONCERT

- You will see everything from jeans to dress attire. Dark suits and dresses are recommended.

- For the opera a tuxedo may be expected.

## FORMAL

- Men: Business suit, black tie, morning coat or tails. Inquire which is required.

- Women: Cocktail suits or dresses.

- Formal attire can be rented easily at a formal wear rental shop.

*Men and women wear wools and tweeds for casual occasions.*

## HOSTESS

- When invited to someone's home, always bring a small gift for the hostess.

- Present the gift upon arrival.

- Gifts are opened upon receiving.

- It is nice to send flowers the morning of a dinner party.

# GIFTS

- Give: Flowers, chocolates, wine, champagne, books.

- Do not give: White lilies, which denote death.

### BUSINESS

- Gifts are normally not exchanged at business meetings or even at the successful conclusion of negotiations.

- It is acceptable but not expected to give a Christmas gift to a British colleague.

- Give: Ties, pens, drink mats/coasters, books, desk accessories, diaries, leather notebooks, paperweights.

- Do not give: Expensive gifts, which may be perceived as vulgar.

## HELPFUL HINTS

DO:

- Be aware that a car is an important symbol of status in England. Having a chauffeur is an absolute sign of success.

- Respect the English desire for privacy.

- Use "Please" and "Thank you" whenever the occasion calls for it.

- Stand when "God Save the Queen" is played.

- Learn cricket etiquette. Quiet behavior is expected; clap for a good play by either team regardless of your preference.

- Phone ahead to arrange a visit to someone's home. Don't drop in!

- Men should be especially polite to women: Open doors, stand when a woman enters the room  and give up your seat on the bus.

- Speak clearly without using slang.

- Always hold the door for a person following you.

- Show respect for traditions and customs.

- Honor rank when entering a room.  Allow higher rank to enter first.

## DO NOT:

- Never insult the royal family or show a morbid interest in their private lives.

- Never ask where a person lives or what a person does for a profession or job.

- Never talk about money.

- Do not violate a queue.  English are outraged by anyone who pushes ahead in line.

- Do not shout or be loud in public places.

- Never stare at people in public.

- Do not handle fruits or vegetables at a market.  Allow the vendor to give you the item.

- Do not be too casual, especially with the English language.

- Do not put your arm around someone's shoulder.

- Do not wander through someone's home or garden.

*The English appreciate reserved behavior.  Never shout or be loud in public.*

## PUNCTUALITY

- Punctuality is impolite for a social occasion in someone's home. Arrive at least 10 to 20 minutes after the stated time. *Never arrive early.*

- If a social invitation reads "7:30 to 8 p.m.," arrive between 7:45 and 8 p.m. If a social invitation reads "8 p.m.," arrive between 8 and 8:30 p.m.

- Restaurant entertaining demands punctuality.

- Be on time for a business meeting but be prepared to wait 10 minutes for English colleagues.

## STRICTLY BUSINESS

### BUSINESS CARDS

- Most businesspeople exchange cards. There is no set ritual for the exchange of cards.

### CORPORATE CULTURE

STRUCTURE: Company organization traditionally is multilayered with a vertical chain of command. The leader has principal responsibility for making important decisions and implementing major plans. The board of directors is the center of power in many companies, and most decisions require the board's endorsement.

A network of committees, formal and informal, exists in larger companies. Consensus is preferred to individual initiative; nonetheless, groups are reluctant to take responsibility for error.

In older companies, business still centers around the "old boy network" with schools, universities and family ties being of great importance. People may be selected for jobs because they are from the right school (such as Eton) or university (Oxford or Cambridge). Newer companies, however, tend to be more progressive in their hiring and promotion policies.

MEETINGS: Meetings are scheduled well in advance and usually have a clearly defined purpose—to reach a decision or an agreement, formulate an action plan or implement a plan or decision. The British tend to get down to business after a few moments of polite conversation. Opinions are welcomed; however, not all participants will necessarily be well-prepared. Presentations should be detailed and understated. Agreement may be slow, and decisionmaking can be adversarial.

*London is one of the world's major financial centers.*

COMMUNICATION: Expect formalities and protocol to be observed in business, especially in London. It's not acceptable to call English businesspeople at home unless they have given you permission to do so or it's an emergency.

- "The City" is the London business community made up primarily of banks, brokerage firms, insurance companies and other financial institutions.

- Contacts are important; business is best initiated through a well-connected third party.

- Relationships in companies are generally arm's-length and guarded.

- Company loyalty is less common than in the past.

## ENTERTAINMENT

- Breakfast meetings, once viewed as a North American bad habit, are now acceptable.

- Most business entertaining is done in a restaurant or pub over lunch.

- Lunch works best for discussing business. Brits will invest two hours if necessary.

- Actual negotiations are not usually carried out during a meal, but business is discussed.

- Business dinners with spouses included are commonly for socializing or for thanking a customer. Do not discuss business at dinner in someone's home unless the host initiates the conversation.

- An invitation to someone's home is more common in England than in the rest of Europe.

- The British are appreciative of a dinner invitation and they are excellent dinner companions. However, don't try to impress British guests with an extravagant dinner; they prefer understatement.

- A British business associate may invite you to watch cricket or a regatta. Both are prestigious events. Wear your tweed sport coat or blue blazer.

---

## APPOINTMENTS

**Office Hours:**    **Monday through Friday 9:30 a.m. to 5:30 p.m.**

**Bank Hours:**    **Monday through Friday 9:30 a.m. to 3:30 p.m.**

- Make business appointments well in advance.

- Avoid July or August (summer holiday period), the week between Christmas and New Year's and all holidays.

---

## ESPECIALLY FOR WOMEN

- The "old boy network" is alive and well in the United Kingdom. Women are accepted but still must deal with old ways.

- Women are becoming more common in managerial positions in the United Kingdom, especially in service industries and public-sector jobs. Women make up 45 percent of the work force despite the fact that maternity benefits and child-care facilities are negligible.

- It is acceptable, but may be misconstrued, for a foreign woman to invite an English man to dinner. It is best to stick with lunch. If making a dinner invitation, a foreign businesswoman should ask her British guest to bring a spouse. If a woman would like to pay for a meal, she should state this at the outset and arrange with the *maître d'* in advance.

- Women may go to a pub unaccompanied. However, women alone may prefer the lounge section in a pub—it is a more plush section of the bar with a more mature clientele. Children are not allowed in most pubs.

- It is considered more ladylike to order a half-pint of lager or beer rather than a pint. Lager and lime is considered a "woman's drink."

- Don't be insulted if someone calls you "love," "dearie" or "darling." These are commonly used and not considered rude.

- Crossing your legs at the ankles, not at the knees, is considered proper.

- Do not plan to make a business visit or schedule any appointments during the following holidays or festivals. Be sure to check for the numerous regional and local holidays and festivals.

| | |
|---|---|
| January | New Year's Day (1). |
| February | Pancake Day (Shrove Tuesday, the day before Lent). |
| March | St. David's Day (1)*, St. Patrick's Day (17)**. |
| March/April | Mothering Sunday (fourth Sunday in Lent), Easter (Friday-Monday). |
| April | St. George's Day (17)***. |
| May | May Day Bank Holiday (first Monday), Spring Bank Holiday (last Monday). |
| June | Queen's Birthday (second Saturday), Fathers' Day (third Sunday). |
| July | Battle of the Boyne (12)**. |
| August | Summer Bank Holiday (last Monday). |
| November | Guy Fawkes Day (5), Remembrance Day (second Sunday), St. Andrew's Day (30)****. |
| December | Christmas (25), Boxing Day (26–or closest working day). |

\* Wales only.
\*\* Northern Ireland only.
\*\*\* England only.
\*\*\*\* Scotland only.

# SCOTLAND

## VITAL STATISTICS

POPULATION: 5.7 million.

CAPITAL: Edinburgh, with a population of 439,000. Glasgow is one of Britain's largest industrial centers, with a population of 733,000.

LAND SIZE: 30,405 square miles, approximately the size of South Carolina.

LIVING
STANDARD: GDP = $13,329 per capita.

NATURAL
RESOURCES: Natural gas and petroleum, small deposits of coal, hydroelectric power.

AGRICULTURE: Barley, cattle, oats, sheep, wheat, fish.

INDUSTRIES: Automobiles, chemicals, industrial machinery, iron and steel, ships, textiles, whiskey.

CLIMATE: Temperate and wet. Summer: 60°F to 70°F; winter generally above freezing.

CURRENCY: British pound sterling (£). There are additional bank notes issued by Scottish banks that are legal tender in all parts of the U.K.

# THE PEOPLE

<table>
<tr><td>CORRECT<br>NAME:</td><td>Scots or Scotsmen.</td></tr>
<tr><td>ETHNIC<br>MAKEUP:</td><td>Mostly Scots. Small minority of Indians and Pakistanis in larger cities.</td></tr>
<tr><td>VALUE<br>SYSTEM:</td><td>Scots value generosity, respectability and are very satisfied with themselves and determined to stay unchanged. They have a passionate love of Scotland. They jealously guard their uniqueness and refuse to go along with English ideas.</td></tr>
<tr><td>FAMILY:</td><td>Scots have a great love of family. While cool and aloof externally, they are extremely sentimental about their family and their country. Most Scottish traditions come from clans that began hundreds of years ago. Clans are made up of families with the same name and common ancestors. Each clan has its own plaid design called a tartan used for shirts, ties, kilts, etc.</td></tr>
<tr><td>RELIGION:</td><td>The official Church of Scotland is Presbyterian. Approximately 30 percent belong to the Church of Scotland. Other religions include Baptist, Congregationalist, Episcopal and Methodist.</td></tr>
</table>

Customs and behavior in Scotland are similar to those in England. However, the following are points to note.

## MEETING AND GREETING

- Strangers are welcomed kindly with a high level of civility.

- To strangers, Scots may appear reserved, noncommittal and in no hurry to impress.

## LANGUAGE

*Scots live in Scotland, drink scotch and speak Scottish.*

- English is the official language. Scots speak English with a soft, almost musical accent.

- A person living in Scotland is a Scot or Scotsman.

- Scots may be called British but dislike "Brit."

- Scotch is whiskey, wool, tweed or mist (persistent drizzling rain).

- Small numbers of Scots speak Gaelic, an ancient Celtic language. Gaelic in Scotland is different from Gaelic in Ireland.

## DINING AND DRINKING

- Make a motion as if signing your name to ask for "the bill" at a restaurant.

- Scots prefer scotch whiskey before dinner. Most drink scotch without water or soda.

### TYPICAL FOODS

- Food in Scotland is simple and delicious.

- *Lamb Stew:* Scottish lamb is world-famous.

- *Scotch Egg:* Hard-boiled egg wrapped in sausage.

- *Haggis:* Famous national dish of heart, liver and lungs of sheep or calf, chopped with suet.

- *Kippers:* Smoked herring.

- *Salmon:* Smoked, grilled, poached.

- *Crawachan:* Oatmeal laced with whiskey, cream and lots of sugar.

## TOASTS

- *Shlante* (SHLAHN-tay), "To your health." Formal and informal. A foreigner is usually not expected to attempt this. "Cheers" or "Good health" would suffice.

---

# MANNERS

- Scots are always polite and courteous.

---

# DRESS

- Never make a joke about or ask a Scot what he wears under his kilt.

- Kilts are worn by men at formal occasions (i.e. black tie, weddings, etc.).

- Casual clothes are appropriate for most occasions.

- Very few hotels or restaurants require jackets and ties.

- Premiere at Edinburgh Festival: Men wear tuxedos and women wear evening dresses.

DO:

- Respect a person's privacy.

DO NOT:

- Do not call trousers or slacks "pants." Pants means underwear.

- Never be loud in public.

- Never stare at anyone.

- Never jump ahead in a queue (line).

## PUNCTUALITY

- The Scots are punctual for social and business meetings.

## STRICTLY BUSINESS

- Scots are suspicious of "go-getters." They are determined and thorough and respect success only when it is achieved over time.

- Scots are known for being skilled businesspersons; they begin negotiating when they answer the phone.

- Fortitude and resilience are Scottish trademarks.

- Scots pride themselves on being internationalists. They interact well with foreigners.

- See "U.K. Holidays and Festivals," p. 477.

# HOLIDAYS
# AND
# FESTIVALS

# WALES

## VITAL STATISTICS

POPULATION:   3 million.

CAPITAL:   Cardiff, with a population of 273,856 million.

LAND SIZE:   8,019 square miles, slightly larger than New Jersey.

LIVING
STANDARD:   GDP = $13,329 per capita.

NATURAL
RESOURCES:   Coal, limestone, slate, copper ore, iron ore, water reservoirs.

AGRICULTURE:   Barley, hay, oats, potatoes, turnips, beef, sheep, dairy foods.

INDUSTRIES:   Aluminum, iron, steel, tin plate, chemicals, electrical equipment, motor vehicle parts, plastics, synthetic fibers.

CLIMATE:   Humid but mild. Rain and fog are common.

CURRENCY:   British pound sterling (£).

# THE PEOPLE

CORRECT
NAME:            Welsh.

ETHNIC
MAKEUP:          Most are Welsh or English.  Many are immigrants
                 from former British colonies and other parts of
                 the U.K.

VALUE
SYSTEM:          Welsh take great pride in their country and their
                 heritage.  They have been part of the United
                 Kingdom for more than 400 years, but have kept
                 their own language, literature and traditions.
                 Welsh love to sing and talk.  Their choirs and
                 glee clubs are famous.

FAMILY:          Families are very close.  The father is the
                 decisionmaker but the mother has considerable
                 influence in the family.  It is increasingly
                 common for young people to live together before
                 or instead of marriage.  The Welsh are
                 homebodies.  Most spend their evenings at home
                 watching television with their families.

RELIGION:        The Church of Wales is the Anglican Church.

Customs and behavior in Wales are similar to those in England. However, the following are points to note.

| | |
|---|---|
| **LANGUAGE** | • English is the official language. Welsh is the official regional language. About 32,000 people speak only Welsh. |
| | • Less than 20 percent of the population speaks both English and Welsh. |
| | • Never call Welshmen "English." Use the name Welsh or British. |

| | |
|---|---|
| **BODY LANGUAGE** | • Don't rub your nose—it's a rude gesture. |

| | |
|---|---|
| **DINING AND DRINKING** | • Welsh food is simple. |
| | • Entertainment is done in restaurants and homes. |
| | • Some restaurants and pubs only serve lunch, which is generally the main meal of the day. |

### TYPICAL FOODS

• *Leeks:* The national emblem.

• *Sewin:* Welsh trout.

• *Mutton stew.*

• *Welsh rarebit:* Melted cheese and butter with beer, served on toast.

- *Bara laver:* A vegetable dish made with seafood.

- *Cawl:* A meat and vegetable soup.

---

- *Lechyd Da* (YEH-hid day), "Good health." Formal and informal.

**TOAST**

---

- Dress is generally informal. In the city, some people dress more formally for dinner.

- Always take a raincoat and umbrella.

**DRESS**

---

- Welsh lovespoons are famous. They are given for almost any occasion.

**GIFTS**

---

- Corporate structure and business behavior are similar to those in England. However, you should be aware of some subtle differences:

- Decisions are made slowly.

- It is necessary to establish a personal relationship before doing business.

- Rank and age are important in business.

- Entertain anyone who has entertained you.

**STRICTLY BUSINESS**

---

- See "U.K. Holidays and Festivals," p. 477.

**HOLIDAYS AND FESTIVALS**

# NORTHERN IRELAND

## VITAL STATISTICS

The smallest of four countries that make up the United Kingdom of Great Britain and Northern Ireland.

Northern Ireland is often referred to as Ulster, but this is not technically correct. All of Northern Ireland lies in Ulster, but not all of Ulster lies in Northern Ireland. Six of Ulster's nine counties lie in Northern Ireland and the remaining three lie in the Republic of Ireland.

POPULATION:     1.6 million (1988).

CAPITAL:     Belfast, with a population of 303,800.

LAND SIZE:     5,452 square miles, about the size of Connecticut.

NATURAL
RESOURCES:     Lignite, fertile fields and pasture lands, peat, sandstone.

AGRICULTURE:     Beef, sheep, hogs, poultry, barley, potatoes, dairy foods.

| INDUSTRIES: | Agriculture, aerospace, aerospace engineering, textile machinery manufacturing, shipbuilding, electrical components manufacturing, synthetic fibers, and the manufacture of forklift trucks and automotive components. More people are employed in the service sector than in manufacturing. |
|---|---|
| CURRENCY: | British pound sterling (£). |

---

## THE PEOPLE

| CORRECT NAME: | Northern Irish. |
|---|---|
| ETHNIC MAKEUP: | Two-thirds have Scottish or English roots. The others are of Irish descent. |
| VALUE SYSTEM: | Irish value friendliness, sincerity and nature. They dislike pretentious behavior. They are honorable. In many respects, life in Northern Ireland is more like that in the rest of Great Britain than like that in the Republic of Ireland. |
| WORK ETHIC: | Irish work hard, but have a slower pace than in North America. |

| FAMILY: | Family ties are very important. However, the traditional role of women staying home is changing. Many now work outside the home. The divorce rate is still very low. |
|---|---|
| RELIGION: | 56 percent Protestant, 44 percent Roman Catholic. |

---

Unionists or Loyalists support Northern Ireland remaining part of Great Britain. Nationalists (the minority) favor Northern Ireland becoming part of the Republic of Ireland.

## CRIME IN NORTHERN IRELAND

A survey carried out in 1989 found that 15 percent of adults in Northern Ireland were victims of crime one or more times in 1988. This compares to 29 percent in the U.S., 19 percent in Great Britain, and 21 percent in Western Europe.

Even allowing for terrorist violence, the murder rate in Northern Ireland is lower than in the U.S. (lower than in 36 of the 50 states) and Canada.

Customs and behavior in Northern Ireland are similar to those in England. However, the following are points to note.

| | |
|---|---|
| • The people are not English. The people are British or preferably, *Northern Irish*. | **NAMES AND TITLES** |
| • Northern Ireland is not the Republic of Ireland. | |
| • Northern Ireland is not England. | |
| • The people are *Irish*, not English. | |

| | |
|---|---|
| • Religion and politics have created conflict in this area for many years. Avoid these topics if possible. | **LANGUAGE** |
| • Approximately 5 percent of the population speaks Gaelic (Irish) in addition to English. | |

| | |
|---|---|
| • Pubs are an important part of social life. | **DINING AND DRINKING** |
| • Northern Irish food is simple. | |
| • There are numerous ethnic restaurants. | |

| | |
|---|---|
| • See "U.K. Holidays and Festivals," p. 477. | **HOLIDAYS AND FESTIVALS** |

# REFERENCES

Aburdene, Patricia, and John Naisbitt. *Megatrends for Women*, New York: Villard Books, 1992.

Acuff, Frank L. *How to Negotiate Anything with Anyone Anywhere Around the World.* New York: Amacom, 1993.

"Alerts & Updates," *Business Europe.* December 18, 1992.

Axtel, Roger E. *Dos and Taboos of Hosting International Visitors.* New York: Wiley, 1990.

Axtel, Roger E. *Gestures.* New York: Wiley, 1991.

Axtel, Roger E., ed. *Dos and Taboos Around the World*, 2nd ed., New York: Wiley, 1990.

*Big Little Denmark.* London: The Danish Tourist Board, 1992.

*Business Traveller's Guide '93 - Copenhagen.* Copenhagen: Business Denmark Publications, 1993.

Bryn, Steinar. *Images of an American in Norway.* Oslo, Norway: Samalget Printing Company, 1992.

*Culturgrams, 1992.* Provo, Utah: David M. Kennedy Center for International Studies, Brigham Young University, 1992 ed.

*Denmark Review.* Copenhagen: Royal Danish Ministry of Foreign Affairs, Foreign Trade Relations Department, 2/1993.

"The Diplomat" Newsletter. Cold Spring Harbor, New York: The Diplomat, 1992.

*The Economist World Atlas and Almanac.* London: The Economist Books, 1991.

*Finland - A Nation Under the North Star.* Espoo, Finland: Lapmap Oy, 1992.

*Finland Fact Card.* Helsinki: Ajatus Publishing Company, 1992.

*Finnish Instruction Manual.* New York: Conversaphone Institute, 1978.

*Fodor's Germany.* New York: Fodor's Travel Publications, Inc., 1993.

*Fodor's Greece.* New York: Fodor's Travel Publications, Inc., 1993.

*The Food of Spain and Portugal.* New York: Atheneum, 1989.

*The French Economy, Facts & Figures.* Saint Maurice, France: Editions Ecorama, 1992.

*Growing Accustomed to Customs.* California: DHL Airways, Inc., 1991.

Hostie, Fanny leJemtel. *Invest in France Report, Issue #50.* New York: Invest in France Agency, 1993.

*Italian for Travellers*. Oxford: Berlitz Publishing Company, Inc., 1970.

*Italia, Travellers Handbook*. London: Italian State Tourist Board (E.N.I.T.), 1992.

*Italy, Europe Tax-Free Shopping*. Varese, Italy: Italy Tax Free Shopping, 1993.

*Just Listen 'n' Learn French*. Lincolnwood, Illinois: NTC Publishing Group.

*Key Facts, Figures and Themes. Northern Ireland*. Belfast: Government of Northern Ireland, 1992.

*Langensheidt Language for Travelers - German Quick and Easy*. Nasspeth, New York: Langenscheidt Publishing, Inc.

*Living in Holland*. The Hague: NUFFIC, 1988.

*Marketing in Turkey*. Washington, D.C.: U.S. Department of Commerce, 1993.

Mole, John. *When In Rome*. New York: Amacom, 1991.

*The New York Times*. New York: New York Times Company.

*The 1990 Information Please Almanac*. Boston: Houghton Mifflin Company, 1990.

*1993 Federal Express World Business Advisory & Calendar*, Clarks Summit, Pennsylvania: Educational Extension Systems, 1992.

*Norwegian Instruction Manual*. New York: Conversaphone Institute, 1985.

Ostrander, Sheila. *Superlearning - German*. New York: Simon & Schuster.

*Shopping in Denmark, Tax Free for Tourists*. Kastrup: Europe Tax-Free Shopping Denmark A/S, 1992.

*Shopping in Finland, Tax Free for Tourists*. Helsinki: Europe Tax-Free Shopping Finland, 1992.

*A Small Treasury of Swedish Food*. Stockholm: The Federation of Swedish Farmers, 1992.

*Spanish for Travelers*. Oxford: Berlitz Publishing Company, Ltd., 1983.

*Swedish Instruction Manual*. New York: Conversaphone Institute, 1984.

*Swedish Language 30*. Washington, D.C.: Educational Services, 1983.

*Switzerland in Figures*. Zurich: Union Bank of Switzerland, 1993.

*A Tax Guide to Europe*. New York: Arthur Andersen and Co., 1992.

*Tax Refunds for Shopping in Austria*. New York: Austrian National Tourist Office, 1993.

*These Strange German Ways*. Hamburg: Atlantik Bruecke, 1984.

*Trade & Culture* Magazine. Baltimore, MD: Trade & Culture, Inc.

*Turkish Republic.* Chicago: Turkish Consulate General, 1993.

*The Wall Street Journal.* New York: Dow Jones & Company, Inc.

*We Danes and You.* Copenhagen: The National Travel Association of Denmark.

*Welcome to Italy. A Guide for Young Visitors.* Italy: Eryica.

*Welcome: Quality of Life in the Netherlands.* Amsterdam: Ministry of Economic Affairs, the Netherlands Foreign Investment Agency, 1992.

*Western Europe . . . A Tax Tour.* New York: Arthur Andersen & Co, 1989 ed.

*World Book Encyclopedia.* Chicago: World Book, Inc., 1992.

*The World Factbook 1992.* Washington, D.C.: Central Intelligence Agency, 1992.

*World Trade* Magazine. Newport Beach, CA: Taipan Press, Inc.

# INDEX